D0887347

ROSSET

ROSSET

My Life in Publishing and How I Fought Censorship

by
Barney Rosset

OR Books
New York · London

Published by OR Books, New York and London
Visit our website at www.orbooks.com

First printing 2016

Cataloging-in-Publication data is available from the Library of Congress.
A catalog record for this book is available from the British Library.

ISBN 978-1-68219-044-9 paperback
ISBN 978-1-68219-045-6 ebook

Text design by Under|Over. Typeset by AarkMany Media, Chennai, India. Printed by BookMobile, USA, and CPI, UK. The U.S. printed edition of this book comes on Forest Stewardship Council-certified, 30% recycled paper.

Contents

Barnet Rosset Sr. and Jr., Chicago, c. 1927.

XX is by no means a typical American, even typical of his own class or his own group, but his specialness is not so unusual as to basically differentiate his problems from those of the other American progressives.

XX was born and raised in Chicago, and spends part of the time of the book in Chicago. Thus he is most deeply a Midwestern American by culture, and he in many ways is an extremely typical American—middle-class style. One of the main character traits to play up is his rootlessness in the sense of not having a sharp national background, a religious stability, or even a constant group of old family friends.

His father is Jewish, but without any ties of culture or emotion to the Jews. He would rather have forgotten the accident of his birth, felt that it held him back more than it did anything else. He believed in the power of money above all else, but at the same time felt that he was trying to do good in the world, but his reliance on his own abilities, his own money, is something XX revolts against. The struggle with his father is deep, from infancy in the competition for his mother, and he cannot take up the same values, unless in the sense that he goes toward opposites.

XX was a fierce competitor in school but not for money, only for prestige of scholarship, athletics, and above all else, girls. Thus struggle to get girls has been a deep-rooted problem, and he felt, rather mistakenly, that he could never be successful. This competition for girls was a very subtle thing, taking many forms, and also being a very chauvinistic thing in that the girl was basically a prize to be sought after, not an important human being.

One important idea in the story and a constantly growing one, is the relationship of XX to women, in that he starts as being quite chauvinistic and slowly grows out of it.

ZZ helps him in this, because she is acutely aware of the position of women and this must be one of their main interacting struggles, but of course just as she slowly pulls him out of his chauvinism he must change her from being a lone wolf who is against men, outside of their sex value, into a woman who can see over the ills of her society and integrate herself into society.

—Barney Rosset, "Notes for an Autobiography," 2006, unpublished manuscript from the Barney Rosset Papers, Rare Books and Manuscripts, Butler Library, Columbia University

For Astrid and for my children
Peter, Tansey, Beckett, and Chantal

Foreword

Some people think my chief claim to fame is having published the first book to be sold over the counter in this country with the word *fuck* printed on its pages in all its naked glory. Perhaps to the mainstream that's all there was to D. H. Lawrence's *Lady Chatterley's Lover*—just fuck, fuck, fuck. I saw the publication of Lawrence's masterwork somewhat differently—as a major victory against ignorance and censorship.

There has been much more to my publishing career, of course, than that. I believe, more fairly, that I should be thought of as the publisher who broke the cultural barrier raised like a Berlin Wall between the public and free expression in literature, film, and drama. My determination to publish an unexpurgated edition of *Lady Chatterley* in 1954 was consistent with my long-held conviction that an author should be free to write whatever he or she pleased, and a publisher free to publish anything. I mean *anything*.

This relatively uncomplicated idea has gotten me into all kinds of trouble with the authorities. The resultant battles have eaten up great chunks of my time and energy, not to mention money, and enriched a whole generation of attorneys. But we broke the back of censorship. I think this is a good time to tell the story of my life—as a man and as a publisher. I will try to explain what shaped me as a crusader against the anti-obscenity laws, and why very early in my life I believed them to be an outrageous denial of freedom. But it seemed that almost nothing I did was greeted calmly and peaceably. How did I get that way? What made me into such a maverick troublemaker?

1

An Irish Ancestry:
From Ould Sod to the New Land

Rebellion runs in my family's blood. We have never shown a willingness to accept unthinkingly what authorities told us was right or wrong, in good taste or bad. The repression of imposed conformity has always been something we fought against, no matter what the odds.

On July 10, 1884, in Carrick-on-Shannon, County Leitrim, Ireland, my great-grandfather, Michael Tansey, was sentenced to death for the murder of one William Mahon.[1] The unfortunate Mahon was a British landlord's man, a gamekeeper on an estate, charged with preventing poachers from unlawfully taking fish and game during a famine year. The Anglo-Irish aristocracy was literally driving Irish tenant farmers off the land, land that the British had seized by conquest and were now leasing back to its original owners at high rates.

Mahon disappeared on the night of October 16, 1879. Because the closed-mouth community offered no help to the authorities, the police were stymied for seven months by what amounted to an unsolved missing person case. Then a local woman, probably out poaching, saw a human hand protruding from a sack that came bobbing up from the bottom of the River Suck. It belonged to Mahon's decomposing body. A postmortem showed he had been beaten to death before being dumped into the cold water.

Most under suspicion in the case were the Tanseys, because Roger Tansey, Michael's teenaged son and my grandfather-to-be, had been accused of poaching by Mahon, and Michael himself had threatened the man.

There were a lot of threats in the air at that time. The Irish Tenant Right League had persuaded Prime Minister Gladstone to back the Land Act of 1870, which recognized that a long-term tenant had certain rights to his holding, including a fair rent. This help didn't amount to much, though, because as a result of the disastrously poor harvest of 1879, tenants couldn't afford to pay any rent whatsoever. The League managed to keep people on their farms and have their rent waived during that famine year, but the following year when the crops were better, landlords demanded payment of rent that was in arrears from the year before. If a tenant couldn't pay he was evicted. And if he refused to leave his house, it was pulled down. In response, violence broke out all over Ireland. Landowners and their hirelings were killed, cattle were poisoned, and property was destroyed, often by dynamite. The British reacted by passing the new Land Act of 1881, which gave more rights to the tenants, but outlawed the Irish Land League and imprisoned its members, including, for a time, Charles Parnell, the greatest Irish leader of his day.

It was in this atmosphere that my great-grandfather was put on trial for the gamekeeper's murder. The police investigation of his death had not been terribly extensive, but that situation changed when a new crime, involving my great-grandfather's other son, also named William, was committed. On March 26, 1882, Weston House, the residence of the gamekeeper's employer, was bombed. Because footsteps at the scene led in the direction of Ballyforan, home both to the Tanseys and a peat bog, the investigation was directed there. Michael Tansey and his sons worked in the bog where, as it happened, dynamite was often used to blast sections of the peat apart. This explosive, used to gain access to peat, a form of low-grade fuel used for heating and cooking, was also a handy tool for terrorism. The authorities persuaded four of the men involved to become state's witnesses.

At the trial, William Tansey and the four "leaders" of the conspiracy received heavy sentences, William getting fourteen years and a co-conspirator, a fellow named Patrick Rogerson, twelve. When William was sentenced, he yelled out, "God save Ireland!"

Trouble did not end there. Bernard Geraghty, one of those who had turned on the defendants, confessed that he knew something about the 1879 Mahon murder and convinced some others to join him in testifying in court. With this new evidence, on January 27, 1884, the police arrested my great-grandfather and his colleagues, charging them with the murder. Michael Tansey was first to be tried. The case against him was strong, and the jury retired for only forty-five minutes before returning with a guilty verdict. Sentenced to be hanged, he made just one request to the judge: Let me shake hands with my wife before I die. The request was granted, but in the interval before the execution was scheduled, a petition to spare Michael's life on grounds that the evidence was weak was signed by 50 men in the district, as well as Parnell and other notables, including many members of Parliament. The appeal was successful; Michael's sentence was commuted to life imprisonment.

His son, William, was released on July 12, 1892, after serving almost ten years of his sentence. In 1895, an ailing 65-year-old Michael Tansey was released from the obligation to labor. He pleaded for the authorities to let him die a free man with his family. Once again a petition was signed by prominent people supporting his plea for clemency. He was hospitalized with a severe case of bronchitis in March 1901, and this seems to have softened the hearts of his keepers.

So my great-grandfather was finally given his freedom. On December 6, 1902, he walked out of the prison gates and returned to his farm in Ballyforan. As time passed, he found it increasingly difficult to report to the police barracks weekly as part of his parole. In October 1907, after making these visits for five years, he wrote a plaintive letter, in which he said he was 77 years of age, weighed down with infirmity and weakness and tottering fast to the grave. He died shortly thereafter.

His family—and therefore mine—had formed part of the clandestine revolutionary movement in Ireland, which eventually ousted their English overlords from much of the country. It is a heritage of which I am very proud.

My grandfather Roger somehow absconded from Ballyforan and, via Boston, found his way to Marquette, Michigan, where he married Maggie Flannery and where his children were born: Barney (nickname for Bernard); Mike; Sarah; my mother, Mary—born July 28, 1891—and a much younger sister, Kate, whom they all called Babe.

Marquette took its name from the French explorer and priest Jacques Marquette. So did the Pere Marquette Railway, which took travelers overnight between Chicago and Marquette. I remember one such run when, in the dead of winter one year before I was ten years old, my mother and I spent more than a few hours snowbound aboard our sleeper car waiting for the tracks to be cleared. In the incredibly cold winters the town's citizens, including Roger Tansey, went out on the ice of Lake Superior and drilled down to the unfrozen water to fish.

After winning an upright piano in a beauty contest in Marquette, my mother was inspired to make a new life in Chicago. While working as a teller at one of Chicago's most prestigious banking firms, the Northern Trust Co., she met Barnet L. Rosset, who seemed to her to be an up-and-coming fellow. They were married in 1920, I know not where, and on May 28, 1922, I was born, the only child they would have.

When my father was eighteen, he was already the secretary-treasurer of the Burton Holmes Travelogues Company, a famous and successful firm pioneering a new book format that made great use of photographs and drawings. Looking back, I believe they were a significant factor in my eventually becoming a publisher. We had a set of these ornately bound books, which I own to this day. I later republished part of one of those volumes, about the first modern Olympics, which took place in Athens in 1896.[2] The layout and design of the

Burton Holmes books made them ahead of their time, and Holmes himself was the author and publisher.

My father, even then, was an independent go-getter. He ultimately left Holmes and went on to start his own certified public accounting firm at the age of twenty-two.

Born in Chicago in 1899 of Russian Jewish parents who had emigrated from Moscow, my father was a capable and smart man. I don't know if he graduated from high school or not, but he excelled in accounting and was certified almost immediately. His sisters, Beatrice and Paulyne, were also very intelligent. Beatrice knew the most about our family history, but she told a different story every time you asked her. On occasion she would say the name Rosset came from the Rosetta stone; another time she would claim that it was French in origin. She was a very good raconteur, who took great pleasure in concocting her fictions.

My maternal grandparents, Roger Tansey and Maggie Flannery, retained their undying hatred for the English. No explanation of this was ever given to me. But I do vaguely remember hearing something about the Black and Tans from time to time. Although my grandparents spoke in Gaelic when they did not wish me to understand, I got the message quickly and never forgot it. British colonialism had brutalized Ireland and its native people. Indeed, Roger had left Ireland with a price on his head. Nevertheless, he was a very gentle man, tall, handsome, and the patriarch of the immediate neighborhood, which was largely made up of working-class people. Roger worked for the city, building and maintaining sewer lines.

I spent part of a year with my grandparents in Marquette, attending second grade at the public school. My father, who deeply loved Roger Tansey, brought him a radio all the way from Chicago, the first I had seen, and we listened to the broadcast of the fight between our hero, Jack Dempsey, and Gene Tunney, who was also Irish—but he was well educated and you could almost think he was English. And on the windup Victrola on our tiny enclosed porch we listened to Caruso, Galli-Curci, and John McCormack. My mother's upright piano was in the living room, but I never heard her try to play it. My shell-shocked Uncle Barney did, though—from time to time, almost like an interloping stranger, he would walk into the house out of nowhere, sit down at the little piano, and play songs from his army days. "Mademoiselle from Armentières" and its "Hinky, dinky, parley-voo" chorus would often float out. Barney was tough and well-known, almost romantically so, as one of the local hobos, meaning he had no permanent residence or employment. I never did find out where Uncle Barney lived. Much later, when Pinter and Kerouac came along, I recognized them. Shell-shocked as he was, Uncle Barney had prepared me. He was their prototype.

While most of my grandfather's neighbors were Irish, when he died there was a general day of mourning. The Swedes, Poles, Finns, and French Canadians who lived on our block all came to pay their respects. It was a day I have never forgotten.

◗◖

In 1929 my father supported Herbert Hoover for president while my mother pulled for Al Smith, and I was strongly on her side because Smith was a liberal with strong welfare policies aimed at helping the poor. Hoover was the standard businessman's candidate. I don't doubt that my father regretted it when the Irish Catholic Smith lost the election and the Great Depression ravaged America.

Illinois was one of the states worst hit by bank failures. Illinois did not have branch banking, and in Chicago each bank had to back itself up or it would close. By that time my father was head of one of those self-standing banks and involved with another. Franklin Delano Roosevelt, after he was elected, declared a "Bank Holiday" to stop panicked depositors from withdrawing their money and plunging banks into failure. Before that "holiday" I remember my father putting $100 bills in his shoes to bring to his bank to pay the people standing in line outside waiting to take out their deposits. When a bank was out of cash that was the end. Many people never got their money out. As a result, another Roosevelt institution was developed, the Federal Deposit Insurance Corporation. For me and many others, FDR was the second coming of Al Smith.

Both of the banks my father had headed closed during that time, but he took over yet another one, the Metropolitan Trust Company of Chicago. After he died in 1954, I closed it by merging it with Grove Press. This astonished everybody, just the idea of merging a bank with a publishing company, especially one like Grove Press, which was already beginning to be known for its un-bankerlike character. And it was the first time that anyone in the state of Illinois had ever given up a charter to run a bank without being forced to. I followed state laws and tried to contact every depositor to make sure they got their deposits back. When some failed to respond, I went to the state office for banking in Illinois and said, "In accordance with your laws, I want you to hold the uncollected money." They were reluctant so I had to sue them at their request to get them to take the deposits.

While my parents and I never lacked in life's essentials, we felt the bite of the Depression like most Americans. Chicago during the Depression was, to put it mildly, a dangerous place to live. This was an era of native gangsters regarded by many people as Robin Hoods. Among them were Pretty Boy Floyd, Ma Barker, Bonnie and Clyde, and John Dillinger. They were people mainly from, let's say, Oklahoma and Texas, and they were robbing banks, the depositories for the rich. They were, in effect, trying to destroy the system. And my hero Dillinger was the most spectacular because when he got caught he often escaped from jail. I thought that he was a fantastic person who, with his cohorts, was my equivalent of the Russian Communist leaders. We were in big trouble and Herbert Hoover was not our solution, so I got my classmates to join me in signing a petition to send to the government—this was my first school, the progressive Gateway School—asking that Dillinger be named to replace Hoover and saying, "Let Dillinger alone, don't arrest him, he's too important! We need people like that at this time in our history!"

Hoover did not take our advice. My family and I eventually lived not far from the movie theater where Hoover's FBI shot John Dillinger. He is a hero of mine to this day.

When I was about ten, we lived on the Near North Side, near Sheridan Road and Diversey. My parents were friendly with Catholic priests who spent a great deal of time in our apartment. My father must have had thoughts about converting to Catholicism, but I never asked him, and he never talked about it. Given the fact that he was Jewish and my mother Irish Catholic, it is significant that I never went to a synagogue, and my trips to the local church were few and far between. There was something about the church that frightened and repelled me—the priests in their black gowns, the nuns so severe in their equally austere habits. I never spoke about it with anybody, but I do remember overhearing my pious Irish grandmother and her friends discussing my not being an observant Catholic. At my parents' insistence I went to church for a while—I would accompany my mother to services, but when she was too lazy to go, or so it seemed to me, I was supposed to go alone. I did that for a very brief time, and then one day when I was still in grammar school I abruptly quit. Since I didn't believe in God, I thought it was all crazy. Not knowing how precocious I was being, I declared myself an atheist at an early age.

As an only child, I felt lucky because my parents' attention was focused entirely on me, while I myself lavished all of my love on my stuffed toy dog, Molly. I was shocked the one time my father told me they had wanted to have more children. I felt hurt and frightened. But at the same time I invented brothers for myself. I had a little roulette wheel that somebody gave me, and it had six numbers, 1 through 6. I became number 3 and my brother was number 4, and then 1, 2, 5, and 6, all boys, were my very close friends and enemies. They became absolutely real people to me, and I hated my brother, number 4. Number 3 remained my lucky number, always. When I played football in high school, my number was 33—we didn't have single numbers. Many years later, when I published Samuel Beckett's *Waiting for Godot*, I assigned it the number 33 in the Evergreen paperback series. This was not by accident.

I was nine when I first went to summer camp just outside of Minoqua, Wisconsin. All of the campers were Jewish except, you could say, for half of me. In my eyes Camp Kawaga was a terrible place. I spent three consecutive, miserable summers there and felt that the place had been organized for the purpose of torturing me. Kawaga was like a pale version of a Marine Corps' boot camp and the rabbi who ran it was the drill sergeant. After that camp, the infantry was almost gentle—at any rate, much more humane. Whenever they had religious goings-on, I would hide under the bed. I was simply frightened. They would have to drag me out, and they did.

My many unpleasant memories include having to jump nude into an icy lake at about 6:00 every morning. Then there were the boxing matches I was pushed into with a kid in the next cabin, named Zippy Lippman, just to see if we could hurt each other or at least amuse the other campers. Poor Zippy was very fat and I was very skinny. I couldn't see very well, and Zippy couldn't move very well. It was like throwing two mangy lions into a den to kill each other.

I had one friend there who, like me, would end up going to the progressive Francis Parker School in Chicago. He was a child genius. His name was Ralph Eisenschiml. His father, Otto, wrote bestsellers about Abraham Lincoln but was a chemist by profession. Ralph wrote piano sonatas and poems for his mother. He was not any older than me, maybe even a year or so younger, but I sort of clung to him. People liked him—they didn't like me. I can remember hearing conversations where Ralph would be asked, "Why do you hang out with that guy? He's so ugly and you're so good-looking." That hurts when you're nine or ten.

We had to swim across the lake to qualify to swim outside a roped-in area. I did it but everybody always thought I was drowning. I never learned the technique of the crawl. I was always just flailing. But I did it. I swam across that goddamn lake, with a rowboat following, waiting to drag me in. I may have never become a good swimmer while at camp but I did learn how to run. They held cross-country races. I would start off slowly, but I was always first at the end. It gave me some pride in myself.

At breakfast all the campers sang songs together. The big hit was "Where Do You Live?" and the lyrics went, "Where do you live? I live in the deep dark woods." That was it, day after day. They served oatmeal and you had to eat it. I couldn't swallow it, and the rabbi's chief honchos would keep me in the dining area for a very long time, trying to get me to finish it. But even when smothered in sugar and butter, the lumps would not go down.

My two counselors, Danny and Flip, were would-be actors from Brooklyn and they called themselves the Bohemians. I never knew what that meant, but they had a song, "We're bohemians, we're birds of a feather, we flock together." I did not know what bohemian living was. Sometimes I envisioned birds flying over a verdant landscape.

At our table Danny and Flip gave each of us kids a nickname. I was "The Sword Swallower" because of the way I used my knife to eat. They were good guys. I had another problem at that camp—I wet the bed. They would get me up at four or five in the morning to go and pee so I wouldn't wet it again. But I did anyway, my would-be saviors could not help me. I would pee in my sleep, get up at six-thirty or seven and wash the sheets in the lake, and hang them to dry. That got me no sympathy from the rabbi and his son.

My parents sent me a Chicago newspaper every day and I made imaginary bets on the horses after carefully studying the racing forms. (My mother got me interested in racing because she constantly took me to the racetracks— Arlington, Washington, Hawthorne, even one little bedraggled track in Aurora, Illinois.) Then the next day I'd look to see if I won or lost. It kept me alive. I even remember the names of some of the horses—Gallant Fox, Twenty Grand, Sun Beau. They were almost as exciting to me as the "Fighting Irish," the football players of Notre Dame, who beat Northwestern, elite Protestants. The hero I remember best from then was Marchmont Schwartz of Notre Dame. Would you have guessed? He was half-Irish, or at least I thought he was.

When after three years my parents finally realized that they had sent me to the wrong camp and I had piled enough guilt on them, they asked, "Where would you like to go?" I studied camps all over the United States and picked one in Estes Park, Colorado, called Cheley Camp.

At Cheley there were more horses than campers. I still wet the bed. One night I dreamed that I was in the latrine peeing, but actually I was peeing in the riding boot of my friend Tom Pancoast who was sleeping in the bunk above me. In the morning, it seems some of my bunkmates had guessed what happened. Maybe they could smell something. They watched as Tom stuck his foot into the boot. He divined instantly what had happened. No expression, no words. He just glanced knowingly at me and walked out of the cabin. I became a pretty good polo player at Cheley. But it can be a dangerous sport. Two weeks later Tom's helmet fell off and another guy accidentally hit him on the head with his mallet. The cut became infected and Tom died. His kindness to me made me feel he really was a divine angel, like Jean Genet's Angel Divine.

Tom's family owned a top-of-the-line hotel right on Miami Beach, the Pancoast, near the Roney Plaza, but unlike the Roney, no Jews were allowed at the Pancoast, not then. We vacationed in Miami Beach in 1932 when Roosevelt closed the banks for four days. Even my father, who had voted for Hoover, was happy. Eddie Cantor sang "Happy Days Are Here Again," and "Roll Out the Barrel" was heard all over, celebrating the end of Prohibition. That year we stayed at a hotel two blocks from the beach, the Bowman. It took in Jews. My mother had to change into her swimsuit at the public facility. With her Irish-red hair and white skin I thought she looked out of place. I felt embarrassed for her.

The next year we moved up, to the Miami Biltmore in Coral Gables, outside of Miami proper. There I saw Ray Bolger and Bert Lahr in the hotel's nightclub. It was the Depression era of "Brother Can You Spare a Dime?" Bolger went on to play the Scarecrow in *The Wizard of Oz,* along with Lahr as the Cowardly Lion. In years to come, Bert's son, John, would work at Grove Press. And in 1956, Bert Lahr himself would perform the role of Estragon in the first American production of *Waiting for Godot*, which opened in a new theater, Coconut Grove, in Coral Gables. When it opened, Walter Winchell proclaimed it a Communist play. The joke of the week was: "Where is the hardest place in Miami to get a taxi?" Answer: "Standing in front of the Coconut Grove after the first act of *Waiting for Godot*." Now the theater proudly celebrates the fact that the first American production of *Godot* was put on there.

I went back to Wisconsin only once after my Kawaga camp experiences, in the summer of 1941 for an American Student Union camp. It was a radical students' American history camp, and we sang songs like "Joe Hill," the ballad of the charismatic labor leader.

I dreamed I saw Joe Hill last night,
Alive as you and me.
Says I, "But Joe, you're ten years dead."
"I never died," said he.

When I later heard Pete Seeger, standing next to Paul Robeson, sing that song in Philadelphia at the 1948 Progressive Party convention, I started to cry.

2

Progressive Educations: Experimental Schools and Falling in Love

My first school in Chicago—where I was studying when I circulated those John Dillinger petitions—was extraordinarily progressive. The Gateway School provided a very innovative curriculum on the north side in a big brownstone mansion. It was a tiny, wonderful place with only ten or twelve students in each class up through, as I recall, the eighth grade. The year was around 1927, and many refugees had already begun to flood in from Germany and other countries to Chicago. Designers and architects of the Bauhaus school were getting to be known there, as well as various others who would influence the evolution of Chicago as a great architectural, art, theater, and medical center.

I remember going with my mother to the first day of kindergarten and feeling that I was being abandoned when she left me—a terrifying experience. I attended Gateway until the middle of the seventh grade. Sono and Teru Osato, my half-Japanese friends, were fellow pupils, and their upper class Irish-French

Canadian mother, Francis Fitzpatrick, was my second-grade French teacher. A great society beauty and debutante in Omaha, Nebraska, she had married a Japanese photographer, Shoji Osato, who would later be interned in Chicago during World War II.[3]

When I was in the third grade we students organized our own Olympic Games. Our concept was, yes, that you ran and jumped, but you also wore Greek costumes and recited poetry. Then we bestowed laurel wreaths on the best poets and athletes. I can remember Sono, with her long legs, being the best runner, wearing a helmet and carrying a sword and a shield. Gateway was that kind of school, shedding light in the darkness at the height of the Great Depression.

As a student, I had a terrible time learning the alphabet, but I could grasp entire words very quickly. I could not write right-handed. Fortunately, at Gateway they didn't teach penmanship; we wrote everything in print characters that looked the same from the left or the right. But in the public school in Marquette, penmanship was of extreme importance, and there I was considered a dunce. They literally put me on a dunce's stool in the classroom because my penmanship was so bad. It made me physically ill to attempt to write with my right hand, so when the teacher would walk out of the room I would switch to my left. That hardly helped improve their opinion of me. Yet I thoroughly confused them when I won spelling bees—how could this kid spell who could not even write?

I was madly in love with a girl in my class at Gateway. Her name was Priscilla Braun. Her family did not like me and I suppose they had reason. I hounded her. A friend and I saved money, 50 cents a week, for three months until we had enough to buy a radio for her from Carson, Pirie, Scott & Company department store. My friend Billy O'Leary's grandmother had her chauffeur drive us in her electric limousine to the store to make our weekly deposit. It was the only electric car I ever rode in. But when we presented the radio to Priscilla her mother wouldn't let her keep it. It was a crushing blow, but worse was yet to come.

During the middle of my seventh-grade school year, we were told Gateway was closing—it had simply gone broke because of the impact of the economy.

It was terrifying, like being orphaned overnight, because that school was our real home. So we had to enroll in other schools. Like most of the Gateway kids, I went to Francis W. Parker, a private school, heavily subsidized by a woman who was a liberal aristocrat. Parker seemed huge after Gateway. There were probably, on average, twenty-five students to a class, up through high school.

I never found out how and why my parents picked Parker for me, but it turned out to have a decisive influence on my life. One member of the faculty, Alfred Adler, had recently arrived from Vienna. He was distantly related to the famous psychiatrist with the same name. He taught foreign languages and psychology and took a personal interest in me. Many years later, in an unpublished interview with Edward de Grazia, Adler recalled, "[Barney] had a very mature way of talking about things. At the same time he seemed to be gnashing his teeth, in a way, at everything. He was able to enjoy life acutely and also suffer acutely about practically everything."[4]

It was at Parker that my long relationship, so to speak, with the Federal Bureau of Investigation began. In the seventh grade I read George H. Seldes' book on Mussolini, *Sawdust Caesar*, which was destined to play a big role in my government files. It made a deep impression on me. I detested Mussolini. Seldes made it very clear that *Il Duce* was powerful and very dangerous. Subsequently, the FBI reported that I was a "fascist" and an *admirer* of Mussolini. The reason for this outright lie remains a mystery. After years of obtaining documents from my huge file through the Freedom of Information Act, I determined that I was only called a fascist while I was in grade school. They tagged me as a "radical" from high school on—"radical" was much more to their taste.

My FBI files also revealed that the bureau had investigated my high school years very thoroughly. In a typical statement made about me by "DELETED," he or she said:

. . . while attending the Parker High School, Subject absorbed many radical ideals of his classmates and some of his instructors. Many of these classmates were reported to be Communists. As a result of this Subject became a member of the American Student Union, read Communist literature, and entertained thoughts that there should not be any rich men in the world. However, Subject did not himself live in accordance with his radical ideals, inasmuch as he had everything he desired, including a riding horse, a highly powered automobile, and spent money freely. . . . Subject's father is a wealthy banker in Chicago and is very much a capitalist. In fact Subject's actions in this regard have nearly broken his father's heart.[5]

Not quite accurate, but not all wrong—we were in fact quite "radicalized" by the time we were in eighth grade. One member of the faculty, Sarah Greenebaum, who taught us in eighth grade, was a marvelous teacher and a genuine progressive. She was certainly a force for "radicalization." She had us study a version of *Robinson Crusoe* that she had written, one quite different from Defoe's narrative. Crusoe was portrayed as a villain who took money, land, and food away from the people he found on the island after he had been cast ashore. But some people on the island wanted a socialist economic system and they overthrew Crusoe. A few of the kids in my class took this unusual story home and, of course, some of their parents read it and got very upset. They were not pleased that Parker had more than a few faculty members who were, like Sarah Greenebaum, a bit *too* progressive.[6]

During the eighth grade I formed a close bond with another student who would become a lifetime friend, Haskell Wexler. In that grade small groups of students each briefly put out their own newspaper. Haskell and I called our paper the *Sommunist*—for socialist-communist—a name we later changed to the *Anti-Everything*. I had an uneasy feeling that some of the parents were annoyed by that first title. But we persisted in expressing our radical views. Haskell later recalled in another unpublished interview by Ed de Grazia that I impressed him because of my endless curiosity and store of information: "He would know the odds on horses. He was interested in Buckminster Fuller when nobody ever heard of him."

Around the same time, Haskell and I became members of the recently founded American Student Union. I was to be a delegate to its 1937 convention, which was held at Vassar College—and its participants were almost all college students! I rode on a rickety, undersized, chartered bus to Vassar together with another eighth grader from another school on the South Side of Chicago, Quentin Young, and students from the University of Chicago and the University of Illinois. (Quentin later became Medical Director of Cook County Hospital and then Health Commissioner of Chicago.) The head of our delegation was Al Rubio, a charismatic, politically knowledgeable and compelling young man. The lovely coeds in our delegation crowded around him. Al was certainly my role model. (I never saw him again until the Chicago Seven trial in 1969, when his daughter accompanied her husband, who was one of the seven defendants.)

Parker had a deep impact on my thoughts about politics, society, and economics. Quentin Young, in conversation with Ed de Grazia, recalled that "There were several teachers at Parker who were highly influential in shaping [Barney's] mind and, I would imagine, stressing the importance of independent thought." He considered Haskell and me zealots from "a group of students in this kind of private, upper-class progressive school."

But many students at Parker certainly did not share my views or those of Haskell and Sarah Greenebaum. One of them was James Bullock Hathaway— very good-looking and a top student. He started the Liberals Club (today it would be called "neo-Liberal"). We would joke about him and other boys in our class who were his best friends and whose names were unbelievable—one was Stuyvesant Van Buren, another was Benjamin Franklin Roselle. All three had definite social and political aspirations. Bullock and Steve enlisted in the Marine Corps in World War II and were killed early in the conflict. Ben survived after suffering a large number of wounds. I liked all three of them but not for their politics. We had a student government, and at one point Bullock and I were the final candidates to be president. And he won by, I think, one vote! Then I was elected president of the senior class. You couldn't have both positions. So for me, it was a fair tradeoff.

Haskell and I were actively involved in politically left causes. Inspired by the Oxford Movement in England (led by such writers as W. H. Auden), we organized a one-day strike of the whole school every year in April, not on Armistice Day but on behalf of peace, taking the entire student body and all the teachers out of our building to parade—peacefully—through the neighborhood. One reason almost everyone joined in the strike is that they feared they would have become unpopular had they not participated.

Bullock, Steve, and Ben were from families connected to the Daughters of the American Revolution. Quite understandably, their parents got upset when there was any hint of radicalism in the air. But they weren't stupid people, those parents. They probably realized that the Parker "radicals" were not capable of doing much real damage. But that didn't make them any happier about it.

The first two kids in our class at Parker who had cars were Haskell and me. It was not exactly your working-class ethic at its best. We were for Republican Spain; we were pacifists; we were Socialist-oriented, and we held the Soviet Union in high regard. We were critical of the capitalist system, but in an abstract way. It did not, however, make us feel guilty about the way we personally lived. In fact, football was just as important to us as politics, if not more so. Haskell and I were co-captains of the football team in our senior year, and Parker almost won the Private School Football League championship.

As I look back at that period, I think that, despite our wealth, our Parker class was the most radical of all the classes from other years, but we marked the end of the era. The shadows of fascism were deepening, which made life even more difficult for American Communists, whose mentor and Svengali, the USSR, had made an alliance of convenience with the Nazis.

One of the sad things I discovered was that communists, instead of believing in that much flaunted "free love" in which they supposedly engaged, were Puritans to the core. I didn't much like the communists, and yet it seemed to me they were at least committed to doing something. They put everything on the line, said they would do anything to accomplish getting rid of racism, monetary inequality, and various other forms of injustice. Whether it was true or not was another matter. They had been doing the same thing for years and years, in the tradition of American radicalism. However, to be frank, I didn't know anything about the Communist Party other than what I had read.

Many of the things Roosevelt did back then were considered to be communist—and are considered communist today by many on the right. There was enormous animosity against him in right-wing economic upper circles. He was called "Rosenfeld" or "Jewfelt." When Jack Ellison, who later became principal at Parker, was interviewed by the Army about me, he said, "Well, if Roosevelt is a communist I guess you could say that Barney is a communist."[7]

The end of the left-wing student movement as a political force came in 1940. It was a dead end. Communist or not, I was a hedonist, no doubt about it. I was lazy and didn't want to spend all my time with a lot of these Marxists, whom I disliked. And it was hard; I always had trouble being around any large number of these people. They drove me crazy. They were so boring.

Despite the climate of progressiveness and radicalism at Parker, not a single black student was enrolled. I can't understand, today, why we didn't make a fuss about that. I found Richard Wright's *Native Son* so compelling. Why I didn't carry that book's message to our school, I don't know. I didn't speak out about it at Parker or when I went to college. We were reading John Steinbeck's *Grapes of Wrath*, James T. Farrell's *Studs Lonigan*, Meyer Levin's *The Old Bunch*, and some older writers, like Frank Norris. But the bitter evidence of racism that we could see all around us that blighted the lives of black Americans did not seem to sink in very deeply yet. That would change.

A very attractive girl in our class at Parker named Nancy Ashenhurst would soon become a problem, a big one. Haskell and I both zeroed in on her. She was all-around fantastic. She was beautiful and she was everything. She was strong. She wanted her own way. Nancy's method of getting things done was to make the boys who were the most important to other people do what she wanted them to do—help her.

Nancy came from a family of very literary people. Her grandfather was Robert Morss Lovett, head of the English Department at the University of Chicago. It was said that he was, at that time, one of the foremost English professors in the United States. He wrote several books and he attracted a great number of unusual students to the University of Chicago and its English Department—a number of writers like Farrell, Nelson Algren, Vincent Sheean, and John Gunther, who were to become famous novelists and journalists.

Nancy was also a leader, especially in anything to do with the theater. She wanted to be an actress, but she desperately wanted to be a director, which was unusual for a girl back then. She made sure that whenever a play was put on at school she was either the director or at least playing the lead. I acted in plays with Nancy and I did anything she wanted. I was her stage manager, her all-around helper. We staged works such as R. C. Sherriff's antiwar play *Journey's End* in 1940, which Nancy directed. She was not really political but if the only people doing theater were left-wing or liberal, then she was too. And one of the driving forces behind drama at Parker was the American Student Union. We were mostly interested in mounting plays if they had some sort of political message; Nancy didn't care if they were political—she just wanted to put on plays. According to Alfred Adler, Nancy "was able to stage a play better than Mr. Merrill, who was one of the drama teachers at Parker . . . I was quite moved by what this girl was able to do. She was, at the age of sixteen, really an adult."

I wasn't truly devoting my life to political action. Instead, I was infatuated with Nancy and certainly was as interested in sex as politics. More so. Looking back, it doesn't sound so sinful, or anti-Communist. I was in love.

3

Off to College, Off to War

It was because of Nancy that I went to Swarthmore College in 1940 and it was because of Nancy that I left after only one year. Swarthmore is outside of Philadelphia, but my outrageous sense of geography made me think it is close to Vassar College in upstate New York, which Nancy had chosen.

During my year at Swarthmore I almost never spoke to a teacher except for an unfriendly but supposedly radical economics professor and an English professor who doubled as the cross-country running team coach and had also edited a selection of American novels put together in a textbook series. This was one of my first adult inadvertent glimpses into publishing. Though the professor whose course I was enrolled in assigned James Fenimore Cooper's *The Deerslayer*, I disdained actually reading it, having discovered a series of books in the Swarthmore library that contained condensations of most of the books assigned to us. I used these whenever possible and slid through the course that way.

I had gone to Swarthmore expecting to play football but there was no way I could play without my eyeglasses. In those days facemasks had not yet been invented, and when I was in high school I had made my own mask with a metal clothes hanger shaped as a guard for my supposedly shatterproof eyeglasses. However, at Swarthmore, where they were aware that I was a high school football player of some renown, the coach was overtly hostile and refused to let me have my helmet wired up. I tried playing for a few days, but whenever I would attempt to catch a pass—or, much worse, a punt—I simply could not do it. By the end of the first week I quit and went out for the cross-country track team instead.

In track I did better and was easily the best freshman. In fact, the English professor/track coach was the only person from Swarthmore, student or otherwise, who wrote to me after my freshman year, my only year there, asking me to return—but for my running ability, not my literary aptitude. As a coach he taught by example and I admired that. Every afternoon, after class, I would go out and run several miles with him leading the pack.

For me, that daily run was part of a strange routine. First, after classes, I would fall asleep in my dorm room, which I shared with a young Quaker whose surname was Love. It seemed to me that every day I had the same dream. I would be lying in bed and someone would come into the room and attempt to strangle me with his bare hands as I slept. From this recurring nightmare I would awaken and find a release through running. Without knowing it then, I believe that when I ran I was experiencing what was later to be known as "runner's high." At some point in the workout, I would find myself moving effortlessly but fast. It was exhilarating and I looked forward to getting that high day after day.

Our perennial enemy was the University of Pennsylvania, and when I won the Penn-Swarthmore freshman cross-country race that year, a few people actually noticed. My downfall came when we went to another town to race against its high school track team. We had been told that this school had a phenomenal runner, a black kid who was reported to run a mile fast enough to have won at most college meets. They were right. There was no way I could keep up with him. By the time I got to the last quarter mile, he had already finished the race. For the first time, I was not the first-place finisher on our team. I came in last. Having seen a touch of "world class," I realized I was not about to be in that category, ever, and it made an important impression on me going forward.

The demise of my running career and the advent of *Tropic of Cancer* in my life are, curiously, very closely related. I had first read about *Cancer* in Miller's own book, *The Cosmological Eye*, published by New Directions in 1939, a copy of which my parents had mailed to me at my request. What Miller had to say about his father was fascinating. Someone at Swarthmore told me the Gotham Book Mart in New York was a good place to buy *Tropic of Cancer*. So I took the train, went to Gotham, and asked for the book. The owner of this landmark bookstore, Frances Steloff, asked me why I wanted it. I said I was a student eager to read the novel. So she reached under the counter and took out a paperbound copy of *Tropic of Cancer* with "Printed in Mexico" on the cover. The price was, I believe, fifteen dollars.

I never found Miller's novel especially sexy. But it was exciting (if also depressing) because it was so truly and beautifully anti-conformist. My paper for class was titled "Henry Miller Versus 'Our Way of Life,'" and it discussed both *Tropic of Cancer* and *The Cosmological Eye*. My essay weighed whether the American way of life was worth defending, and concluded, reluctantly, that it was. I wrote, "I do not think that we should take Henry Miller's advice too seriously and bomb ourselves out of existence but some of his criticisms are quite valid. . . ." Concerned with freedom of expression in view of the imminent threat of world fascism in 1940, I concluded:

> Perhaps the place of the writer in our civilization is temporarily disappearing. If we become completely Fascistized the writer can give forth nothing creative. Writers must have a liberal society . . . or they are stifled. . . . Of course Miller could not help but feel the sadness and emptiness of the life around him, but of this he said, "Everyone has his private tragedy now. It's in the blood now—misfortune, ennui, grief, suicide. The atmosphere is saturated with disaster, frustration, futility. . . . However, the effect upon me is exhilarating. Instead of being

discouraged, or depressed, I enjoy it. I am crying for more and more disasters, for bigger calamities, for grander failures. I want the whole world to be out of whack, I want everyone to scratch himself to death."[8]

My professor, Robert Spiller, in his quiet Quaker way, commented on my paper, "Perhaps the jaundice is in the cosmological eye itself, not in the world it sees." He gave me a B minus. Mediocre grade or not, that college essay would later turn out to be instrumental during the most important of all the obscenity trials I instigated through the years, about which more later.

When Nancy returned to Chicago to study at Northwestern University I followed her back home, where I enrolled in the University of Chicago in 1941. I was that obsessed.

Every morning I would set off from my house and drive to pick up Nancy, but we never made it to school. Instead, we parked somewhere and necked. This was a foreboding sign. It was as if we had reversed our ambitions and maturity back by three years or so and ignored the future. Looking back, it seems as if Nancy did not wish to start a crippling fight with me by making a clean break, and I was terrified to move aggressively towards her for fear she might thrust me aside. Thus, for months we slowly choked in a sickening miasma.

I saw classmate Bullock Hathaway only once after our graduation from Parker, and that was in the summer of 1941 at what was to be our only class reunion. One of the girls in the class gave a party at the Belden Stratford Hotel, only a block from Parker. I was told Nancy was going to be there and I was very excited about the chance to see her. We had been quarrelling. I was to meet Steve Van Buren at a nearby bar beforehand. He was late and by the time he arrived I had already had several drinks. I was not drunk but I was definitely not sober. It was a lovely summer evening and I wanted so much to have Nancy with me.

At the party, Bullock and Nancy were together. Haskell had gone to California. I was madly excited by Nancy from the moment I stepped into the ballroom. Bullock existed only as a person who had momentarily come between us and was not to be taken too seriously. I did not know how to approach her. I wanted to tell her I loved her. I wanted to shout it out in front of everybody. I told her that she was looking well, that her dress was pretty, that she was a wonderful girl. I also tried to insult her in childish ways. I did not stop drinking and remained suspended in a state of semi-intoxication. I had no basic strategy and as it got later I grew more desperate. I wanted to do something to bring her to me, and at the same time I thought it was impossible. She had not been unfriendly but she remained insulated with her usual calm, and I seemed unable to penetrate it.

When she and Bullock left the ballroom, I followed. Several of us, including Nancy and Bullock, got into the elevator together to descend to the ground floor. When the door opened I tripped Nancy a little bit as she stepped forward. I may have also said something. She had a large purse in her hand, which she swung around with great force, hitting me solidly on the side of the face. I was stunned. Almost blacking out for an instant, I came to with my fists swinging. A blow caught her squarely on the jaw and she flew back against the wall, but did not fall down.

Immediately I realized what I had done and I panicked. The only answer seemed more action and I headed toward Bullock, who was doing nothing, standing on the staircase leading to the front door. I got to him and pushed him down several stairs. Before I could leap after him, several elevator boys, doormen, and friends had hold of me. I stopped cold. My anger dissipated, replaced by a terrible sense of shame.

I had wanted Nancy more than anything in the world, yet I had walloped her in the jaw. Everything was wrong.

Nancy lived a short block away. She and Bullock left together as I was still apologizing to her. Bullock came back, and he, Ben Roselle, Steve Van Buren, and I set out for a bar. Ben and Bullock started quarrelling immediately and kept it up for the rest of the night. I became the peacemaker.

There was no belligerence left in me. I wanted to talk to Nancy, to tell her over and over again how much I loved her. Finally I called her from the bar. I was afraid. I had never conquered the uneasiness I had always felt with her parents, and I did not like thinking about them as I dialed their number.

DIversey-7340 rang a couple times. Mr. Ashenhurst picked up and said, "Hello, Barney. Nancy is all right, don't worry about her."

He had not even waited for me to say hello. He did not sound mad at me. He said that he would tell her I called. And then, "Goodnight."

I turned to my friends at the bar and resumed drinking. I remember later careening down the outer drive with Steve, trying to jump out of the car, pounding Ben on the head with his shoe—all at the same time. Bullock and I kept our truce, but it was just that—a truce.

I never passed a single course or took an exam at the University of Chicago, but I didn't flunk any, either. I got all incompletes. That actually saved me later because it automatically allowed me back into school after the war.

When Nancy decided to try her luck in the theater world of New York, I headed for California and Hollywood. I went to UCLA, with the idea of studying film-making. I also went there to get as far away from Nancy as was geographically possible, because Alfred Adler told me that I was going to die if I did not. This was the same man who, secretly, had gone to Nancy's parents two years earlier and suggested they arrange, in a very discreet way, to vacate their apartment for a weekend so that Nancy and I would find her bedroom a most convenient and natural place to spend our first night in bed together.

For me, UCLA was a desolate place. There I was again totally isolated. My classes were unmemorable except for a psychology seminar, where the professor and I were in solid accord against the rest of the class. He and I agreed that Marshal Tito and his Communist partners in Yugoslavia were fighting the Germans and that General Dražă Mikhailovich, his mortal enemy, was Hitler's ally. Somehow the US Government had failed to notice that then. As a psychology professor, he was very cool, advising us students not to worry about the exam, to take some amphetamines beforehand, and simply enjoy it. This might produce gibberish, he explained, instead of proper test answers, but so what? He was fired. Not only was he the best teacher I encountered at UCLA, he is the only one I remember at all. And I did take the pills.

One day, after months in Los Angeles, a student, Pearl Glazer, came up to me and said, "Haven't I seen you somewhere before?" I said, "I hope so." And she went on, "Yeah, we went to a meeting together in Philadelphia. Must have been 2,000 people. Some kind of a very left-wing thing."

She introduced me to everybody she knew, so all of my first acquaintances in Los Angeles were from Philadelphia, including Joseph Strick, the mildly radical filmmaker-to-be who was studying physics or some science at UCLA. A little later, he married a girl whose uncle, the director Herbert J. Biberman, was one of the Hollywood Ten. They were all very much into the left-wing Hollywood group, who at that time were riding high. They were talented and making money. Later, all were blacklisted, finished. Joe and Haskell eventually made a marvelous film together about Los Angeles called *The Savage Eye*. Ben Maddow, usually a good film writer, wrote the script, which was not good. But if you view this film silently, it's incredible to this day. It showed everything about the real Los Angeles of that era.

Eventually I met other people in Los Angeles, but mainly only offshoots of the Philadelphia transplants. A group of us volunteered to pick tomatoes for the war effort. The farmers hated us. There we were, working for nothing to get the crops in, for the soldiers. We were "premature anti-fascists." It was a weird, weird period.

In the FBI's dossier on me there is a list of books I had mailed to somebody. I suspect that the father of a sorority girl I had met reported on me to the FBI. We were giving her radical publications like Marshall Field's New York newspaper *PM*. She was intelligent but naive and she had never in her life been exposed to anything quite like this. A lovely girl, I really liked her. One day I drove her to Mexico, just for the hell of it. We went for lunch and ended up in Baja California.

By the time we got back it was four in the morning and her family almost went berserk. Nothing "bad" had happened but her father almost killed her, and then she was gone. They took her out of the university and sent her to Arizona.

During the first eight months of the war, when I was a student at UCLA, its reality finally began to sink in. The government came closer to drafting my age group and I had to begin thinking of what I was going to do. I took an ROTC course because it was required. I did miserably. I hated it but I passed. For a while I decided that I wanted to finish college and I tried to enlist in some sort of reserve, which was supposed to enable me to do so. During this time I tried to enlist in the Marines and they turned me down. Then I tried to get into the Royal Canadian Air Force. Same thing, bad eyes. I had even memorized the chart. No luck. Haskell was already in the Merchant Marine. By then, Nancy's search for her place in the theater had proved fruitless and she had returned to Chicago. Was it absolutely necessary for me to go back home to enlist—or was it to see her? Who can say?

So in the fall of 1942 I got in the car and drove to Chicago to enlist in the US Army. I was designated to be in the infantry. They would take anyone who could walk. My father was relieved about my joining the Army. When I suggested going into the Merchant Marine he had objected strongly, saying it was not respectable. But he did not want me to be in the Army either, instead suggesting the Quartermaster Corps. That was the place to be. You might end up in a nice office and learn something. Maybe you could even help a general and travel around with him to quiet places. I did not want to be in the Quartermaster Corps.

After a two- or three-day stop at Camp Grant, outside of Rockford, Illinois, I was deployed to a camp in Oregon to the 96th Infantry Division, a newly activated unit, which was then being filled with new recruits. My train trip out there ended several days later on a cold rainy night on the sidings of

Camp Adair, near Corvallis, Oregon. We stepped down from the cars of the train and slogged through the mud to barracks. I felt alone and miserable.

I spent eight months in the 96th, most of them at Camp Adair. They placed me in a line company of an infantry regiment. Most of the time, I served as a squad leader in an infantry platoon. I lived a double life. I tried hard to be a good soldier but it was difficult for me to adjust to military discipline. I struggled to salute and say, "Yes, SIR." Making a full field pack and stripping an M1 rifle were mysteries almost impossible to solve, but there was help available. Most of the men with me came from the South—if you include Texas, Missouri, and Indiana in that mix. Perhaps ten percent of the regiment was illiterate. It made me truly happy when I was ordered to teach these illiterate soldiers in my off-hours how to read and write and how to sign their paychecks. They, in turn, helped me cope with problems involving my weapon, gear, and other things. I rarely left camp. I read military manuals and learned about intelligence and tactics. I had the potential to become a good infantry soldier, but it never flowered.

My feet were my curse. They were not made for the infantry. I was in above average physical condition when I arrived. I could do everything but march long distances day after day. The more I marched, the worse my feet got. They developed infections and time after time I was dispatched to the hospital, which I hated with a passion. The moment I was admitted I began asking for my discharge and to be sent back to duty, and always managed to get it approved before I was really healed. One day I marched until one foot was swollen so badly that my shoe would no longer go on. The next day I wore galoshes, with a shoe inside only on my good foot. The day after that I was sent back to the hospital.

I gained a certain amount of respect from the officers for my persistence, but my performance was badly hindered. My best skill seemed to be in solving tactical field problems involving single squads. My squad was as good as any, not only in the company but maybe even the battalion.

While I was still at Camp Adair I got a letter from Haskell. He had been torpedoed off Murmansk and returned to Chicago, where he was warmly welcomed and praised. After apologizing for not having written to me right away when he returned home, he explained that, after he survived his ship's being torpedoed, his ongoing service in the Merchant Marine had taken him to warmer regions— and another torpedo attack. He wrote me:

> We were up in Egypt for a month. Saw a little of the Nazi aircraft, met with our allied soldiers and airmen and had an informative and rip roarin' good time despite interruptions. We unloaded up there incidentally, so when we were banged in the ass off South Africa we were empty—much to the sub commander's chagrin.
>
> This letter is for a special purpose and not to let go with a wild west story about our exploits. Nancy and I are going to be married next Saturday. We're going back to the coast and in a week or so I'll be shipping out again. That's it in a nutshell.
>
> Except for a couple of things: the nature of my work, my political convictions make it important for there to be a deep comradely spirit between husband and wife. Nancy and I have not yet reached this point but she has developed marvelously and shows a sincere interest in the labor movement. This development I know is due primarily to your influence.

Haskell also phoned to tell me this. There I was, stranded at Camp Adair, in the Army. The news struck me dumb. It put me into a catatonic state. I had been writing to Nancy regularly from my lonely outpost in Oregon and she had never once given me a hint. I thought they were making a terrible mistake in getting married and I said so. When I called Alfred Adler in the middle of the night to break the news, he simply predicted the marriage would not last. He took the news in what I thought was a very nonchalant way of dealing with such an important problem. But he also later wrote that

Barney and Nancy would not have had a good marriage. No, not at all. He would have pushed her around. He wanted to force her . . . to have certain leftist interests that she didn't have. When Mao Tse-tung appeared, Barney said, "That is something! You should get yourself interested in it." And I found that rather childish.[9]

Adler's prediction about Nancy's marriage to Haskell proved to be accurate. I don't know how many years they were together but it was long enough to have two children. After their divorce, Nancy went back to teach drama at Francis Parker. I don't really know what happened there, but I believe she was asked to leave; I think everybody thought it was very sad. Although Haskell called me when they were about to be married, he didn't when they were getting divorced. On the other hand, he did call me on the day she died in 1952. There is no doubt that my star-crossed relationship with Nancy had a profound impact on me and my relations with women during the rest of my life.

In Oregon, I maintained my lifeline to home. Late at night, in the incessant rain, I would leave my barracks and trudge to the phone booth to call Chicago. Then I would wait for an hour or two until the call was put through. This went on night after night. My father began promising me things—and I asked for them. He was going to have me transferred, he was going to get me to a better climate, into Officer Candidates School (OCS), anywhere but where I was. Sometimes I resisted his proposals. On one day I was determined to stay and fight out the war with my company. The next day I wanted out.

Three possibilities shaped up. I could get placed into a limited service group and finish out the war as a technician of some sort; I could go to OCS; or I could get into the college Army training program. But as much as I hated the whole mess, I refused to abandon the Army.

I wanted badly to go to an OCS but there were few openings. My father had a friend at the White House, Charles K. Claunch,[10] who could work minor miracles, and he worked quite a few of them on my behalf, or on my father's behalf. The Quartermaster OCS was one of the last still accepting new candidates and I, fortunately, was one of those selected. I reported to division headquarters where, within a few hours, I appeared before a board of approval and moved over to the Quartermaster barracks. Ironically, it was with real sadness that I packed my barracks bags. Only later in China would I come as close to being an integral part of a group when in the Army as I had been in that infantry company.

While I was waiting for my orders to go to the Quartermaster training center in Camp Lee (now Fort Lee), in Petersburg, Virginia, I secured my license to operate large trucks. I enjoyed that part of the work. We moved both personnel and materiel from Oregon up to Washington by road convoy. I had bought an old car, an Oldsmobile convertible, which had been garaged in Chicago, and I took it to OCS with me. I could only use it on weekends, but what an asset it was. I found myself going into town more frequently. Though I tried to escape at night to find a neighboring town where other soldiers weren't hanging around, I never was able to find one.

My first days in OCS were a nightmare. I was convinced I could not get through it. I was unprepared, had hay fever like never before, causing my eyes to swell shut when I was asleep. I had to stumble to the latrine in the mornings to get hot water to pry them open. But after I got through this first difficult period, my hysteria subsided. Maybe there was a chance for me after all. What work demanded mental skill was simple, and as for the physical military demands on me, this was ground I'd covered thoroughly in the 96th Division. I concentrated on staying in the background. The hay fever made seeing and breathing a continual torture, but my foot problems had prepared me for that kind of ordeal. I could accustom myself to suffering a little more than those around me.

The weekends were unexpectedly pleasant. I had never before been in the South and I did not expect a good time during my off-moments. I was proven wrong. We were allowed to leave camp Saturday afternoon and did not have to return until Sunday night. The first weekend I went to a USO dance in Richmond, and in an unusually easy manner for me I met a native Virginian girl, the first I had ever known. While she came from a very genteel family and had been properly brought up, she was willing to kiss and drink and provide a little affection. That was all I needed to forget the camp and school for a while.

Our early North/South antagonism ended up as self-mocking enjoyment. I learned that there were some nice white Southerners. My problem was that I found two of them—one prettier, warmer, more intelligent, and less racist than the other. But each week I changed my mind as to which I preferred and of course thereby lost them both.

My father and his White House friend, Claunch, were busy working on my behalf in the interval of time I had free before reporting for my first orders as an officer. I did not want to serve in the Quartermaster Corps. To me, it was part of the pencil-pushing war. Because of my early interest in motion pictures, I had hazy ideas about making films, but I did not know exactly where films were made in the Army. My father began making inquiries. Eventually his (and my) maneuvering worked out. I was transferred to the Signal Corps.

My first major stop was Boston. I went there on a 60-day loan from the Photographic Center in New York. I reported to the film distribution center of the 1st Service Command, where I had to learn something about film distribution. I started by taking a course in how to run and service projectors. My homework was to read manuals on film distribution. I lived in a fine hotel in Boston. Life picked up, especially at night.

When the course ended, I left Boston reluctantly and found myself spending 60 days of temporary duty in my first film library building, at Camp Patrick Henry, a high-security embarkation camp back in Virginia. The library, which housed training films covering everything from basic infantry tactics to how to avoid getting venereal disease, was a gloomy shambles. A lazy sergeant and a WAC were my helpers. It was like starting OCS. I wanted out.

But this time things went better. Film distribution was organized on a vast, competitive basis in the army. Each service command was rated on the number of film showings it held per soldier. I was sent to show films in camps that had been doing badly. I thrived on competition, and I did a good job. I reorganized my library, managing to make many improvements in all of its functions, and was proud that my camp shot up toward the head of the list for the country.

The Signal Corps Photographic Center next placed me in their school in Astoria, Queens. The heads of the school were a little baffled by me because, compared to my fellow students, I had no experience or technical knowledge. The other students seemed to be unusually informed about directors like Frank Capra and John Huston—and some actually knew them personally. The place was riddled with politics. Big shots' sons abounded. The Hollywood atmosphere at the school, which had once been the home of Paramount Pictures, had penetrated everything.

First I was assigned to a still photography class. I was always two jumps behind the other officers, who had been professional photographers in peacetime. But I was not criticized too severely and I quickly acquired some skills. It was nice living in New York. I had my Oldsmobile and a suite, directly over a nightclub, at the old Belmont Plaza Hotel on Lexington Avenue.

The school started a new motion picture class, and my little group of officers was enrolled. We were taught cinematography on a very simple level. One important thing the teachers insisted on was that a single static view of an object does not give it film life. You have to see it from a distance, from a medium view, and up close.

Technical problems beset me as usual but I was learning the things I most wanted to learn. We were sent on picture-making sorties, sometimes on our own, and other times in teams of two or three men. One day I shot film at a Coca-Cola bottling company. Another day I took shots of trucks being loaded on ships. Several times I went to Central Park to photograph seals in the zoo and pigeons. I also was assigned to film at Coney Island.

Being almost completely literary in point of view, I did not really know anything about the visual world. I knew little about painting or composition. Now I started to understand the power and wonder of visual media. I wanted to know all about films—but up to then my method of learning was to read about the subject.

One of the things I liked about filmmaking was the immediate connection you had to your work. You took your camera out, photographed a story, and two days later saw the result on the screen. And the idea of editing was appealing—being able to sit in a room and handle the material without having to go out and be in contact with people: you could play with them without their interfering. Editing promised to be the best end of the business, but the school taught us very little about it. We were being trained as field camera crews. The film would be edited in the United States at the studio. So we were left to editing within our cameras, a skill that would later inform my work at Grove Press and *Evergreen Review*, as I mentioned to friends more than once over the years.

One of my instructors at the film center, a lieutenant, was particularly annoying. He was very neurotic and was supposedly suffering from shell shock after a tour in Italy, which was probably true. One time I sat in his office for several hours waiting for my daily story assignment. The morning was almost gone when he finally told me to go out to a swimming pool and photograph whatever was going on there. It was not even being used. I was disgusted by this useless assignment and made it obvious. He was furious. He had his revenge; only a few days later I received my orders for overseas duty. I was not really disturbed by this; I wanted to go. The school gave me a mark of "satisfactory" in my record—the worst I was to receive as an officer.

My embarkation camp or "staging" area was about ten miles from Marysville, California, and it was a bleak hole. Far inland, the camp was like an oven in August. I hated it—and I hated the waiting. Waiting is something that you spend a lot of time doing in the Army.

Finally our outfit was put on alert, but I did not know where we were going. We were to board the train without being told our ultimate destination. I had already decided we were headed for China, although there was no evidence to support my notion. I just wanted to go there. My copy of Edgar Snow's *Red Star*

Over China was always with me. Then one of the men in our shipment found out that the train was being stocked with provisions for a week. We were certainly not going to a town in California. After a train ride that seemed to last years, though it was really only about six days after we left Northern California, we came to a final stop in a camp in Virginia where, after a week of cooling our feet, we were pushed aboard a ship loaded with 2,000 or more troops.

We still had no idea of our destination, and our voyage was a particularly bad one. Twelve of us—ten doctors and two photographers—were crammed into a minute cabin without portholes. The tension steadily increased for over three weeks. I was extremely irritable but some others were even more so. A young doctor, one of my bunkmates, lost a card game and threw the cards all over the floor of the cabin. I told him he was a crazy bastard. He lifted his fist and tried to wallop me in the jaw. That enraged me but I did nothing more than hold onto him until some of the officers who were in the cabin with us were able to stop the fight.

The voyage went on for forty days, down the Atlantic to the Panama Canal, across the Pacific and the Equator, and around Australia, and on to India, where we finally made port in Bombay. I got off the ship for an evening furlough before we officially disembarked, and lapped up as much whiskey as I could. When I got back onboard I was drunk but happy.

4

China:
The Forgotten Theater

We disembarked in Bombay. The trip by train across India was somehow beautiful and sometimes sad. About ten of us, almost arbitrarily assembled, went from Bombay to Calcutta in four days. The coaches were divided into five classes: I, II, III, Intermediate, and IV. Our coach was class IV. It had wooden benches and was stiflingly hot, but I didn't notice the discomfort. I liked India. I tried to learn Hindustani words out of a guidebook and practiced them on little children who ran up to the train. I stared out at the villages, at the women kneeling beside flat baskets filled with rice and bananas, and suckling babies who would never get enough milk. At one stop when I was on guard duty—we had to watch out for thieves—the train's conductor and its engineer invited me into the station for a cup of tea. When we returned to the platform the train was gone. However, the next train, which we boarded, somehow caught up to mine, and I was able to resume my guard duty post without my absence having been noticed.

After traveling for four days and nights, we awakened one morning to find ourselves on a desolate siding in the middle of nowhere. The heat was *unbearable*, but still the five psychiatrists who were in my group were afraid to get out and look around—without orders. So, along with a homeopathist who by now had become my friend, I left them in the train car and walked down a dirt road lined with very tall coconut trees. A number of coconuts dropped to the ground within a few feet of us. Then we spotted the "perpetrators," monkeys, who were throwing them at us. The enemy barrage was sustained for several kilometers until we stumbled, quite accidentally, on our new camp—a US replacement camp, thirty miles outside of Calcutta.

Camp Kanchrapara was a sweatbox. We were to stay there, living in uncertainty until our individual assignments came through. We lived in tents and ate horrible food while camp commanders invented things for us to do while we bided our time. Way too many men stationed here sweated each day and froze each night as jackals stole our shoes from our tents and rooted in our garbage.

I sneaked away as often as possible to Calcutta, where there were incredibly elegant brothels occupying some temporarily vacated palaces. One Indian girl, a successful courtesan/prostitute, became very friendly with me. I took her out to a film one afternoon, a highly unusual venture for an American officer. The English civilian audience included a goodly number of dowdy middle-class English women who seemed a bit disconcerted by the sight of me and my consort, in her elegant but understated sari. Earlier, I had photographed her putting it on aided by two extremely helpful English women who were her daytime servants in her suite at the palace/brothel.

Finally, orders came for me to report to the 164th Signal Photo Company in New Delhi, our company headquarters for China, Burma, and India (CBI). Officers here lived in better quarters than they did in the States. The food was good. There were big hotels and social functions. However, New Delhi reminded me of Washington, DC, and I didn't like it any more than I did its American counterpart.

The 164th had one unit in China, another in Burma, and a third in India for the entire CBI theatre. When I arrived in Delhi, rumor had it that one of our officers in China had committed suicide so I volunteered to replace him. The war had been progressing very badly for the Allies in Southern China and it looked as if there might have to be a mass evacuation. I wanted to get there before it was too late. It was my chance to engage in what for me was the compelling part of the war. Edgar Snow's *Red Star Over China* was getting closer. They printed my orders, and I packed.

After waiting at an airbase, a steaming hole, for two days, I boarded one of the ungainly, underpowered C-46s for the plane ride over the Himalayas to China. Taking off from Assam, India, for Kunming, my unit's Chinese HQ, in December of 1944, I was still a raw, semi-trained second lieutenant in the Signal Corps Photographic Service, twenty-two years old and with only a few dreams to cling to. Squashed under the weight of my equipment, I struggled onto the airplane and sat on the metal floor next to some uncommunicative Chinese soldiers. I leaned back in the curve of the bare fuselage, hugging a heavy parachute, which was a totally foreign object to me. We were in a death crate, a hulk of a cargo plane barely sustained by two undersized motors. As we puffed oxygen through our masks, the planet's highest mountains glowered beneath us and loomed on both sides.

As we reached our destination, behind the door of the cockpit, the third red-alert light shone as we descended, a sure sign that Japanese Zeros were tailing and using us for cover as they bombed the runway. On landing, I scrambled from the airplane into the night's bewildering disorder—no contacts, no commanding officers, no what-to-do-next. My GI parachute stayed on the runway where I dropped it and ran. Somehow I arrived at a dimly lit, wooden shack crowded with Chinese patrons drinking hot yellow rice wine. Apparently, I had left the Kunming air base. The next thing I remember was waking up with a hangover in our outfit's billet, the headache rendered irrelevant by the fact that I was in the China of my dreams.

The 164th Photo outfit was small and it shared a hostel in Kunming with another non-photo company. Our commanding officer was a Bostonian with traces of culture and sensitivity. It was quickly obvious that he wanted to get me out of Kunming to fill the hole in the lineup as expeditiously as possible.

Other than the rumor about suicide, I really never learned how or why the deceased officer whom I had come to replace had died, and my instinct was not to probe. He told me the 164th was sending me to Kweiyang (Guiyàng), the other end of the line. He did not tell me very specifically what to do or how to do it. I was provided with a weapons carrier, which was a small but sturdy four-wheel-drive truck, some equipment and supplies for a still-photo field laboratory, a co-driver who was a young American GI, and written orders directing me to Kweiyang.

Having my directive, I drove eastward on the only road, unpaved, toward Kweiyang, the capital of Kweichow (Guizhou), the adjoining province and a main place of concentration for Chinese civilians fleeing before what still seemed to be the oncoming Japanese army. I named my weapons carrier "Foto Moto" and painted the name in large letters on the front radiator. The truck was the equivalent of a big strong mule, not nimble but willing, and I was literally driving it toward the oncoming Japanese.

Or was I? What nobody said to me my last night in Kunming, and what was most likely not known, was that the current Japanese offensive had halted just short of the outskirts of Kweiyang, circling part of the city from the East, North, and South just as I was rolling in from the West. Going in our direction there was no traffic to hinder us. It turned out to be an historic moment in the history of the Sino-Japanese War, marking, I believe, the deepest penetration into China by the Japanese during all of World War II.

Arriving in Kweiyang after a dizzying ride on dirt roads and hairpin curves, I went to the main American enclave. It consisted of the remnants of a beautiful inn, plus odds and ends of additional buildings. In it was an incredible concentration of Army brass—at least seven West Point grads, all of them full colonels and a one-star general. What they were doing there I never really learned.

As if they had expected me, Chinese servants wearing the white jackets of another era took my gear and escorted me to a small, second-floor room whose paper-parchment walls barely made it to the ceiling. On the rafters there was a continuous noisy, and often visible, traffic of rats. I spread my sleeping bag on the bed, which filled most of the room, and went out into Kweiyang.

New Year's Eve, 1944. The dirt streets were crowded and lively with an air of hope and desperation. There were rumored to be Chinese bounty hunters in the crowd, paid by the Japanese to pick off Americans, but my thoughts were not of them. There was space in my parchment-walled room at the inn for a girlfriend whom I had only to find and lead back. And I found her! We had our own New Year's Eve, feeling, holding, and experimenting. The fact that we were almost completely surrounded by the Japanese seemed to make no impact on our celebration.

In the morning I discovered we had an audience on the other side of the thin parchment wall. A certain Father O'Donaghue, Catholic priest and Maryknoll missionary, had heard me sin. My Irish Catholic mother's influence made me erupt in shame, but the good father heard my silent confession and absolved me. He would remain a staunch friend throughout my time in China.

I was trying to figure out how to put together a photo lab in Kweiyang when I came across a rather thick pamphlet lying in the dirt. It was a manual, not new by any means, published by the US Navy. And, miracles of miracles, it contained detailed, easily understandable instructions on how to build a photo lab under field conditions.

Soon after my arrival, I made a new friend, Meredith "Muddy" Rhule, who was an American naval officer in the Office of Strategic Services (OSS). The Chinese OSS people whom he commanded were situated on both sides of the Japanese lines—shuttling back and forth on search and destroy missions. Muddy was a stocky, fearless, bull-necked cop from Springfield, Illinois. He also had been a professional wrestler and a sharpshooter before his demolition training.

Rhule trained his Chinese demolition teams to act with precision. Their mission was to penetrate Japanese-held areas and destroy anything of potential value to the Japanese Armed Forces. Now we had to destroy weapons in order to keep the Japanese from using them against us. With Rhule I became a sort of unofficial OSS man, without the knowledge of my HQ or his, helping him get his men to their areas of operation and then back to home base. I covered many miles of Chinese roads with Muddy Rhule and his cadres, all the while doing unofficial and unpaid work on behalf of the OSS.

Perhaps it would be appropriate to say a few words here about why I was rejected by the OSS. This is something I didn't learn about until many years later when, through the Freedom of Information Act, I was able to access files and learned I was being investigated even in 1945. Here is a report by Lt. Bordwell ascertaining whether or not I was a good candidate for the Secret Service:

FOIA Document #25
[In CIA Ltr OTO 8/29/75 this is Document 177.]
MEMO OTO 2/27/45 According to CIA Cover ltr OTO 8/29/75 this is "Released."

HEADQUARTERS
OSS SU DETACHMENT 202
X-2 Branch

MEMO:
FROM: 2nd Lt Paul H. Bordwell.
TO: LT (jg) Arthur H. Thurston, USNR.

1. It was requested by Major Harding that I make an inquiry re the wire from Washington on 2nd Lt. Barnett [*sic*] Rosset of the 165th Signal (Photo) Co.
2. On the morning of the 27th of January I called on his commanding officer and frankly told him why I wanted to know the whereabouts and availability of Rosset. His commanding officer was most obliging and gave me a rather complete story on Rosset.
3. It seems that Rosset is a 22 year old officer who in most instances seems to act round about the age of 17 rather than 22. He is not particularly mature. It also seems that his father is some New Deal "bigwig", to quote the CO, and that this attempt to get him into OSS has been going on for quite some time. . . .

4. At present Rosset is in charge of a Field Photographic team consisting of himself and several enlisted men, operating out of Kweiyang. At the immediate writing, Rosset is strictly speaking not available due to a shortage of personnel. However, three or four additional officers are in the process of being shipped in, in which case, the CO is willing to release Rosset.

5. From a personal point of view of his CO, Rosset certainly would not be fitted for any intelligence work. One, he has had no experience whatsoever; two, he is far too immature, and three, he does not impress you as being too intelligent.

6. In summation, from his CO's point of view, it might be said that the said officer is under the impression that the entire scheme is one of "dirty politics."

Instead of taking me into the OSS, they suggested in another memo that I be transferred to another photographic unit.

Now the Chinese followed the Japanese—who were self-propelling themselves back home, toward the East. My Signal Corps Photo team's job was to record this strange retreat. Apparently, Chiang Kai-shek held to the dictum of the ancient philosopher Sun Tzu, who wrote in his *Art of War* that the acme of skill is to subdue the enemy without fighting at all. There were supposedly 20,000 or more Chinese troops with mobile artillery "pursuing" the enemy, yet a few Japanese soldiers with machine guns held them off again and again.

One night in the middle of a burnt-out village, Corporal Cedric Poland, a truly invaluable member of our photo unit, and I stopped at a desolate, destroyed road intersection to sleep. We tied our hammocks between the jeep and its trailer. Occasionally, in the darkness, we could see ghostlike figures moving around in the ruins of the buildings but nobody came close to us.

Hordes, literally thousands, of rats scurried directly under our hammocks to cross the dirt road.

There had been rumors of Japanese re-infiltration. Nervous, I began keeping my gun very close to me. We had not eaten after we stopped. I had brought along a large number of cans of fruit, and stood shirtless in the hot gloom, wolfing down some pears. The place smelled of death.

Morning light brought reality with it. The homeless wanderers who meandered through the refuse no longer looked like Japanese soldiers. We started off, looking for the most forward American liaison team. On one stretch we found perhaps twenty dead Japanese cavalrymen and their horses. They had either been ambushed by guerrillas or strafed by the 14th Air Force—both groups later claimed credit. The open areas were covered with growing corn, and it was perfectly quiet. It was almost like being on a dirt road in Iowa in the summer. Only the stench of the dead ruined such daydreams.

Bridges became increasingly difficult to cross. They had been destroyed and then repaired in the flimsiest fashion. Poland and I were thankful that we had switched to a lighter jeep, having left "Foto Moto" back in his stable. We came to a town that we knew was very close to the front. It had once boasted a British consulate whose roof was now gone, and with one fallen wall that exposed the remains of the rooms. A few other buildings were intact, but most were smashed and debris blocked the streets. We crept forward, got stuck, backed up, and slowly made our way through town. The people were gaunt, and they hardly seemed to notice us, although we knew that not many Americans could have preceded us there. Eventually, we made our way to the US Liaison Team's headquarters located in a half-battered-down house on the town outskirts.

There we were informed that, the day before, an American inspection team made up of an American colonel, a Chinese colonel, a Chinese interpreter, and an American captain had arrived in a jeep wanting to see the front. The liaison team warned these sightseers that they were already very close to the Japanese, but the American colonel had not been impressed. He wanted to see some fighting, so they set out in their jeep again, looking for Japanese along the unpaved highway to the last point held by Chinese regulars. A Chinese squad leader tried to stop them, but no Japanese gun positions were in sight, and no one heard any gunfire. Ignoring the warnings, the colonel continued on.

Another jeep drove up to our little group. In it were Teddy White, the famous *Time* correspondent, and a *Life* photographer. They seemed happily relieved to see us and we sat around in the broken-down little courtyard. There was one embarrassing moment for me, though, since before he had been identified, I asked him, "Do you know Teddy White is coming?

He replied, "I am Teddy White."

After talking for a time, we all started out for the place where the inspection team from Washington had last been seen.

We arrived at their last known position and made no further progress for two or three days. Water had to be boiled in big gas cans, and the day's heat was compounded by the fires. I was filthy. My clothes clung to me, and it was a tremendous effort to shave. At night we listened to the Air Force radio, which was powered by hand pumping.

The Air Force liaison officer and his men rode with Poland and me in one jeep, while White and his photographer followed us in theirs. We had passed more burnt-out bridges but nobody was around and we saw no jeeps. A burnt-out building stood to one side of the road, and a little stone shed was on the other. Rice paddies ran up to the side of the road, bordered with damp gullies. Mountains rose a few hundred yards off to the side. We got out of the jeeps and looked for farmers to talk to. At the foot of the hills were a few small villages. The first one was completely deserted. The Japanese had lived in it; we found scraps of uniforms and rifle cartridges. Narrow pathways ran between the mud buildings. The enemy had just left. Maybe he still lurked around the corner.

Cy Poland was an absolutely reliable and extremely capable soldier, and most amazing of all was that he was a cousin of my old Chicago love, Nancy Ashenhurst. Anyway, Cy went back with his two or three men and me to where the jeep had stopped and examined the nearby building. I walked into the barnlike structure and immediately a horrible smell washed over me. There was a pile of straw in one corner. A hugely bloated, burned corpse lay on top of it. I couldn't tell if the body was Japanese, Chinese, or American.

We decided that the shreds of uniform left indicated that it was Chinese. Then we left the area and drove back to our temporary camp. We had found a body, but we had not found our missing men. We probed further the next day, but White was no longer with us. He had gone back to Kunming in order to send his dispatch back to *Time*.

The rest of us stood in a little group on the road and there our search ended. One of the men kicked at a pile of dirt in the gully, and suddenly a cadaver was uncovered. Maggots swarmed over the face, and the skull was almost completely devoid of flesh. A few feet away we found another corpse in the same condition. Poland and I photographed the remains.

Trying to make identifications, we decided the first was the Chinese interpreter, and the second the American colonel. As it turned out, we were wrong. The American colonel and his aide, an American captain, had been captured alive. We gave our film to the infantry liaison people and moved on. A week later the missing American colonel wandered back into an outpost. He had escaped, he said, but the captain had not.

Shortly after these events, I wrote a letter home from Kweiyang on quite another subject. An incredibly sad one it was:

April 14, 1945

The news of the death of President Roosevelt came as a terrible shock yesterday. It was just about the worst news since the war began. I think that Roosevelt was the greatest American since Lincoln, and if ever the world needed him, it is now. Truman is faced with a tremendous responsibility and I hope that everybody co-operates with him. . . . The news of the tremendous advances against Germany continue to flow in and it seems impossible now that the war can last much longer in Europe.

While FDR did not live to see it, the end of the war was getting closer. Every night we pitched our hammocks a little farther down the road as we headed for the big city of Liuchow, which had once been the site of the biggest American airfield in China. As we neared, Chinese troops encountered a small number of entrenched Japanese. But the Chinese did not seem eager to engage the enemy at close quarters and contented themselves with firing at the enemy position with artillery. Had the Chinese commanders made a real push they could have prevented some of the damage the Japanese were doing to the town and its people. But the generals were taking no chances with their personal safety.

We felt compelled to make a move. Didn't the saying "save face" start here? By deciding to walk toward the Japanese, we thought, we might shame the Chinese into following us. Stilwell had done that when crossing the Salween River into Burma, but Stilwell was a four-star general who knew what he was doing. We believed the Japanese only had small arms and we could walk quite a way before moving into their range. A railroad track cut across the area in front of us, on a rise, providing cover almost up to the Japanese entrenchment. It was an extremely hot day, and we did not want to carry any unnecessary objects, including weapons. A little while later I was most sorry we had left them behind. The Chinese glared at us as we walked nonchalantly out, but they said nothing. Soon we were between them and the Japanese. We came to the railroad tracks and halted. Once past the tracks, we would be within range of the enemy rifles. However, thick foliage on the other side of the tracks hid us as we crossed. We raced over the top of the abutment and into the trees on the other side, creeping cautiously for a few moments, still advancing on the Japanese.

Then bullets began cracking over our heads. We dove into tall grass and stopped dead. We did not know if the shots were meant to hit us or not, but began to wonder what exactly we were doing. We didn't have so much as a penknife among all of us. The Chinese could no longer see us and had no idea how close to the Japanese position we were. A Japanese soldier could have easily strolled down and put us out of our misery.

Next morning, the way was clear for an Oklahoma Sooner dash into Liuchow. We got up very early in a drizzling rain and learned that the Japanese had abandoned their position and Chinese scouts were setting out to explore the road. Our decision was made. This had to be it. My photographers, including the Air Force officer and me, hurriedly packed up and moved out. We caught up to and passed the lead element of Chinese scouts. No consultations now. We could see the hill was empty and we did not want to be stalled. The flat surface of the airfield soon appeared in the distance, surrounded by a barbed-wire fence. Here we followed the wire until we found an opening. The remains of the building installations were on the far side of the enormous field whose dirt runways were pitted with four-foot-wide holes. Glancing down into one of these holes, I thought it looked as if the Japanese had dug them with the intention of putting mines in them and then left without completing the job.

The July 9, 1945, issue of *Time* magazine featured Teddy White's report on the recapture of Liuchow, which was now a horrible, terror-stricken shambles. Few buildings remained intact. Fires smoldered and death hung heavy over everything. Very few people were in the streets and those were literally in a daze. A large river bisected the city. All of its bridges had been destroyed. We drove along the Liu River's edge, photographing the destruction. We found a family huddled in the center of the road. Two little children lay there, apparently near death. Their parents had been shot in the legs. Through a combination of words and gestures, they told us they had been attacked by the Japanese. Unfortunately, we had no medical resources and could not even give them rudimentary treatment. I hoped that we might find someone who could help them, but looking around at the destruction everywhere made me realize there was little possibility of doing so.

We needed to cross the water to get to the main center of town, and a boatman offered to take the four of us in his small sampan. A crowd on the other bank stood waiting for their great American liberators, namely, us photographers. Waving flags, they cheered at the edge of the boat landing. The Chinese slapped us on the backs. Disillusion had yet to set in. That would take a few days.

The first night back on the airfield was uneasy, but nothing happened. In the morning we explored our surroundings. The wrecks of several planes were neatly lined up in a bay adjoining one runway. The Japanese had lived up to their reputed cleverness. They had camouflaged destroyed American fighter planes to look like Japanese Zeros. Their ruse meant to draw fire had worked; these decoys were riddled with bullet holes and torn up by American bombing and strafing.

The next day a captain from the Corps of Engineers and an enlisted man landed in a little L-5. The captain had not been out of the plane for five minutes before he discovered the first land mine. In fact, his plane had passed right over it when it landed. We were dumbfounded. The Japanese had planted American fragmentation bombs with detonators everywhere. We followed the captain and he pointed out the ugly noses of one frag bomb after another. He walked to the edge of one of the holes, but stopped before he got to the lip. A bomb was planted there, too. The Japanese had expected us to do just as we had done, lured by our curiosity into mortal danger. The enemy had purposely left their excavations empty and positioned mines in the loose dirt around their brims.

The captain and his helper set to work clearing off a strip for future landings. They crawled on their stomachs up to the mines and softly brushed away the dirt. Then they attached fuses and lit them one by one to destroy them. We photographed the first few attempts, but retreated when the fuses started sputtering. I jumped into the jeep and drove it more than a hundred yards away. One of the mines sent shrapnel screaming past my ears even at that distance. In the end, it turned out that there were thousands of mines on the field and it took weeks to clear them. I returned by plane to Kunming with the exposed film, remembering I had earlier looked down into one of those holes and feeling grateful I had not set off a mine and been killed.

I was recommended for a Bronze Star. Then the citation was disapproved by Lieutenant General George E. Stratemener. I have no specific idea who I might have annoyed. Does it happen very often that a recommendation is annulled? I do not know, but it was nice to be recommended. I thought what I had done was very reckless. I didn't know any better, I had acted spontaneously. Nobody told me about mines. What does a photographer have to know about landmines?

5

"The Liberators": Shanghai and the Return Home

From Liuchow an Air Force plane flew us to Shanghai, a place I already knew through dreams—it was my secret Chicago. I had earned the right to go there after dodging cholera and malaria, after slogging through the mess created by the corrupt and crooked Chiang Kai-shek regime. We landed in a drizzling rain at a Japanese-held field and three of my 164th photographers and I were taken to a Japanese-driven pickup truck parked on a runway. The war was still on but it was with a new script. I had switched consciously from Edgar Snow's version, *Red Star*, to Malraux's *Man's Fate*.

Standing in the open back of the truck, the four of us were driven into the city. There was nobody to be seen for blocks. Then we began to notice people in the streets, gawking at us and, as I gradually realized, cheering—we four in American uniforms, standing in the rain, represented again the US liberating army. The truck took us to the Bund, the waterfront area of Shanghai, to the

Cathay Hotel—one of the most beautiful hotels I had ever seen. Outside the Cathay, Bubbling Well Road and then Nanking Road were lined with people who applauded as we entered the hotel. The Japanese manager met us in the lobby. I was in a fog, dazed by this strange transition in a war that still had a few days to run. The manager led me to my suite, knocked, and an imposing Japanese officer in an immaculate white uniform answered, bowed to me, and left, turning over his luxurious suite to a twenty-three-year-old American lieutenant.

On the day before, I had slept on an airfield in the cholera-stricken heat bath of Liuchow. Now with the press of a button I was ordering trays of Canadian Club, ice and soda from room service. Out on Bubbling Well Road the girls were walking arm in arm, while American officers were still imprisoned in the YMCA practically next door and would be kept there for at least a few days to come. The latter were delighted when we brought bottles of scotch to their cells. But we were free and they stayed in jail.

We were invited to a party at a Soviet club. It was a dinner in a richly appointed hall with a portrait of Stalin at one end and Lenin at the other. There were many beautiful women in attendance. As the night progressed, I found that most of the Russians there, many of whom were Jewish, didn't like Stalin or Lenin, for that matter. At the end of the evening, I asked one of the girls if I could take her home. She pointedly told me to watch out for the German Jewesses I might meet in the ghetto. They were all prostitutes, she warned.

I had learned that perhaps 20,000 German and Austrian Jews were still confined to a ghetto, now known as the Shanghai Ghetto, not far from our hotel. The next day we stumbled on some of them at an afternoon dance/picnic they were holding in Hongkou Park. They stared at us and at our American uniforms as though we were apparitions, and we were equally shocked to see them. Within what seemed a short time a young man came running up to me with a small package that he insisted upon giving to me. It was a Rolleiflex camera still in its original box. I think he must have returned to the ghetto to pick it up. The band stopped playing and we found ourselves joyously embraced by men and women, young and not so young. A short while later we heard a voice call out from the podium, "Break it up, it's curfew."

"No more curfew," I said, "the war is over." My new friends were not quite convinced.

I picked out one young woman, Ilse Hammer, a very attractive, dark, German Jewish girl from Berlin. We went and sat on a bench together, defying the curfew at dusk. The streetlights lit up, and along came a tall, turbaned Sikh rifleman in the International Settlement Police, a vestige of British Rule that the Japanese had maintained. This was the test. My new friends and we Americans, shaking, watched as the Sikh strolled up. He saluted me and said, "Good evening, Sahib."

He hadn't tried to arrest us, he merely wished us a good evening. The constabulary already recognized their new clients.

It soon became apparent that Ilse was also adaptive. A former law student from Berlin, she unlocked Shanghai for me. Despite the curfew maintained in the ghetto, she had made the French Concession her domain, her special place, that chunk of Paris where one drank at turn-of-the-century bistros on the Avenue Joffre.

I was definitely more fascinated by her than disapproving. Ilse made me think of Valerie, the temptress in Malraux's *Man's Fate*, which was set in Shanghai. But who then was I? Sometimes I was her lover and protector. At other times, I was waiting, anxious and excited, for her to return from some unexplained rendezvous.

"Tony" was Ilse's Shanghai name. She worked at the Roxy, a somewhat disreputable nightclub, as if there could be such a thing in wartime Shanghai, located on Tongshan Road alongside several other little nightclubs. The club was set back from the sidewalk, in a clump of trees. Its small electric sign was scarcely noticeable. A clean paved walk led up to the door, where a turbaned Sikh doorman stood. Inside, a long hallway led to the main part of the club. A bar was partially enclosed in a niche in the far corner of the room. A three-piece band softly played old American tunes almost constantly. A small dance space was carved out from the nest of tables and a few couples were sometimes dancing. It was not crowded.

The night I met her, Tony was sitting at one of the tables waiting for someone like me. I asked her to join me. She led me over to a booth in the quietest part of the room. Her low-heeled shoes and simple beige dress seemed made more for a walk through the park than this dark nightclub. Her hair fell down over her neck in a thick wave, softening her slightly sharp features and giving a touch of tender youthfulness to her big sad eyes. The dark rings under them were not noticeable in the smoky air. I liked Tony, very much.

A voluptuous young blonde sat by herself in a corner. Tony said that she was her girlfriend Trudy. The music stopped and the musicians retired to the bar and Tony's friend came over to our table. At three in the morning an American marine sergeant entered the club and announced that the closing hour was approaching. For the moment, he constituted the honorary and complete military police force of Shanghai. After spending the war in a Shanghai jail, he had been released to the heaven prepared for all good Marines. Nobody took his warning very seriously and he downed two shots of rum before shaking hands all around and leaving.

Tony and Trudy began talking about themselves. They were Jewish refugees from Berlin. Shanghai was the only port left open to them when they fled Germany before the outbreak of the war. Tony was not so eager to talk about the past. She had just entered law school in Berlin when the professors began their diatribes against the Jews. She had tried to ignore the problem, but it began to be impossible. One day she insulted a teacher. Her friends, including the head of the school, smoothed things over while she packed her books and left. After that the problem was how to leave the country. Her mother was not willing to go: Germany was her homeland, and she owned property there. Tony's father, separated from the family for years, wrote from Switzerland, constantly urging her to leave. There was a friend, the son of a rich shop owner. They decided to get married and escape together. Hans was still a boy, but it was easier for a married woman to travel. They took a train to Italy, and at the German frontier they were searched—and robbed—by the German frontier guards. It was a battle to get on a boat, any boat. However, their honeymoon voyage was provided, free of charge, on a luxury-style Japanese ship that took them to Shanghai, the only port they knew in the world still open to them, from an Italian port on the Mediterranean.

The Italians and especially the Japanese operators of the luxurious tour ship were friendly and cooperative.

In Shanghai, Hans became a drummer in one of the bedraggled little nightclub bands, but his mind never left Berlin. Tony started out as a salesgirl in a store, and then the jobs were gone. She had to join her friends in the bars, living off commissions on drinks, and whatever else one felt it necessary to do. Tony divorced Hans after a year in Shanghai, but she said he kept coming to her with every new problem this jungle of a city threw against him. She spoke unemotionally about her mother. It was almost certain that she had died in a gas chamber, but no letter ever came to clarify the past.

At closing, it was pouring rain outside. The bearded Sikh was still standing on the walk. Tony and Trudy and I emerged into the night, the two women with their bicycles in tow. I asked if they wanted pedicabs, the rickshaws pulled by bicycles. Trudy said no and, wishing us a good night, rode off. Tony and I waited a moment for a soaked, bare-legged pedicab driver to pull up. Tony took the bike she had and put it on the pedicab and off we went.

Back at the posh Cathay, Tony stood in the middle of the large bedroom, making no move to take off her dripping, shabby raincoat. I tried to comfort her but suddenly she was crying. She said she had to leave. It was too late for breakfast. She could not make a date. If I wanted to come to the Roxy, that was my business. She worked there. I took her back downstairs to her bicycle. It was still pouring, but she did not hesitate to go out. We stood in the rain while she unlocked the wheel of her bike. Then I asked her again: tonight at six in the lobby of the hotel. She said maybe and swiftly pulled away from the curb and winged down the Bund, past lines of sampans and steamers tied up at the docks. I saw her disappear over a bridge, standing up on the bike, peddling determinedly and naturally.

The next afternoon the American brass was beginning to arrive. Several colonels were standing at the hotel desk waiting to be assigned rooms. They wore combat boots and carried carbines slung over their shoulders. I walked to a big chair near the street entrance and sat down. Probably Tony would not come, but I could not give up hope.

Painted, pretty, white Russian girls sauntered in and out. Some had just said goodbye to their Japanese friends; all of them were picking out their American officers. Allied internees, fresh from the detention camps, pushed timidly in, as if they were still not quite sure that freedom was legal. I saw barbed-wire fences and years of enforced boredom stamped on their thin faces.

At a quarter past six, Tony arrived. Her light cotton dress and flat-heeled shoes made her look strangely and pleasingly out of place in the luxurious lobby. She pulled the bicycle with her and there was a shy smile on her face. I put my arm around her waist as we walked out of the hotel into the dying August day. A badly spelled sign was going up between the Cathay and the hotel near it. WELCOME VICTORTUOUS SEVENTH FLEET.

Our pedicab was like a hansom going through Central Park. Shirt-sleeved crowds flowed along beside us in rickshaws, bicycles, automobiles, and on foot. Nobody was in a hurry. The office workers were going home. The International Settlement was free, and the atmosphere vibrated with relief and indolence. As much as I had thought about Shanghai, through the eyes of Malraux, I was not prepared for the blocks of semimodern structures, the broad streets, the great enterprises. The Fiaker Restaurant to which we went was Viennese. Big photographic panels of Vienna lined two walls of the quiet, half-empty place. A waiter carefully drew the cork from a bottle of dry white wine.

In my imagination I could see Tony in Vienna, lost in a fairy dream at the opera, and later holding her father's hand in a café, sipping hot chocolate covered with a cloud of cream. Tony had no desire to revisit her bad memories of what had happened in Vienna, but she took a photograph from her worn wallet and put it down in front of me. A tall dark man held a little girl at his side. The paper was yellow and frayed, but the German script was still legible. The last words were "*geliebte* Ilse" ("I love Ilse").

Now it was good to leave the restaurant and go out into the city. With the whole night spread out before us, we walked along the boulevard in the warm, yellow-lighted evening, watching the twisting and rolling shadows cast out by the heavy old bicycle at our side.

On the roof of the Cathay there was a cabaret with an open-air terrace. We sat up there leaning on the railing, flush with the top of the sky, Shanghai pancaked beneath us. The lights of Bubbling Well Road and the Bund intersected each other. Small lamps flickered from sampans on the river and the British racetrack etched out a black oval in front of the Park Hotel, nearby.

Once in my room adolescent modesty disappeared. We undressed and embraced. Love was gentle in the humid half-dawn. There was a feeling of closeness and wakeful peace.

At six or so she moved away from me and I watched her through half-dreaming eyes as she pulled the cotton dress down over her thin, lithe body. Then she came over to the bed and kissed me, in a soft rubbing way, across the mouth and cheek.

She was gone before I could pull her back. But after that she would stay the night. We didn't have to go to the Roxy, where she had had to urge drinks on me and colored-water cocktails on herself.

Shanghai was made even stranger by the mute corps of stylish, surprisingly tall, white-uniformed Japanese soldiers, who drifted around zombie-like. One rainy night, cycling alone, downhill along the waterfront, my newly obtained bicycle spun out from under me and I landed hard on my back. I looked up from the wet brick road to see a large company of white uniforms surrounding me, faces regarding me with blank, inert hostility. I rose nervously and remounted my bicycle in this enemy throng, which slowly and uncertainly parted as I began to roll. I picked up speed and crossed the Waibaidu Bridge, on my way to meet Tony.

One day the US Army G-2 colonel attached to the Chinese Combat Command gave me a welcome task—to help a US Navy lieutenant commander seize evidence of the collaboration of Chiang Kai-shek—Chancre Jack—with the Axis. Some Italian seamen who had fought on the Loyalist side in the Spanish Civil War, then been jailed in Shanghai after reaching there by ship from Spain and were now released, had occupied the Italian Embassy. I quickly collected my photographer's case full of Signal Corps microfilming equipment, bedrolls, carbines, and a bottle of whiskey wrapped in a towel. My photographers and

I joined the Italians in that embassy for three days and nights, reassembling and photographing the shreds of documents that Mussolini's fleeing diplomats left behind. The Malraux environment still enveloped me.

In late October the phone rang in my suite at around 4:00 a.m. and an American officer's voice instructed me to be downstairs with all my possessions in one hour, for transport back to Kunming.

I was ordered to return to New York via India. In shock, I woke Tony. One hour! I gathered everything I owned, including two Chinese bicycles, a treasure in and of themselves, and sacks of Japanese occupation currency. I then took Tony downstairs and got her a pedicab. I heaped clothes, all the money I had, and the bicycles on top of her. And only then told her I was leaving—now it was shades of Humphrey Bogart and Ingrid Bergman's *Casablanca*. Tony and I parted, only this time the roles were reversed. I was stunned and confused.

Auf Wiedersehen, Shanghai.

This time there were no bombs dropping on the Kunming runway—the war was over and I felt like a postwar casualty. I had run into a wall higher than the Himalayas which lay just beyond. My Burma Road had reversed itself. I felt bruised and abandoned.

At least the Chicago Cubs, *my* boys of summer, were in the World Series, a solace for me if I could only find a shortwave radio in our compound. Across from two low stonewalls at the end of a large parade ground stood a radio shack. I was starting alone across the field on that dark October night when machine guns opened at both ends, shooting at each other. Tracer bullets lit up the landscape. I was hunched in that exposed position when I saw an oh-so-welcome GI truck, with its four double wheels in the rear, sitting in the middle of the field. I crawled under it and lay there all night. As always, the Cubs lost.

Kunming was under curfew due to the antics of Chiang Kai-shek's henchmen, but the next night I "liberated" someone's jeep, an unusual act for me, and found the bar/brothel, Girls of All Nations, outside of Kunming. In a desperate mood, I got one of the Girls from one of the Nations and drove her around aimlessly, from large roads to small roads, then off-road, and across a field, finally making love to her on the cold ground at the bitter dead end of my China journey.

●‿

Shanghai Dec 21, 1947

Ilse Hammer
674/59 Tongshan Rd.
Shanghai 18/China

Dear Barney, what a real surprise your X'mas card had given me. I was pretty sure that by now you completely had forgotten about me. It quite flatters me to know, that occasionally you remember me.

It might interest you to hear, that by March of the next year I will enter USA for good. I think that San Francisco will be the first port I am going to be sent to. If I can find a job there in the first week, I may stay otherwise my community will send me to some smaller city.

There are not much news to tell. Right now I am working at the 9 floor of the Cathay-Hotel (you remember?) the place is named the "Tower". You must have certainly heard about the silly exchange we have here. For one American Dollar you get now Shanghai Dollar 160.000—CNC, soon we will have to count in millions again like the time you had been here, while we had still Japanese money.

It has become very cold lately, and all I am dreaming about is a heated room in Frisco and a nice bathroom with hot water all day and night. But I am sure that those dreams will come true soon and that makes me a bit warmer already.

It would be nice to hear a little more about you, what are your plans? Are you married already? If you don't find time to write to

Shanghai to me, you can always write to San Francisco "Hicem" that is an international organization.

I wish you a very merry X'mas and happy New Year also for your family.

Do sometimes remember,

your Tony

Yes, Tony, I do remember you! For the rest of my life, I will remember you, my Ilse, my Tony.

The trip home from Karachi in December of 1945 took twenty-two days. Our ship, a converted luxury liner, was the sister ship of the *Lurline*, the small but elegant cruise ship that my parents and I had taken to Hawaii in the winter of 1937. It was quite pleasant compared to the miserable forty-two-day voyage out the year before, even though, after crossing the Indian Ocean, the Red Sea, the Suez Canal, and the Mediterranean, we ran into tremendous winter storms in the Atlantic. A Christmas we had anticipated spending at home was improvised at sea. Nevertheless, the atmosphere was light, almost gay. We were on our way home.

When we ran into colder weather I stuck it out with my khaki uniforms. I would wear one suit for several days and then heave it overboard. I knew I would be leaving the military and by getting rid of them I lightened my baggage and my mood.

We reached New York at dawn December 29, 1945. Many of the men got up early that morning and stood on the deck in the gray light as the ship turned toward the harbor. Still down in my cabin, standing at the porthole, I watched the Statue of Liberty loom up out of the dark. I stared at the old icon and cried.

Soon a small boat drew up alongside ours. Peering at it down below in the fog, I saw a woman standing on the deck before a microphone. She began singing, accompanied by either a record or a small orchestra concealed from view. I do not know what she sang, but it made me cry again. For a second we were a boatload of conquering heroes, back from the war.

The sky grew lighter and I went up on deck to look at Manhattan. The skyscrapers seemed isolated from their moorings, floating like ghost ships in the sky. The piers jutted out into the black, solid waters. Then I saw the signs painted on the ends of the piers, and on their sides, and splashed on buildings overlooking the water—WELCOME BACK, JOB WELL DONE.

A speedboat approached our ship, its occupants waving at us. The light was still rather dim, but in a few moments I was certain that two of them were my parents. I waved, but they didn't see me. As the other soldiers learned that my parents were aboard this little boat, they tried to point out where I was standing. To my acute embarrassment, this went on for several minutes, but finally they saw me, and we waved back and forth.

The ship bumped to a stop against a pier, and we went back to our cabins and completed the odds and ends of packing. The feeling of excitement and release had returned. The porthole in my cabin was quite close to the gangplank. Looking out, I saw my mother. She looked so much older. For a moment, I felt sick, hurt. Orchids and a mink coat could not distract from the impression of how much her face had aged.

Not expecting to leave the ship for some time, I was delighted to hear my name called out. I was to report to the gangplank. The officer there had orders to let me pass. He checked off my name as I shouldered my val-pak and disembarked.

I was officially and completely back in the USA.

After embracing my mother and dad, we started down the pier. It was the meeting of those who had been apart for a long time and yet it oddly seemed as if I had just come back from a two-week vacation. The way they met me was very special, but otherwise everything was the same. We hustled to the exit and into a waiting limousine. My father told the major, to whom we were giving a ride, what a great guy I was. I was happy, uncomfortable, and bored, in that order, after thirty minutes in New York. I learned it was the former fire chief of New York who had fixed things with the Transportation Corps people for my swift debarkation.

Dad wanted me to go back with them to Chicago—that evening. I did not want to go. There was nothing for me in Chicago. I knew nobody there whom I wanted to see. Nancy had been taken from me long ago. The only girl who cared about me was in New York—Gale was a Southern girl I met in the spring of 1944 in New York. She was the first woman I knew who really enjoyed sex, without inhibition. We had had an affair, intervals of intimacy over a long period of time. She had come out to see me in California just before my long train ride and embarkation for duty overseas.

My mother agreed with me: it was silly for me to go rushing back. I felt more relaxed with her than with my father, more able to talk about personal feelings. Yet whole areas were blocked out. In the end, it did not occur to me to tell them to leave without me. So I went with them, back to Chicago.

On New Year's Eve going into 1946, I had barely been in Chicago for a day. I didn't know exactly what I would do that night, but I did want to be with somebody I could associate with my past.

The only person available to fill that role was my old Parker school classmate Benjamin Roselle, who had been wounded numerous times and had been written about in the *Saturday Evening Post*. Ben had lost part of a leg while fighting with the Marines on one of the South Pacific islands. I learned that he had come home from the hospital shortly before I arrived, so I called to see if he wanted to go out on New Year's Eve. He did. He suggested that we pick up Lucia Hathaway, whose brother, Bullock, had also been our classmate at Parker. Ben, Bullock, and Steve Van Buren had been inseparable friends since grammar school. As I said before, of the three, only Ben had survived the war.

I didn't know how to dress for the evening. By law I had to wear my uniform until I was discharged. I did not have many decorations. There were two overseas stripes on my sleeve and a few ribbons, one of which had two battle stars. Not wanting to present myself as a war hero to Ben, that New Year's Eve I didn't wear any. I was thankful that I did not because Ben wore none, either, not even his Purple Heart.

There had not been any real closeness between us during our high school days, but an emotional finish to the baseball game played between the junior and senior boys on "Field Day" had sent us off to college with a feeling of warmth and friendship. The game had ended when Ben banged out a hit, bringing me home with the winning run.

Now I was to meet Ben at his parents' apartment. They received me very warmly. We talked about Ben, who was still getting dressed. His mother told me people were amazed at how well Ben was doing. They had expected to see their son buried. Their joy at finding him alive, if barely, had not worn off. Then Ben came in. He looked very tall and heavy in his unadorned uniform. It was hard for me to relate him to the Ben of our high school days, but before long he had resumed much of his old, familiar identity. He was cheerful, and not overwhelmed by his injuries. My uncertainty about how to talk to him dissolved.

Lucia Hathaway lived on the same street, one block farther from the lake. The streets were icy and it was not easy for Ben to navigate. I was pleased that Lucia was going out with us, but I dreaded seeing her family because I didn't know what to say about Bullock. Mr. Hathaway opened the door and greeted us. We walked through the dining room into the living room, where the Christmas tree was still standing. Mrs. Hathaway was waiting for us there. She called to Lucia upstairs.

Then suddenly I noticed something in the dining room. It was completely dark except for one light, which illuminated a life-size portrait of Bullock in his Marine Corps uniform. He seemed to jump right out of the wall at you. The Hathaways' hopes for the future were enshrined and entombed on their dining room wall. It had the atmosphere of a chapel. Mr. Hathaway took me gently by the arm and led me up to the portrait. I mumbled things about the picture, about Bullock, anything that came to my mind. Mr. Hathaway started talking. I have no memory of what he said. I only knew that I should be quiet, graceful. I wanted to get out of that house. Its air was filled with death.

Lucia came down. Her face was beautiful with big, glowing, dark eyes. Her black hair was combed close to the head. She was as quiet as ever, but full of life. I liked her immediately.

I had no idea whether or not to wish the Hathaways a Happy New Year. Do you give salutations to people in mourning? We escaped down the front steps. I was surprised that they had been so warm and so eager to share Bullock's shrine with me as one of his companions. I could never escape the feeling, when I was among the faded aristocracy of the Midwest, that I was an alien Jew. But when I was with the upper crust of Chicago Jewry, I felt equally alienated.

I wondered how to treat Lucia. I felt my being alive was an insult to her dead brother whom she had loved so much. I could not talk about Bullock with her. It was as if I were afraid he would punish me from the grave through her.

At our favorite bar, the Tin Pan Alley on Rush Street, we toasted the New Year. Lucia, Ben, and I did not have much to say to each other. We just drank and tried to be funny. Finally, we took Lucia home, and Ben and I continued on alone.

A feeling of belligerence began growing in me when I returned to Chicago just a day or so earlier. Civilians seemed hostile. The war was over and they were tired of soldiers. But I still hadn't been discharged and I had to stay in uniform. I felt surrounded by enemies in every bar. I wanted to explode. With Ben at my side I could walk down the street and snarl because he was at my side. No civilian could cast aspersions on him because he had been so badly wounded.

Now, at the end of the night, I felt weak. The fury had drained out of me. I was angry at being back in my father's house, at being in the military, at not having a girl, at being an inferior being. But now I was finished for the night. Happy new year, soldier. Welcome home.

6

Joan Mitchell:
The Beginning

Soon after my return from China, I again dropped into my favorite bar, Tin Pan Alley. Huddled in one corner, playing wonderfully, were the blind pianist and singer Laura Rucker and a great old jazz drummer named Baby Dodds (whose memoir of coming up the river from New Orleans I would later publish in the first *Evergreen Review*). At the end of the narrow bar there was a staircase, and that night I saw this attractive girl walking down the stairs from the ladies' room.

She was Joan Mitchell. The moment I saw her I knew I was going to marry her. I knew immediately that she was the one who could choke off any flames that might still be flickering for Nancy. All I remember is that I went up and I spoke to her and that was it. A few days later, I started asking her out.

I had known Joan in high school but had paid little attention to her at the time because I was a few years older and very infatuated with Nancy. Still,

I admired Joan, followed her skating career, and was aware she was a painter. I didn't really know her well, but she was always there in the background. When she was in the tenth grade, I took her to see *Citizen Kane*. I also tried to make her more receptive to radical political ideas.

Joan was a great athlete, and she was pushed by her mother to become a figure skater. Although she did not have the grace and agility of a ballerina, she did become one of the two or three best young skaters in the country and spent many hours practicing at Lake Placid, New York. This took her away from Parker a good deal, which aggravated the school's faculty tremendously.

In fact, almost none of the teachers at Parker liked Joan because she was definitely difficult. She was very abrasive towards the teachers, openly critical. When she did happen to be around, Joan was an instigator of trouble. The Parker teachers wanted to throw her out. Fortunately there was an art teacher who thought Joan was a marvelous art student. He recognized her talent. He stood up for her, protesting vehemently. He won out, and she stayed. Alfred Adler, our foreign language and psychology teacher at Parker, later recalled, "She became a very different kind of person after she left Parker for college, more likeable, more sociable."

Joan's family lived two blocks from where my family ultimately lived. Both of our parallel streets dead-ended a block north on North Avenue. Between us lay the elegant and grandiose home of the Catholic Archdiocese of Chicago. Her family lived in an apartment with a view of Lake Michigan. "I carry it around with me," she said later, and her paintings are full of water—water by turns calm and chaotic, like her life.

The Mitchells were a wealthy and well-known family. Joan's mother, Marion Strobel, was the daughter of Charles Louis Strobel, a major architectural force and, along with Louis Sullivan and others, a pioneer in the use of steel in building construction, which made it possible for the new generation of world-famous architects just coming into their own in Chicago in the 1890s to use steel and stone in combination, now a common practice in modern architecture. His work was crucial to the construction of Chicago Stadium, which lasted many years and was the only stadium in Chicago.

Marion Strobel was involved in so-called high-society, and at the same time she was an esteemed poet and an editor of *Poetry* magazine as well as a close coworker of *Poetry*'s founder, Harriet Monroe. She knew many important writers and poets, from William Carlos Williams, who wrote a poem for her, to Karl Shapiro, who later, at her insistence, was the editor of *Poetry* for a period of time. The fact that he was Jewish impressed me. Karl also wrote the introduction to *Tropic of Cancer*. Another editor of *Poetry* was William Jay Smith, who was of American Indian heritage. Like Shapiro, he became a friend of mine. He introduced me to Jean Genet and Grove would later publish the selected writings of Jules Laforgue which he edited.

Joan's father, James Herbert Mitchell, was a dermatologist from a small town in Illinois, and he had become quite famous in the Chicago area. He had high connections in the Presbyterian Hospital, then the fanciest in Chicago. (He treated Al Capone for syphilis.) Eccentric and cranky, he was a very nasty person in many ways. Joan told me that he kept bottles of gin in with her underwear and was constantly slugging from them on the sly. Still, she spent a lot of time with her father, who took her to the Art Institute from an early age and painted watercolors with her. He was cold, and as demanding and competitive as her mother, who I always felt did not like me because I was Jewish and therefore persona non grata.

In 1942, at sixteen, Joan entered Smith College. She left after two years to study full time at the Art Institute of Chicago. She spent the summers of 1945 and 1946 in Guanajuato, Mexico. In Mexico she met the painters David Alfaro Siqueiros and José Clemente Orozco. You can see their influence in her painting at that time. I went to Mexico in 1946 and drove her back home, speeding down hot, two-lane highways. We stopped at grungy motels and dim cantinas, then crossed the border and pushed north through the lushness of the American Midwest.

My love for Joan was not like my love for Nancy Ashenhurst. I did not have the same mad, wild longing for her. But Joan was an exciting and talented artist, sexually sophisticated, an achiever, and someone I wanted to make my life with. New York was where we had to be. Joan wanted to study Abstract Expressionism with Hans Hofmann (she would attend one class with him and never go back). And I wanted to go into films. So I moved to New York in January 1947.

My sad, beautiful childhood friend Teru Osato had been diagnosed with cancer, which was to bring on her death within not too many weeks. She asked if I would like to take her apartment in Brooklyn by the East River, next to the Brooklyn Bridge. I agreed immediately and asked Joan to move from Chicago and live with me when she finished her term at the Art Institute. She said yes. I don't know how shocked her parents were by anything she did. She had always been a free spirit.

(From Chicago, Joan to Barney)
February 10, 1947

I love you and your drawings and your letters [. . .]

I started a tremendous painting because life was so wonderful too and I dreamt about you all night and found it difficult to sleep—(the pillow kind where it almost became you and then is only a pillow) and I kept remembering the Saturday I spent at 1540 similarly half awake only you weren't a pillow and the fucking, oddly enough, I remember only as a side line—I miss you terribly—much more than 2 weeks & 3 days worth and at times I feel turned inside out and there are no substitutes at all for Barney—the rank and file has nothing to offer in this case [. . .]

Why do you mean so God damn much to me—not why but what in the hell am I doing away from you [. . .]

Of course I'll be your Valentine—it was a nice Valentine—but none of this one-sided stuff—you have to be mine [. . .] I want to be really happy—I'm sick of missing you—write me more—draw me more pitchas [sic] and be my Valentine.

In June of 1947, Joan graduated from the Art Institute and was awarded one of its traveling fellowships. She was planning on going to Paris, but postponed the trip until the following year and settled into the Brooklyn apartment with me. Helped by Francine Felsenthal, a friend from the Art Institute, she took the station wagon I had borrowed from a filmmaker and moved all of her belongings to Brooklyn.

In New York, her painting would develop toward Abstract Expressionism, inspired in part by the work of Wassily Kandinsky and Arshile Gorky, later by the work of Willem de Kooning, Mark Rothko, Franz Kline, and Jackson Pollock. She spent most of her time visiting galleries and museums, notably the Museum of Non-Objective Painting (later the Solomon R. Guggenheim Museum). She was also caught up with me in the production of the film I would go on to make, *Strange Victory*.[11]

The following June of 1948, Joan left for Paris, sailing from New York on a Liberty ship, the *S. S. Ernie Pyle*—a ten-day voyage. Staying with friends, the artists Zuka Omalev and Louis Mittelberg, she explored the city until she found a studio on the Rue Galande in the fifth arrondisement. The small Left-Bank atelier overlooked the Greek Orthodox Church of Saint-Julien-le-Pauvre and Notre Dame, on the other side of the Seine.

(From Paris, Joan to Barney)
July 5, 1948

Schmuckie darling—
    Je suis ici and very confused—very lonely—very lost—and lots & lots of french poodles—all sizes— [. . .]

My room is tiny but beautiful—Tomorrow I look for a studio—I'm exhausted—didn't go to bed last night—went to a party or rather a "salon" [. . .]

it's all so confusing—but two beautiful letters from you—write me there for a while (To me)—I live in Montmartre—right Bank—surrounded by black market Arabs— . . .

Your letters—what can I say—I love you—I miss you—and maybe I'm just homesick or maybe I've just never been in this position before and maybe it's good—maybe too it's difficult to bridge gaps with people and maybe I'm not so dumb as I feel—but one doesn't go around here with an inferiority complex or any complex at all I guess and one isn't an American if one can help it— [. . .]

I must learn French quickly—I must start painting—I mustn't feel so damn inadequate— [. . .]

I think tomorrow it will all be filled with moons & stars—I think it must be only first day displaced depression—there's much that's like Mexico here— & Havre was the first reality of war I had seen—horrible in the dawn [. . .]

It's tomorrow night—that is Saturday and today was better—in fact Paris is beautiful—I saw all the things one is supposed to see— [. . .]

God—no one knows Orozco or Kollwitz or Posada [. . .] —they know Klee sort of—Paris is provincial in a way I guess— [. . .]

Chauvinism here is very subtle but there is much—subtle in the sense that one is expected to be a female woman—as well as the pants & smoking in the street things—and strangely enough here you think of N. Y. as the center of art—everything modern really is there plus things like Kepys butter & American coffee are essential—the people are so poor—I didn't expect it—where are you—I love you so much—and I think it's worse being here without you than in New York—It's not a city to be alone in—I suppose I must be strong like all these other people—but fuck—I hate seeing Zuka & Louis together—I hate going to bed alone—and here too I walk along the street with my puss in the air looking at the studios (whole blocks of them) and wishing we lived in one— [. . .]

Miss me un peu—I can't imagine loving anyone else—ever—& my love to your ear—

Juana

⬤ ⬤

(From Paris, Joan to Barney)
July 9, 1948

Darling Schmuckie

Christ how I'm missink [*sic*] you—really—at times life at 1 Fulton St seems like a dream—Gluton [our cat]—you & the bridge—it doesn't seem real—like it happened—and anyway you make up your impression of a place starting with the person you love and building around it. How was Nancy—J'ai peur de cette fille—tu comprende—you fucked—no you necked—well a little—no no—which makes me think of Gale—of N.Y.—of you—when please will S.V. [*Strange Victory*] be finished—you must have seen the first print by this time—good?—of course—what I'm asking is when will you be here—I'm lonely—and writing you makes me think of it more and I don't want to think of it more because I don't know why I came in the first place and I haven't all this Promethean strength one is supposed to have and I don't know what to paint next week because I guess I'll begin then and there are no bridges and God I wish you were lying against me now, warm (it's about 45° here)—just being real. Really Barney I don't feel whole without you, something's gone and I keep looking up and down the streets for it—what have I done—lots & little I guess besides rereading your letters at every other café. . . I didn't get in the Momentum show which doesn't surprise me.

Maybe the paintings weren't finished enough. I don't know—sometimes I'm no longer sure if I can paint [. . .]

Right now I'm cold—where are you Schmuckie—why can't I write you what I'm thinking. I think so much of the war when I'm not thinking of you—of people with courage & no stockings, of the collaborators that are all over now, of the confusion [. . .] Sometimes I think something will happen to you and I get frightened—sometimes I think I'll wake up and find you and feel you—and make eggs & bacon & English muffins—and then I think I'm spoiled—but really spoiled and feel guilty—but still the reason for things is gone when I remember that there's nothing to come home for and no one to take a bath for and no one to be bitchy in the morning for. Bring blankets. And how is Sager [Dr. Clifford Sager, my psychoanalyst for many years] & Gluton and the other gulton—soft & sleeping among the holes in blue shorts—

I love you darling—& don't be depressed like you sound—just finish the thing and come quickly and we'll go swim in a blue sea—& fuck on yellow sand—without your letters I'd go crazy—bush is crying—J.

I went to see Joan in Paris for the month of August 1948. I took my new Jeep station wagon with me on the plane, loaded after an all-day nightmare. Then it was back to New York to get *Strange Victory* on its rocky road to an opening.

Another period seemed to end. I had wound up my film, and there was a new life with Joan, America was heading into a war in Asia, and a blanket of suspicion hovered over the country as the Cold War slammed down a barrier between the Soviet Union and the United States. Anyone with a radical background was threatened with exposure and persecution. It was a good time to get out. At the end of the year I would follow Joan to Europe.

7

Partings and Beginnings: Joan, the Hamptons, and Early Grove

In Paris, after Joan and I returned from a miserable trip to Prague, where we went to sell the rights to *Strange Victory* at the end of 1948, I watched Joan's paintings become more abstract and more violent. She was doing good work in abominable conditions. Our studio was freezing. It was impossible to heat. We both had colds and later Joan developed bronchitis. Paris in summer was delightful, full of sunlight and flower and leaf; in winter it was like a dreary gray cell with a view. The only warmth came from Joan's paintings: views of the river, the bridges, figures, and interiors of the studio. Still, our days were punctuated by coughs.

Finally Joan's bronchitis was serious enough that I took her to the American Hospital in Paris. The doctor advised that she move south. I was delighted. We packed up. I knew where we were going—straight to Provence, a place called Le Lavandou, where we sublet a villa from our friends Sidney and Joan Simon.

There was time for a trip to Spain in the spring of 1949, where, at my absolute insistence, we visited Guernica, the setting for Picasso's great painting. We were depressed by the condition of the country under Franco even though we had expected it. The Guardia Civil was everywhere, along with ragged peasants, aging prostitutes, child delinquents, and gorgeously dressed members of high society. I had been too young to join the Spanish Loyalists in their defense of Madrid in 1939 but now I was able to offer up feelings of adoration for those like Ernest Hemingway and Paul Robeson, who had joined, and above all, my greatest love and grief for my most revered heroes, the International Brigade.

We stayed almost half the year at Le Lavandou. Joan was painting nonstop, moving into her own space, increasing the size and brilliance of her work. By the end of that time, we decided to get married and return to America. Soon after our wedding in Le Lavandou on September 10, 1949, we sailed for New York. The long stay in France had been an important transition for us both.

In New York we went straight from the ship to the Chelsea Hotel, where we stayed while looking for a place to live. The Chelsea was a beautiful building on the outskirts of nowhere—West Twenty-third Street between Seventh and Eighth Avenues—and had been and was still the place for poets, composers, and artists of all kinds to live, congregate, and express themselves.

Residing there at that time were such people as the documentary filmmaker Robert Flaherty and the composer Virgil Thomson, who had encouraged *Strange Victory* by suggesting composers and instrumentalists. A bit later the independent filmmaker Shirley Clarke ensconced herself in a group of former maids' rooms out on the roof, accessible from a fire escape. She filmed *The Connection*, Jack Gelber's play, which was produced by Judith Malina and which we much later published at Grove. And Maurice Girodias, the French publisher who was to play a big part in my life, was later a longtime tenant.

Joan and I finally moved into our first Greenwich Village living space, 267½ West Eleventh Street in late 1949. If you walked from our place to Hudson Street and crossed you ran more or less smack into the White Horse Tavern. That site gained much fame, a bit later, because of the nightly presence of Dylan Thomas, the greatly talented Welsh poet who died "from a massive insult of alcohol to the brain" at St. Vincent's Hospital, only a few blocks away. It took him far too short a time to achieve the necessary saturation to kill himself. The Irishman Brendan Behan, whom I got to know, publish, and regard with real affection, followed Thomas step for step, succumbing to the same trap as his fellow artist.

Our apartment was a strange little one-room house, with a basement, which had been planted down in the middle of a garden behind a brownstone. Maybe it had been meant for a maid or for a children's playroom, but it was our living space—and Joan's studio. Some friends from Chicago who were handy helped us insulate the basement, and there we were.

Going out from our narrow entrance lane and turning left on Eleventh Street, you came in less than a block to Seventh Avenue and the Village Vanguard. We got to know Max Gordon, the proprietor, and his wife, Lorraine, very well. We spent hours at the Vanguard with the likes of Pete Seeger and his folk group. One night the great South African singer Miriam Makeba came on stage, fresh from the shebeens of Soweto and Johannesburg. It was at the Vanguard we saw the tragicomic Lenny Bruce warning us there was a cop in a raincoat in the audience; and then Miles Davis playing his horn facing the wall one night because the audience annoyed him; Jack Kerouac spinning a bizarre, more than slightly drunk monologue; and Huddie Ledbetter, Lead Belly himself, just out of a Southern prison, escorted by Alan Lomax, singing his new song "Goodnight, Irene."

In April 1950 I worked as a volunteer at the American Association for the United Nations, while trying (unsuccessfully) to get a job at the UN. At that time I was also doing volunteer work—a version of an internship, you might say—for the new Socialist magazine, *The Monthly Review*. Grove Press might never have existed but for an act of carelessness on my part that resulted in my losing that job: I got a parking ticket on my car while I was distributing freshly printed copies of the magazine to some workers at a building near Union Square. I paid the parking ticket myself. But the editor, Leo Huberman, good leftist that he was, decided that a bourgeois like me, who got parking tickets while delivering the goods, was not the person to help people on the left side of the spectrum, and I was fired.

During the summer of 1950 Joan and I traveled to Haiti and Cuba, then on to Yucatan and Mexico City. After we returned home we concluded that 267½ was a bit too small for a painter whose canvases were growing larger by the week, so we decided to move. Just before we were supposed to move, Joan had an acute attack of appendicitis at 4:00 one morning and Dr. David Barsky, who had helped create the first mobile hospital units during the Spanish Civil War, the war that never ended, rushed her over to Beth Israel Hospital and operated immediately. He looked in on her a few hours later, and then went to jail to begin his sentence for refusing to answer questions before the House Un-American Activities Committee.

Then we packed up our stuff and moved into two floors of a nice brownstone at 57 West Ninth Street, setting up the living room on the top floor as a studio. Reached through an inner staircase, it was a large room with a vaulted ceiling, large fireplace, windows and glass doors, terraces at each end. And no heat.

Back in Chicago, I was used to moving from one apartment to another, but I had never really lived in a *house* until I found Greenwich Village, where, as I write this, I have lived for sixty years. The Village had a unique ambience. It had elements of my childhood in Chicago—the importance of the Irish and the Jews—but also a strong Italian community and culture. And of course there were the writers, the artists, the theater people. Hey, Eugene O'Neill's plays were staged here. And real communists gathered in Union Square (see the film *Reds*). Disparate souls were joined together in this place. I had found my home.

In 1951, thanks to the GI Bill, I enrolled at the New School for Social Research, only three blocks from our apartment. I worked hard and enjoyed myself there. Among my professors were Wallace Fowlie, Stanley Kunitz, Meyer Schapiro, and Alfred Kazin. It was their inspiration and the Village atmosphere that propelled me on to graduate with a BA, something that at Swarthmore, the University of Chicago, and UCLA I had failed to do.

Meanwhile I was doing work for the Council of Living Theater and the film producer Lester Cowan. I wrote reports on the Stella Adler and Sanford Meisner schools for acting. In December 1951, in Wallace Fowlie's course at the New School, I submitted a partial film script based on the novel *Le Grand Meaulnes* (*The Wanderer*) by Henri Alain-Fournier. I was crawling my way toward a career that I thought might still be in film, though soon it would take a different turn. My old friend Haskell Wexler had moved to Hollywood, undergoing his own transformation into a great mainstream filmmaker—but like me, never abandoning his political orientation, or at least its spirit.

Joan's work flourished. In October of 1950 she had her first solo exhibition in St. Paul, Minnesota, with thirteen paintings created in Le Lavandou and New York. But we were slowly growing apart. She rented another studio in a marvelous clone of a Paris studio building on West Twelfth Street, and it occupied her attention more and more. She began meeting and making friends with other artists, like Willem de Kooning, socializing with them, sometimes at the Cedar Street Tavern on University Place, where all the artists drank and argued endlessly.

I remember Joan and de Kooning having long discussions about different kinds of oil paints. Joan and Bill were very traditional in their likes and dislikes. Quality was what mattered most. They thought it incredible, but amusing, that Jackson Pollock was using a commercial paint, Duco. For Pollock, anything was possible, but it was not for them.

I thought Jackson Pollock was a great artist. To me, he was almost frightening in the sense that he seemed extraordinarily quiet and tense. Though he was gentle, I felt an incipient violence in him. The only violence I actually ever saw was leveled against himself or an inanimate object, except for one night when he got into an argument at the Cedar bar. With whom? Franz Kline and Bill de Kooning. I was sitting at a table with the three of them, listening to their talk, then suddenly they were arguing. Pollock stormed off to the men's room and I heard a loud crash. The owner told him to leave—not forever, just a month, maybe, like a fine for a basketball player who had crossed a forbidden line. When we saw Pollock peering inside the bar window, we went out to console him and soon were all happily saying good night to one another. Even in this instance Pollock didn't hurt anybody, just the bathroom door.

Joan and I were sinking, much as I desired to stay with her. She became confrontational and combative, and, though we were sometimes extremely close, it was impossible to maintain an intimate relationship. By the spring of 1951 she had slipped away from me, moving out of the apartment into a studio building at 51 West Tenth Street. She exhibited that year in the Ninth Street Show, organized by Leo Castelli and held in a vacant storefront at 60 East Ninth Street, and was represented in the Whitney Museum's 1951 Annual Exhibition of Contemporary American Art.

I wrote in my journal on Thursday, May 8, 1952:

My stomach feels uneasy and weary. Last night was with Joan. The last night that we may well spend together while we are still married. It is supposed to be all over tomorrow. First we talked with Bob, Howard, and Alfred about doing a book motivated by Bob's film THE LIFE OF CHRIST made from Durer's woodcuts. I felt that Joan was un-cooperative and hostile but perhaps it was all me. The whole idea had seemed so good a few days ago, but it suddenly collapsed last night and I ended up agreeing with Joan. We all went to the Bocce to eat, and then Joan and I talked for hours at a bar, arguing, recriminating, crying, and so on. Finally we came home, Joan remarking at the door that she was being a high class whore, but in she did come, and we had a wild, brutal time in bed, ending in almost tenderness as I switched off my hostility near the end.

That was 3AM. Now it is noon. Joan is still asleep. I have been up since eight, and I am sitting in the downstairs room, waiting for her to wake up. I have been on the verge of panic all morning. After bitter conversation with my father about becoming thirty on May 28. He made all the money he says. It is his. I am in it only as a tax deduction. And then the conversation shifts, as before. It will go my way he says, and then we stop. He is drinking, as usual, though it is still morning in Chicago.

Joan goes to Dr. Fried this afternoon, and I go to Sager. Between us we will pay forty dollars to speak a combined hour and a half or so. It has been going on for so long. When was the beginning, somewheres [sic] back there so many months ago, when will be the end and is there an end.

We divorced in 1952, not with a moan or a whimper, but with a sense of relief. Now we were free to be friends, and we remained friends. I bought her a poodle in Paris when our divorce was finalized and had the dog shipped to the US. I named the dog Georges du Soleil—and I took her to the airport to meet this "young man." Georges was impossible and Joan loved him desperately. That same year, she had her first solo show in New York at the New Gallery. I spent many hours getting her catalog written by the surrealist writer Nicolas Calas, and printed. She was a part of me—no matter what.

Our relationship slowly dissolved, but in a rather beautiful final act, Joan, with the help of her Art Institute friend Francine Felsenthal, encouraged me to enter publishing. Together they helped me take the very first step.

Francine lived on the Lower East Side in a sixth-floor walkup, one room after we knocked out the wall. There was a girl next door in the only other apartment on the same floor, Susan Nevelson, whose ex-mother-in-law was the sculptor Louise Nevelson and perhaps Susan's best friend. Beautiful Susan made a living by sketching fashion models for retail store ads. Later she became, for a brief moment, a lover, and afterward was still my close friend. A photo she took of her daughter is on the cover of *Evergreen Review*, No. 6.

One fateful day in late 1951 Francine brought me copies of the three titles published by a moribund little company, Grove Press: *The Confidence-Man* by Herman Melville, a new collection of the religious love poetry of Richard Crashaw, and a book of the writings of Aphra Behn, who was said to be the first feminist author. Francine told me that her friend, John Balcomb had, with a partner, Robert Phelps, formed a company and published those three books. The company's name was Grove Press after the West Village street where Balcomb lived. Having publishing the three titles in 1949–50, they had run out of money and stopped. Balcomb's wife Cynthia had put up the initial money but would not put up any more. She and John were getting divorced.

I looked at the books and all three intrigued me. In the Aphra Behn book the following statement was printed: "The function of the GROVE PRESS, as we understand it, is to publish the kind of books that other publishers publish books about—those 'unexpected' masterpieces of the past and present that have been more read about than read simply because they have been hitherto inaccessible to the general reader." And the back of the title page stated: "Grove Press editions are edited by John Balcomb and Robert Phelps and are published by the Grove Press, Inc., at 18 Grove Street, New York City."

The first book the Grove Press partners had done was the closest to being a simple reprint, meaning, it contained no new editorial material. *The Confidence-Man: His Masquerade* was a lithographed copy of the Dix, Edwards & Co. edition of 1857. It had been out of print for 60 years before they revived it.

The jacket flap of *The Verse in English of Richard Crashaw* stated that Richard Crashaw "has left what is probably the most exultant body of religious verse in the English language. . . . Crashaw opened every stop, and celebrated his belief with all the emblazonry of the Baroque instinct at its fullest."

In true Balcomb/Phelps style the jacket went on to say, "In most cases Crashaw left at least two very different published versions of each poem, and it would be an extremely dubious undertaking to establish a single 'definitive' text. The present edition therefore has brought together the complete texts of the first and last versions of all the poems published during and immediately after Crashaw's lifetime."

The third, *Selected Writings of the Ingenious Mrs. Aphra Behn*, had an introduction by Robert Phelps, who quoted the author as saying, "If I must not, because of my sex, have this freedom [to be a writer], I lay down my quill and you shall hear no more of me, no, not so much as to make comparisons, because I will be kinder to my brothers of the pen than they have been to a defenseless woman, for I am not content to write for a third day only. I value fame as much as if I had been born a hero; and if you rob me of that I can retire from the ungrateful world and scorn its fickle favors."[12]

Phelps wrote of Behn, "She is chiefly regarded as a novelist, or at least as a writer of narratives, and due recognition is given her method of creating reality by the immediacy of her own avowed, witnessing person. . . . She had a genuine, natural gift, that of a tale-teller."

Was I interested in meeting Phelps and Balcomb? Yes, I was. I reached out to embrace Joan's idea of my becoming a publisher. My documentary filmmaking days were no longer appealing. The film business hadn't worked for me. That world was too big, too expensive, with "strictly business" interests too deeply embedded. I was ready to segue naturally from studying Proust, Rimbaud, and the like to publishing them and authors like them. Since the Village was now my home it would become the home of my Grove Press as well.

Like his mentor Ezra Pound, Balcomb was a highly literate, eccentric person. His apartment was crammed with stacks of newspapers and magazines. We met there and made plans to continue Grove Press as partners. I then had to go see Robert Phelps, who lived in Woodstock, to ask whether he would sell his share to me, or whether he would join us. It turned out to be easy to make an agreement to buy Phelps's interest in Grove Press for $1,500. So, with my father's help, I became John Balcomb's partner, and there we were, in business. The negotiations took place during September through December 1951.

Beyond those first three books, Balcomb and Phelps had set in motion work on a fourth book, Matthew Gregory Lewis's gothic novel, *The Monk*. They had already set the type—no small task in those days before computers—but had been forced to abandon it for lack of funds. Now the project was alive again. But it wasn't long before I began to see that Balcomb and I could not coexist. He had a headstrong personality, set in his version of Ezra Poundian ways. I respected Pound as an astute critic and poet and felt almost personally aggrieved when Pound (who had made pro-Mussolini radio broadcasts during the war) was arrested by the American army in Italy, impounded, so to speak, in a cage as if he were a dangerous, perhaps rabid, animal. I could abide Pound, but I simply couldn't abide Mr. Balcomb. He was at my mercy in a sense, because he was without money to continue publishing on his own. So, again with my father's help, I bought him out, too, for about the same amount paid to Phelps. I don't remember my father ever saying what I should do. I think he knew it was hopeless to try to tell me. So he provided the $3,000 required to buy the company and the inventory.

Now I was free to go on alone.

I had taken a real liking to Lewis's *The Monk*, this strange, sadistic, weird story of a girl who enters a monastery dressed as a monk and seduces the head of the monastery, who himself, in a lustful passion, murders another girl, and so on. And I was interested in the history of Lewis himself, who was an eccentric eighteenth-century Englishman from a family of considerable wealth. I decided to go ahead with its publication.

Balcomb had hired a professor to do a kind of variorum edition of the book, with all sorts of scholarly notes about the different editions published and changes made across the years, a pedantic exercise that repulsed me. I eventually did publish the original edition and the variorum changes in a very small hardcover edition, but was able to get an introduction from John Berryman, an excellent poet and littérateur (also rather psychotic, as Lewis had been) to write another introduction. Berryman admired *The Monk* on its own creative merit and he was able communicate that feeling.

Berryman wrote that *The Monk* was "one of the authentic prodigies of English fiction, a book in spite of various crudenesses so good that even after a century and a half it is possible to consider it unhistorically; and yet it has never quite become a standard novel. Several reasons for this must be its intermittent unavailability, its reputation for eroticism, its not being reinforced by excellence in Lewis's other imaginative work, so that it has had to stand alone."[13] Berryman went on to explain that Lewis's father had secured him the post of attaché in the British embassy at The Hague when Lewis was not quite nineteen. Out of boredom with Dutch society, he began composing the novel and finished it in an astonishingly short period of time.

> The book created a sensation instantly. . . . It was attacked, defended, parodied, plundered, dramatized, opera'd, adapted, translated, imitated. . . . On coming of age in July 1796 [Lewis] was returned to Parliament . . . (taking the seat, oddly, of the author [Thomas Beckford] of Vathek) and when a second edition was called for in October he not merely put his name on the title-page but added "M.P." This was oil to fire.

Hauled into court, Lewis was forced to expurgate the text. Berryman quotes the author as saying, "I have to accuse myself of high imprudence. Let me, however, observe that *twenty* is not the age at which prudence is most to be expected."

So there were at least some semi-rational reasons for buying Grove Press. Here was a small but existing enterprise with a flair that lifted it above a mundane commercial effort. It fit my way of thinking. When Balcomb left, I was on my own and my first "dirty book," *The Monk*, would soon emerge from the printing press.

The additional copies of the first three books which I had printed, and later, the English imports that followed, were stored in my apartment at 57 West Ninth Street. Along with other titles I was beginning to publish, they took up so much space and were so heavy that the floors were on the verge of collapse after a year or two. The original books I had bought from Balcomb and Phelps were all contained in a few small trunks and suitcases, probably a few hundred copies of each title, but more and more were being added all the time. The originals

I took to a bindery and had them rebound into hard covers. Later, unsatisfied with the way they looked, I stripped off the unsold hardcover's bindings and put the books back into paperback format—and also changed the design of the covers. I was very influenced by James Laughlin's publishing house, New Directions. The original Balcomb/Phelps Grove covers were unattractive and without coherence. The new covers were plain yellow wrappers imprinted with black type—sort of a cross between the publication style of books in France and that of New Directions here.

Another important influence on me in the early days of Grove was Anchor Books, a trade paperback line at Doubleday, created by Jason Epstein. We became friends and shared ideas about publishing. When Jason left Doubleday because the firm would not let him publish Nabokov's *Lolita*, we decided to undertake a partnership and buy the American franchise on a trade paperback line published by a British publisher, Penguin, and its US subsidiary, then based in Baltimore. Before the Frankfurt Book Fair, Jason and I went to England and made an offer to the owner, who turned us down.

Shortly after this, Jason joined Random House where he created another trade paperback line, Vintage, that became and remains enormously successful.

The first book I published after *The Monk* was an edition of Henry James's *The Golden Bowl*, and I got Richard Blackmur, a famed Jamesian critic, to write the introduction. Publishing *The Golden Bowl* was Joan's idea. It was her favorite of all of James's books. She had found a copy in France and discovered that it had not been in print since 1925. We approached Scribner's, who still owned the copyright. They sent an elderly and distinguished editor, Whitney Darrow, down to my office to see if we really existed. The copy of *The Golden Bowl* that Joan gave me was the actual copy we used to print from by photo-offset, and Francine did the illustration for the cover. I went on to publish seven or eight more of James's novels, all out of print when I picked them up.

So Joan actually had a lot to do with Grove in the beginning. But I also knew Horace Gregory at that time, and he was a big influence on me, too. Horace was a Jamesian scholar as well as quite a good poet.

Early on, I became aware that English publishers were publishing many good books that weren't being done in America. Having read and catalogued various books and authors that interested me, I traveled to England and approached publishers such as Faber and Faber, Chatto & Windus, and a few others, and ended up taking on a number of British writers. Little did I know then how unusual were my friendly, helpful overtures to the English publishers.

In 1952 I took a course in publishing at Columbia. Saxe Commins, onetime senior editor at Random House, was the professor. I learned a great deal, but mainly I met book people—each session had a great visiting lecturer, each a leader in his or her area of publishing: advertising, editing, and so forth—people such as Ian Ballantine of Ballantine Books. But I also met students, among them Donald Allen, the first of the editors who would work with me at Grove. Donald had been an English teacher at Berkeley, and during World War II he had served as a specialist in Japanese for Naval Intelligence.

At first Don appeared to me to be the prototype of the effete intellectual snob, albeit the brightest one ever. But when I got to know him better, I came to admire his daring and uncanny good judgment. I brought him to Grove early on and considered him a very important addition. For a while we comprised a publishing company with an editorial staff of two.

In 1953 Don moved next door to me, into a basement apartment at 59 West Ninth Street, a brownstone with a garden behind it. I soon rented the floor above his apartment for an office. It was the new Grove's first home away from home. One door away, to be exact. An easy commute.

As Grove grew, our editorial and administrative staff expanded. When Richard Seaver returned from his years abroad in 1957 where he'd been a student and one of the editors of *Merlin*, he worked first for the publisher George Braziller. I was finally able to persuade him to join Grove in 1959. Dick's knowledge of European literature helped him make invaluable contributions to Grove during the twelve years he was with us, working on manuscripts of French writers like Marguerite Duras, Alain Robbe-Grillet, Eugène Ionesco, and the Marquis de Sade. He translated many books from French. I once said at a speech (when I was receiving the PEN American Award for career achievement) that if I ever had a brother, I would have wanted him to be Dick Seaver. Eventually Dick would become the managing editor of our journal *Evergreen Review.*

About this time Fred Jordan, who had come to work at Grove in 1956, took on more editorial responsibilities in our book publishing division. Like Dick, Fred was essential to Grove's development. He read German (English was his second language), which was crucial in dealing with work by authors like Rolf Hochhuth, whose play *The Deputy* was about the role of Pope Pius XII with respect to the Jews in Europe during World War II. I acquired a copy from our German publisher friend, Heinrich Ledig-Rowohlt, and also the rights. Fred had managed to escape from Vienna when the Nazis took over and made his way to England. During the war he served in the British Army. We were introduced by a freelance Grove salesman, Felix Morrow, who knew Fred and mentioned him to me. Fred got in touch with me and soon joined Grove, working in sales and then editorial—and stayed with the company for more than thirty years, before he left to run another publishing house, Pantheon.

Other long-term employees at Grove included Judith Schmidt, who was my assistant for many years. She could write letters in my voice—and she made good friends with many Grove authors, which, among other things, made them feel at home when they came to our office.

Harry Braverman, another Grove editor, was involved in a major book published by Grove in 1965, *The Autobiography of Malcolm X.* I remember being in my car when it was announced on the radio that Malcolm X had been shot. The next day I seized an opportunity because I heard that Doubleday had his autobiography under contract but did not want to proceed with publishing it. Doubleday himself was quoted as saying he was afraid that the company's employees might be endangered. I went to the agent for the book, signed it up, and then got Alex Haley (who later wrote *Roots*) to put the final touches on the manuscript quickly so it could come out as soon as possible. (Haley had compiled the text from lengthy interviews with Malcolm X.) The book turned out to have enormous political and social impact.

After it was published, I went to my son Peter's school to give a talk on how a book got published (I think Fred Jordan and Dick Seaver came along with me), and when I was finished with my talk, I asked if there were any questions. One of the students, a big, rather imposing young black kid, put his hand up and said, "It's the most important book you ever published, isn't it?"

I wasn't prepared to say yes, so I simply said to him, "You're asking me to choose between my children. I can't."

In fact, as time would tell, many people would feel that a number of my "children" were the most important books I had ever published, including, I might add, our erotica. Richard Gallen, our lawyer for Grove, once said, "Barney's business was always on a precipice. There was no one editorially doing what he was doing at that skill. In terms of drama, European literature, avant-garde literature, sexually provocative literature—there was no one doing it in America. No one."[14]

Perhaps his statement was too sweeping, but there were people like Laughlin, who in publishing Henry Miller left out *Tropic of Cancer*, or Alfred Knopf, who took on D. H. Lawrence's *Lady Chatterley's Lover* but suppressed a crucial chapter. Those things were not being published in this country because of threatened and actual arrests, just as *The Autobiography of Malcolm X* was almost kept from publication because of Doubleday's fears. I never let any of that stop me.

I had always been drawn to books that were considered risky. When I was at Swarthmore in 1940–1941, I asked my parents to send me 50 books, all of which were published by New Directions or the Modern Library. And before that, when I was in Chicago attending high school, I went to Marshall Field & Co. to get books by John Steinbeck, James Farrell, and other writers considered too daring for young students to read, writers such as I. F. Stone, Nelson Algren, Pearl Buck, Edgar Snow, and André Malraux. So when I later found myself making "risky" decisions as a publisher, I was just being who I had always been.

While Harry Braverman was working on the Malcolm X book, he brought in a young editor named Gilbert Sorrentino to help him—essentially, Harry used this occasion to train and work with Gil as an editor. Gil was also an innovative poet and fiction writer. Grove eventually published his remarkable comic novel, *Mulligan Stew*, in 1979, after it had been rejected by numerous other houses.

Jules Geller was another important editor for us. He had been a Trotskyite in World War II and a conscientious objector. He would also eventually act as a leader in the fight against a group of protestors that tried to unionize Grove, about which more later. Skilled at tactics, Jules drove the union people crazy.

Morrie Goldfisher handled our publicity for quite a few years. He was very good at his job and very much part of the inner circle. We also had one book designer, Roy Kuhlman, who did our covers and jackets for many years. He helped make Grove books stand out because of the distinctiveness and effectiveness of those designs. Joan's approval of his work greatly strengthened my belief in Roy's talent. I am proud that he was named to the Art Directors Club Hall of Fame.

In 1967 we made Grove a public company, something that was done by a number of other book publishers at about the same time. Grove had come a long way by the end of the decade. When we started out, there was just Don Allen, my second wife Loly (Hannelore Eckert), Howard Turner, John Gruen, and me. Grove soon needed more space and more editorial help, particularly after *Evergreen Review* was launched. The staff grew to about thirty-five people in the editorial, sales, and administrative side of Grove, and many of them worked with us for a long time.

Evergreen Review originally came out in 1957 as a quarterly. It went bimonthly in late 1959, became a monthly in April 1964, and was mostly distributed in bookstores, although there were subscriptions. Later, when we started the Evergreen Book Club, we linked it to a subscription for the *Review*.

The first issue featured eight pieces along with a portfolio of photographs by Harold Feinstein, printed on coated paper. Some of our contributors were regular Grove authors—Samuel Beckett's short story "Dante and the Lobster" and his poem "Echo's Bones" were included—and certain pieces had some connection to my past, for instance, Baby Dodds' reminiscences of his career as a jazz drummer. (Dodds is the drummer I saw performing as 1945 turned into 1946 at my favorite Chicago bar, Tin Pan Alley, when I returned from the war.) We also published Mark Schorer's "On *Lady Chatterley's Lover*," of course, which would become the introduction to the unexpurgated edition of the novel that Grove was to publish. I wanted to tie *Evergreen Review* to Grove Press as much as possible, and it would turn out that the two entities strengthened each other in immeasurable ways.

Don Allen's relationships with people like Lawrence Ferlinghetti of City Lights Books (founded in 1953 and the first publisher of Allen Ginsberg's *Howl* in 1956) and a wide variety of poets, particularly on the West Coast, led directly to the second issue of *Evergreen Review*, "The San Francisco Scene," and indirectly to one of our landmark books *The New American Poetry 1945–1960*, which Don edited. The anthology included many of those poets who had been featured in *Evergreen,* No. 2, among them Ferlinghetti, Robert Duncan, Michael McClure, Jack Spicer, Gary Snyder, Jack Kerouac, and Philip Whalen. Poets from the Beat generation included Ginsberg, and the "New York School" poets were widely represented—John Ashbery, Kenneth Koch, Frank O'Hara.

The New American Poetry was one of the many books we published that opened up a wider market in the educational sector because they were used widely in college courses. We even began to put out a separate catalog just for that market. Dedicated sales promotion by Nat Sobel and Morrie Goldfisher did a tremendous job in making political poetry and erotica work their way into the halls of academe.

Our book club operation grew steadily. The acquisition of Mid-Century Book Club in 1966 strengthened the Evergreen Book Club; at one point we had over 50,000 members. Grove's best year was 1969, when our net revenues were more than $14 million. This was a huge leap from 1959, when our revenues were less than $1 million.

In addition to the continuing sales of books by authors like Samuel Beckett, whose centrality to Grove grew and grew over time, from *Waiting for Godot* forward, as well as certain others, Grove's revenues continued to rise. Not everything sold well initially, *Godot* among them. For example, Grove had published a book by a psychiatrist named Eric Berne that had sold perhaps two thousand copies. In 1964 we published his new book, *Games People Play,* which for quite a time sold very poorly, so I was inclined to drop it. I told this to one of my fellow participants in group therapy, where we mingled with young psychoanalysts in training and he said, "Don't do it! Keep it going!" So I decided to start doing direct mail ads in the *New York Times* and elsewhere, and that slowly got the book going. It finally broke through and stayed on the *New York Times* bestseller list for 109 weeks. Ultimately more than five million copies were sold.

At its largest Grove had its own warehouse, which was located on the far West Side. And our book club operation was in a separate building. The warehouse was unionized by a comparatively left-wing union, one we got along with quite well. In fact, they made an extraordinary concession—Grove would be allowed to move its warehouse location if need be. (Unions did not want a company to be able to move out of the state, or the country, simply to get out from under the union.) So when it came time for us to shift our warehousing, shipping, sales, and distribution to Random House in 1971, there was no problem.

During my years at Grove its location never went beyond more than ten blocks from where it started—we remained in Greenwich Village. Over the years we moved a number of times, first from our space on West Ninth Street to 795 Broadway between Ninth and Tenth Streets. Grove's offices there were over a clothing and hot dog stand. There were other publishers in the building, including Sheed and Ward and Fred Praeger, whose firm I believe had CIA connections. The two of us used to talk about it and laugh. In 1959 Grove moved to 64 University Place (over a grocery store) and then to 80 University Place (between Tenth and Eleventh Streets). In 1967 we relocated to 53 East Eleventh Street (where we established both the Black Circle Bar and Evergreen Theater, not your usual amenities for a publishing house), and then to 214 Mercer Street after renovations were completed in 1970 at a cost of $2 million. After that building was sold in June 1972, Grove moved back to East Eleventh Street and ultimately to 196 West Houston Street, the southern boundary of the Village. This was the site of both my home and Grove's offices.

After our lack of capital and debt load forced me to sell the company in 1985, I had my final real estate experience at Grove. I had found us an excellent space in the Puck Building, a magnificent Romanesque Revival building constructed in 1885, located at 295 Lafayette Street (at the corner of Broadway) in the SoHo section of lower Manhattan. It once housed the printing facilities of the long defunct *Puck* magazine. The new owners had other ideas. They wanted to move Grove's offices uptown. But Grove (which subsequently merged with Atlantic Monthly Press to form Grove/Atlantic) ended up right back in the Village, at 841 Broadway, only a few blocks from Ninth Street—where everything began.

Apart from the Village, there was another place that became an integral part of my life and, in the years to come, a delightful working refuge for members of the Grove Press family.

I first went out to East Hampton in 1950 with Joan. I thought it quite beautiful, especially the ocean beaches, and I wanted to go back, even though Joan was slowly fading out of my life. Three Mile Harbor in the Springs community of East Hampton was a center for the New York artists who were to become the leaders of their generation, not only in the United States but in the world. Motherwell, Pollock, Krasner, Kline, de Kooning, and Rothko painted out there, along with many other important artists.

A couple of years before I married Loly at New York's City Hall in August of 1953, I bought Robert Motherwell's house in the Georgica area. It had been designed for Motherwell by the French architect Pierre Chareau. I knew nothing about Chareau at the time but Loly and I had read about the house, actually a Quonset hut from World War II, in *Harper's*. It had been built in 1946. Now Motherwell was planning on moving, so Loly and I went to have a look at it. We drove around until we found the house, as I related in an interview published by *Pataphysics* in their 2001 *Pirate Issue*, "this strange-looking thing stuck in a pile of sand. When they had first built it, they had not bothered to cover the construction pit, and only a few young saplings had been planted. It looked hopeless. We loved it immediately."[15]

In order to let us see the interior of the house, as I went on to say, the real estate agent had to break a window. We were charmed and amazed by the originality of the place. We asked the agent how much it would cost to rent for one season. Adding up the main house (the Quonset hut), the studio (also a Quonset hut) and the cinderblock house, it came to eight or nine thousand dollars. We said, "Well, how much would it cost to buy it?" He said, "Twelve thousand." That included the two acres of land not far from the ocean. It sounded ludicrous even then, early on in the real estate boom. Later that year I brought my father and mother to look at it and they were stunned—"You bought that? You paid twelve thousand dollars for *that*?" We had, and it became our beloved home, a transformed Quonset hut.

I have never been to Chareau's Maison de Verre in Paris, supposedly one of the most important examples of twentieth-century French architecture, but I've seen many photographs of it. You could perhaps tell that the East Hampton house was by the same architect because of the way metal and glass were used in its design. The furniture in the house had been designed by another modern architect, Frederick John Kiesler. He was about five feet tall and we called him the Little Genius. I knew Kiesler well and liked him very much. Like Chareau, he was never able to get a major project in this country. The Museum of Modern Art, however, exhibited a full-scale model of Kiesler's Endless House. He designed furniture that was unique, made from plywood. It looked like Jean Arp paintings. In the Endless House the furniture formed part of the walls. In Motherwell's house, you could turn the Kiesler pieces upside down, it didn't matter: a table could become a chair—equally satisfactory. When we moved in, the living room had Kiesler's work in it but Motherwell took it all back. Sad for us.

I think Motherwell had wanted to leave the house because he was unhappy personally. His Mexican wife, Maria Emilia Ferreira y Moyers, had left him, and later he married Betty Little who, I was told, was very stiff, very bourgeois, very conservative, the wrong person to live in a house like that. So Motherwell bought a brownstone in New York. (He would later marry a third time, to the painter Helen Frankenthaler.)

It was very difficult when we first moved out there with our baby, Peter. It had snowed heavily and it was freezing. The first night there was snow down to the ocean, and I almost drove into the water by accident. Then, during the summer, people began showing up and everyone said, "Oh, my God, it's impossible. It's as hot as a furnace." The house was surrounded by burning sand and there were no trees for shelter. The metal roof absorbed the heat. I fixed this by draping soaker hoses over the roof. Then I put in a couple of exhaust fans—simple, inexpensive things that also helped to bring down the temperature. Years later my son Peter and I wood-shingled the metal roof. No self-respecting architect would have ever thought of that, let alone have done it. As the years passed we planted a lawn, and the trees finally grew over the house and joined at the top. It got to be very comfortable and beautiful, albeit strange.

Motherwell had done things to the original house that had lessened the impact of the original plan—put in a partition toward the end of the room where there was a fireplace, defeating its purpose and spoiling the craziness of the place. As soon as I moved in I ripped that out of the center of the ground floor and relocated it at one end.

I made several major changes to the studio Motherwell had used, next to the house, greatly improving it. The ceiling had no insulation and there was a concrete floor. It wasn't really livable. Motherwell painted at night, so light wasn't important to him. The studio had a southern exposure—not ideal—so we put some corrugated plastic transparent panels in the roof, letting in more light. Robert Rosenberg, a wonderful architect who lived out there and became our best friend, designed an addition to the studio—a little roofed terrace that encircled a tree, and a photo lab (Loly was a photographer), a kitchen and a bathroom, and a linoleum floor in the main area. You could live in it and paint: it was a self-contained unit.

In the third unit, the cinderblock structure where Chareau had lived, I took the bathroom out of the center of the one rectangular room and made an interior pool, very beautiful, with windows on all four sides. We also put a dome in the ceiling where the toilet had vented out. The cinderblock unit had the same kind of floor as the main house: three-inch circles of wood cut from tree trunks and embedded in concrete. The number and size of the rooms was changeable. Chareau had placed wooden screens on wheels and thus created moveable walls.

Making any adjustment to the original design was always a difficult decision. We mulled it over for years every time we needed a change, trying to conform to Chareau's original concept, and I think (with the possible exception of the shingled roof) we held true.

In the late 1960s we made a film there, released in 1970, that Norman Mailer wrote, directed, and starred in, a chaotic violent film called *Maidstone*. Norman at the time prided himself on Indian arm wrestling. That was one of the big things in his life then, along with punching people out. But many other, more peaceful, people stayed with us. We threw lots of parties. Everyone loved the house.

I had a vision of all the Grove people living out there in East Hampton—and they did, or almost. I searched out houses that were abandoned and bought them. We moved them on large dollies to another location I had bought, and rebuilt them. I even bought a tiny church, which we hauled to a new site and transformed into a little theater. We chopped one wall off lengthwise and used it as a stage with a big wooden outdoor plaza surrounded by trees. We called it Evergreen Theater.

After living in the Chareau house for thirty years, it had become part of me. Then I moved away in 1980 in part because I had gotten divorced again, for the third time, and thought a change was necessary. But it was the stupidest single act of my life. The new owner tore the house down a couple of years later. I have never been able to bring myself to drive past where it once stood.

●⌣

Living in East Hampton, Loly and I found ourselves in the midst of a wonderful social scene, very nurturing to artists. I've never experienced anything like it before or since. It was not quite the Cedar Tavern in the Village, but it was as if the bar had suddenly added several new layers of personality.

Soon after we moved there, we were invited to a party for Jackson Pollock at the house of someone we didn't know, Alfonso Ossorio. There was a big crowd that night at his estate, the Creeks. Ossorio, a formidable and iconoclastic artist who had been born in the Philippines, had an exquisite sensibility and a lot of money, and he helped other people financially, especially Pollock. The artists, for their part, certainly weren't wallowing in money, but some of their friends were hardly poor. It was a highly unusual group of people, who seemed to cover all the creative ground—Pollock, Pollock's biographer Jeffrey Potter and his wife, Penny, Bill and Elaine de Kooning, writer Harold Rosenberg, artists Warren Brandt, Paul Brach, and Miriam Schapiro, the architects Robert Rosenberg, Frederick John Kiesler, and Paul Lester Wiener, and Wiener's wife, Ingeborg ten Haeff, a very good painter herself. Leo Castelli, the gallery owner, lived across the road from our house. Amongst those who later became my close friends were the writers Berton Roueché, who wrote the *New Yorker*'s annals of medicine, and Joe Liss and his wife, Milly. There was a kind of extended family feeling that I didn't know could exist.

To me Pollock was a little bit apart. He wasn't somebody you could be chummy with, as you could be with de Kooning. Actually, I felt much closer to Pollock's wife, Lee Krasner. We thought of him as a great artist of the period, whether or not anybody knew what he was doing. Certainly Joan thought he was great—he and de Kooning and Kline, and of course I saw painting through Joan's eyes whether or not I was married to her or even in her proximity.

I think it took the artists a long time to understand that they were becoming successful. I can only think of this as being related to the Depression in some way. The older artists had never had money, didn't own things like cars. Franz Kline had never had a car, but when he was living in the "Red House" (so called because it was painted bright red) in Bridgehampton, in the early fifties, he bought a car for $150, a huge Lincoln convertible. It looked to me like a steam locomotive. As I recall, he and Pollock took it out on the road and hit more or less the first car coming toward them, head on. That night, the artist Ludwig Sander, an ex-GI like me, came to my place and told me that Kline had to appear in court for demolishing the other car, which had about six people in it—all uninjured, thank goodness. Franz said that the only thing he owned was his Lincoln, and he was afraid they would take it away from him, so I agreed to buy it for that same $150. In court, the judge let Franz off with a warning. Even the law enforcement people in East Hampton looked kindly upon artists, and Jackson was a recipient of that forgivingness more than once. So I gave Franz back the gorgeous car and he returned my check.

8

Samuel Beckett

One day in the early 1950s, the mailman brought me an unexpected letter from Sylvia Beach, asking for an appointment. For many years she had been the famous proprietor of Shakespeare and Company, the leading and legendary English-language bookstore in Paris. She had been close friends with James Joyce and published his *Ulysses* in 1922. She had also known Samuel Beckett for many years. During our meeting she spoke about Beckett in the warmest terms as a writer of great importance whose day would surely come.

Her words sounded a magical note to me.

When I had read Beckett's pieces in *Transition Workshop*, edited by Eugène Jolas in Paris, I was still a student at the New School. Jolas had Beckett listed under the category of "paramyths." Other writers listed in the same genre included Kay Boyle, Ernest Hemingway, James Joyce, Franz Kafka, Katherine Anne Porter, Gertrude Stein, and Dylan Thomas. And of course there was also Henry Miller.

After the meeting with Sylvia Beach, I saw an article that told of the opening in Paris on January 5 of that year of a play by Samuel Beckett called *Waiting for Godot*. I somehow got a copy of *Godot*—it had only been published in French, the language in which Beckett had written it—and I read it. My immediate response was, "Here is a kind of human insight that I have never before experienced. I want to publish it." I set about finding Beckett's New York agent, Marion Saunders, and made one of the earliest Grove Press contracts. The contract itself was with Beckett's French publisher, Les Éditions de Minuit, the first of many I was to sign with them. It called for an advance of $1,000 against royalties.

About this time, after I had read *Godot*, I asked Wallace Fowlie, a specialist in French literature who had been one of my professors as well as my friend at the New School, to give me his opinion of it. I believed him to be a far more conservative reader than I. But he more than confirmed what Sylvia Beach had told me and what I myself had concluded. He told me that Beckett would come to be known as one of the greatest writers of the twentieth century.

I had the same sort of feeling about two more "French" writers we contracted for in that same year: Eugène Ionesco and Jean Genet.

June 18, 1953
New York

Dear Mr. Beckett,

It is about time that I write a letter to you—now that agents, publishers, friends, etc., have all acted as go-betweens. A copy of our catalogue has already been mailed to you, so you will be able to see what kind of a publisher you have been latched onto. I hope that you won't be too disappointed.

We are very happy to have the contract back from Minuit, and believe me, we will do what we can to make your work known in this country.

The first order of the day would appear to be the translation. I have just sent off a letter to [*Merlin* editor] Alex Trocchi telling him that the difficulties did not seem as ominous from here as they evidently do from there to him at least.

If you would accept my first choice as translator the whole thing would be easily settled. That choice of course being you. That already apparently is a satisfactory condition insofar as the play is concerned. . . .

I explained to Trocchi at great length, and probably with great density, why I thought it better for *Merlin* not to publish the first act in advance of book publication. It seems to me that a whole act hardly comes under the heading of an "excerpt" and might really serve to take a little of the edge off of the book publication. I suggested instead that they publish excerpts from the novels whenever pieces are ready, and join me in putting the play out as a book as soon as conveniently possible. I hope that you will join me in this idea. *En Attendant Godot* should burst upon us as an entity in my opinion.

As for the translation of the novels, I am waiting first, to hear from you, what you advise, and whether or not you will tackle them yourself. If your decision is no, and I do hope that it won't be, we can discuss between us the likely people to do it.

Sylvia Beach is certainly the one you must blame for your future appearance on the Grove Press list. I went to see her with your work on my mind, and after she talked of you . . . I immediately decided that what the Grove Press needed most in the world was Samuel Beckett. I told her that, and then she suggested that I make a specific offer. I certainly had not thought of that up to the very moment she took out a piece of paper and pencil and prepared to write down the terms.

A second person was also very important. He is Wallace Fowlie. At my request he read the play and the two novels with great care and came back with the urgent plea for me to take on your work. Fowlie is also on your list. His new translation of Rimbaud's *Illuminations*, and a long study of them, is just now coming out. . . .

Chatto & Windus have not one single copy of your book on Proust. If you ever come across one I would much appreciate it if you would let me borrow it. Proust is my particular passion and I would so much like to know what you have, or had, to say about him. . . .

This would seem to be an already indecently long letter, so I will close. If you would give me your own address we might be able to communicate directly in the future.

Sincerely,
Barney Rosset

June 25, 1953
6 rue de Favorites
Paris 15me

Dear Mr. Rosset

Thank you for your letter of June 18. Above my private address, confidentially. For serious matters write to me here, for business to Lindon, Ed. de Minuit, please.

Re translations. I shall send you to-day or to-morrow my first version of *Godot*. . . .

With regard to the novels my position is that I should greatly prefer not to undertake the job myself, while having the right to revise whatever translation is made. But I know from experience how much more difficult it is to revise a bad translation than to do the thing oneself. . . . I translated myself some years ago two very brief fragments for Georges Duthuit's *Transition*. If I can get hold of the number in which they appeared I shall send it to you.

I understand very well your point of view when you question the propriety of the publication in *Merlin* of Act I of *Godot* and I have no doubt that Trocchi will appreciate it too.

My own copy of my *Proust* has disappeared and I really do not know where to suggest your looking for one. It is a very youthful work, but perhaps not entirely beside the point. Its premises are less feeble than its conclusions.

With regard to my work in general I hope you realize what you are letting yourself in for. I do not mean the heart of the matter, which is unlikely to disturb anybody, but certain obscenities of form which may not have struck you in French as they will in English, and which frankly (it is better you should know this before we get going) I am not at all disposed to mitigate. I do not of course realize what is possible in America from this point of view and what is not. Certainly as far as I know such passages, faithfully translated, would not be tolerated in England. I think you might do well to talk to Fowlie about this.

Sylvia Beach said very nice things about the Grove Press and that you might be over here in the late summer. I hope you will.

Thank you for your interesting catalogue. I shall certainly ask you for some of your books at a later stage.

Thanking you for taking this chance with my work and wishing us a fair wind, I am

Yours sincerely
Samuel Beckett

July 13, 1953
New York

Dear Mr. Beckett,

It was nice to receive your letter of June 25 and then your letter of July 5.

First, I must tell you that I have not received your translation of *Godot*. I am most anxious to see it. I would like to plan on publication of the play for 1954, either in the first or second half of the year, depending entirely upon completion date of the translation. I would think the ideal thing would be to coincide publication with performance, but that is ideal only and I would not think it wise to indefinitely postpone publication while waiting for the performance.

As to the translation of the novels, I am naturally disappointed to hear that you prefer not to undertake translation yourself. I can well see your point, however, and it would seem a little sad to attempt to take off that much time to go back over your own books but I hope that you will change your mind. . . .

As to the obscenities within the books, my suggestion is that we do not worry about that until it becomes necessary. Sometimes things like that have a way of solving themselves.

I do hope you locate a copy of *Transition* with the fragments translated by yourself.

I do plan on going to Europe in the fall, and I will certainly look forward to meeting you then.

Yours sincerely,
Barney Rosset

July 18, 1953
6 rue des Favorites
Paris 15me

Dear Mr. Rosset

. . . In raising the question of the obscenities I simply wished to make it clear from the outset that the only modifications of them that I am prepared to accept are of a kind with those which hold for the text as a whole, i.e. made necessary by the change fro[m] one language to another. The problem therefore is no more complicat[ed] than this: Are you prepared to print the result? I am convinced you will agree with me that a clear understanding on this matter before we set to work is equally indispensable for you, the translato[r] and myself.

Herewith *Transition* with my translation of fragments from *Molloy* and *Malone.*

Yours sincerely
Samuel Beckett

July 31, 1953
New York

Dear Mr. Beckett,

Your translation of *Godot* did finally arrive. . . . I like it very much, and it seems to me that you have done a fine job. The long speech by Lucky is particularly good and the whole play reads extremely well.

If I were to make any criticism it would be that one can tell that the translation was done by a person more used to "English" speech than American. Thus the use of words such as bloody—and a few others—might lead an audience to think the play was originally done by an Englishman in English. This is a small point, but in a few places a neutralization of the speech away from the specifically English flavor might have the result of enhancing the French origins for an American reader. Beyond that technical point I have little to say, excepting that I am now extremely desirous of seeing the play on a stage—in any language. . . .

I read the fragments by you in *transition* and again I must say that I liked them very much—leading to the continuance of my belief that you would be the best possible translator [for the novels]. I really do not see how anybody else can get the sound quality, to name one thing, but I am willing to be convinced.

By all means, the translation should be done with only those modifications required by the change from one language to another. If an insurmountable obstacle is to appear, let it first appear.

I will look forward to hearing about progress towards a translation.

Yours sincerely,
Barney Rosset

August 4, 1953
New York

Dear Mr. Beckett,

I am putting aside *Watt*, which I received this morning, to write this letter. Fifty pages poured over me and I will inundate myself again as soon as possible. . . .

After the sample of *Godot* went back to you, the first part of *Molloy* arrived and I was most favorably impressed with it. I remember

Bowles' story in the second issue of *Merlin* and it does seem that he has a real sympathy for your writing. If you feel satisfied, and find it convenient to work with him, then my opinion would be to tell you to go ahead. Short of your doing the work yourself the best would be to be able to really guide someone else along—and that situation you seem to have found.

Again a mention of words. Those such as skivvy and cutty are unknown here, and when used they give the writing a most definite British stamp. That is perfectly all right if it is the effect you desire. If you are desirous of a little more vagueness as to where the scene is set it would be better to use substitutes which are of common usage both here and in Britain.

I am happy to be reading *Watt* and I hope to see more of *Molloy* soon

With best regards,
Barney Rosset

September 1, 1953
6 rue des Favorites
Paris 15me

Dear Mr. Rosset

Thank you for your letters of August 4th and July 31st both received yesterday only and also for the translation from *Godot*. . . .

It is good news that my translation of *Godot* meets with your approval. It was done in great haste to facilitate the negotiations of Mr. Oram and I do not myself regard it as very satisfactory. But I have not yet had the courage to revise it. . . . I understand your point about the Anglicisms and shall be glad to consider whatever suggestions you have to make in this connexion. But the problem involved here is a far-reaching one. Bowles's text as revised by me is bound to be quite unamerican in rhythm and atmosphere and the mere substitution here and there of the American for the English term is hardly likely to improve matters, on the contrary. We can of course avoid those words which are incomprehensible to the American reader, such as *skivvy* and *cutty*, and it will be a help to have them pointed out to us. In *Godot* I tried to retain the French atmosphere as much as possible and you may have noticed the use of English and American place-names is confined to Lucky whose own name might seem to justify them.

Yours sincerely
Samuel Beckett

Shortly after this exchange of letters,[16] my wife Loly and I went to Paris for the first of many meetings with Sam Beckett. We embarked for Europe on the small but elegant French liner SS *Flandre*, aboard which I was seasick before we got out of New York Harbor.

As I wrote in an essay published in S. E. Gontarski's *A Companion to Samuel Beckett*, my first meeting with Beckett took place at the bar of Le Pont Royale Hotel on Rue Montalembert, almost next door to Gallimard, France's largest literary publisher: "Beckett came in, tall, taciturn and wearing a trench-coat. He was on his way to another appointment, he announced, and had time only for a single quick drink. 'He arrived late,' Loly remembered, 'looked most uncomfortable, and never said a word except that he had to leave soon. I was pained by his shyness, which matched Barney's. In desperation, I told him how much I had enjoyed reading *Godot*. At that, we clicked, and he became warm and fun.'"[17]

The other appointment forgotten, the three of us went to dinner and to various bars, ending up at Sam's old hangout, La Coupole, on Boulevard du Montparnasse at three in the morning, with Beckett ordering champagne.

14/12/1953
6 rue des Favorites
Paris 15me

Dear Barney and Loly

Sorry for the no to design you seem to like. It was good of you to consult me. Don't think of me as a nietman. The idea is all right. But I think the variety of symbols is a bad mistake. They make a hideous column and destroy the cohesion of the page. And I don't like the suggestion and the attempt to express it of a hierarchy of characters. A la rigueur, if you wish, simple capitals, E. for Estragon, V. for Vladimir, etc., since no confusion is possible, and perhaps no heavier in type than those of the text. But I prefer the full name. Their repetition, even when corresponding speech amounts to no more than a syllable, has its function in the sense that it reinforces the repetitive text. The symbols are variety and the whole affair is monotony. Another possibility is to set the names in the middle of the page and text beneath, thus:

ESTRAGON
I'd rather he'd dance, it'd be more fun.
POZZO
Not necessarily.
ESTRAGON
Wouldn't it, Didi, be more fun?

VLADIMIR

I'd like well to hear him think.

ESTRAGON

Perhaps he could dance first and think afterwards,
if it isn't too much to ask him.[18]

But personally I prefer the Minuit composition. The same is used by Gallimard for Adamov's theatre (1st vol. just out). But if you prefer the simple capitals it will be all right with me.

Could you possibly postpone setting of galleys until 1st week in January, by which time you will have received the definitive text? I have made a fair number of changes, particularly in Lucky's tirade, and a lot of correcting would be avoided if you could delay things for a few weeks. . . .

The tour of Babylone *Godot* mostly in Germany (including the Gründgens theatre in Düsseldorf), but also as far as the Milan Piccolo, seems to have been successful. . . . Marvellous photos, unposed, much superior to the French, were taken in Krefeld during actual performance. One in particular is fantastic (end of Act 1, Vladimir drawing Estragon towards wings, with moon and tree). It *is* the play and would make a remarkable cover for your book. I shall call at the theatre this afternoon before posting this and add address of photographer in case you are interested in purchasing the set.

Best wishes for Xmas and the New Year.

Sam

That was the same Beckett who a year later would write me: "It's hard to go on with everything loathed and repudiated as soon as formulated, and in the act of formulation, and before formulation . . . I'm horribly tired and stupefied, but not yet tired and stupefied enough. To write is impossible but not yet impossible enough." It was the same lovely, courtly Beckett who had written:

ESTRAGON: I can't go on.
VLADIMIR: That's what you think.

The problem of who was going to translate *Godot* into English was a thorny one. Perhaps when Beckett wrote in French, no one looked over his shoulder, and he could achieve a more dispassionate purity. Perhaps he was also angry at the British for failing him as publishers. His novel *Murphy* and a short story collection, *More Pricks Than Kicks*, had achieved little notice in England. Perhaps Beckett felt he was too lyrical in English. He was always striving to strip away as many of his writer's tools as possible before finally ceasing to write altogether—taking away tools as you would take away a shovel from a person who wants to dig.

Because Beckett was never satisfied with any of his English translators, I kept trying to persuade him to do the job himself. It's my belief he always wanted to go back to writing in English, and he did, for the most part, from then on. But I felt he needed to be encouraged. Sam finally came to the only possible conclusion. He did the translation of *Godot* himself. The novels trailed behind.

"It's so nice where we are—snowed-in, quiet, and sootless, that I think you might like it," I wrote my new author in January 1954 from our East Hampton bunkerlike Quonset-hut home. The letter concerned the page proofs of *Waiting for Godot*, the work that would change the course of modern theater.

Formal at first, our correspondence quickly warmed. Sometimes Beckett typed, at my rather brash request, and sometimes letters were written in his almost indecipherable tiny script. In a world where writers switch publishers at the first shake of a martini pitcher, our transatlantic communications seemed to float on a sea of tranquility and trust.

Grove published *Waiting for Godot* in 1954, as well as Jean Genet's *The Maids* and *Deathwatch*.

I introduced Beckett to Joan Mitchell in 1956. They hit it off at once, the craggy droll writer and the attractive young painter. Joan loved writing, poetry especially (she would illustrate books of poems by Gary Snyder, James Schuyler, Frank O'Hara, and many more). Beckett was fascinated by art and had many artist friends. Both were heavy drinkers.

Joan had spent many off-hours at the Cedar Street Tavern, where talk, drunkenness, and occasional physical violence punctuated the evening. De Kooning would yell insults at O'Hara as he came in with Joan—the artists were macho, and few women, all of them highly competitive, were part of the club. Joan held her own, she could out drink and out talk most of the men. Joan had developed as an artist, moving onto larger canvases and finding her own style as an Abstract Expressionist. Her painting was becoming unique, and before she was thirty she had achieved her own style, fluid and violent, characterized by a wild flow of paint.

We had kept in touch, our friendship growing stronger since our divorce. She had begun spending part of the year in Paris, probably for self-protection and also to get away from the intrusive atmosphere of the New York art world. In Paris she met painter Jean-Paul Riopelle, with whom she would maintain a relationship for over twenty years. By 1959 she decided to move to France permanently, but still kept her apartment on St. Mark's Place in New York City. She took a studio at 10 rue Frémicourt and began a new creative thrust into dark disintegrating nature and into her inner moods. She had major battles with Riopelle, which might include the slashing of each other's paintings.

At Le Dôme, Beckett would get together with Joan, Riopelle, Bram van Velde, and Alberto Giacometti. He also became a regular visitor to Joan's studio, where he spent hours, and they would frequently go off drinking together at local bistros. Joan told me that she and Beckett were discussing an illustrated edition of his radio play *Embers*. She painted a few watercolors for the book but then abandoned the idea, feeling that the play was perfect on its own. Beckett grew to depend on Joan for companionship and talk, and the talk often dwelled on loneliness and death, with glimmers of humor in the darkness.

As I wrote in Gontarski's Beckett anthology, Suzanne Déchevaux-Dumesnil, who would not become Sam's wife until 1961, had been his strongest supporter for many years. She was his manager and practical organizer, tending to his every need, protecting him from the world, and vigorously promoting his career. Tall, handsome, and austere, she was even more reclusive than he, never, as far as I know, learning English, and walling herself off from his friends. I remembered her making an attempt to study English at Berlitz when we first met, but it seemed to go against her grain, and I never actually heard her speak anything but French.

During the German occupation of Paris, Sam and Suzanne, who were part of the Resistance and were in danger of arrest by the Gestapo, went to the South of France and hid out on an isolated farm near Roussillon, in the Vaucluse, to which Beckett specifically refers in *Godot* as well as mentioning one of the local farmers by name. There in the Vaucluse the emptiness and monotony of the days stretched on until it must have seemed like an eternity to Beckett.

For three years, Beckett and Suzanne were mostly alone, and I get the feeling of their being bored with each other, not knowing how to pass the time, and wondering what they were doing there and when the hell they were going to get out, and not wanting ever to see each other again, and yet not being able to leave one another. The heart of *Godot* must be inextricably intertwined with all of this. In one exchange between the protagonists Estragon has gone off and is beaten up. Upon his return there is this exchange:

VLADIMIR: You again! . . . Come here till I embrace you . . . Where did you spend the night?
ESTRAGON: Don't touch me! Don't question me! Don't speak to me! Stay with me!
VLADIMIR: Did I ever leave you?
ESTRAGON: You let me go.

While Beckett clearly indicates an all-male cast for *Godot* (he even refused permission to two top American actresses, Estelle Parsons and Shelley Winters, to perform it in 1973), I believe he had taken that very real situation—he and Suzanne on an isolated farm, waiting—and converted it into an eternal predicament, a universal myth. I thought the latent sexuality became much clearer in the New York 1988 Lincoln Center production of *Godot* with Robin Williams as Estragon and Steve Martin as Vladimir. They accentuated the male/female sides of their characters in important ways.

Beckett's life with Suzanne seemed to have had the despairing yet persevering, separate yet joined, quality in many of his other plays as well. In *Endgame*:

HAMM: . . . Why do you stay with me?
CLOV: Why do you keep me?
HAMM: There's no one else.
CLOV: There's nowhere else.[19]

Beckett was very precise about his stage directions, including the look and size of the sets, and I believe that the configuration of his and Suzanne's two Paris apartments reflected their deepening impasse as graphically as did his instructions for the settings of his plays.

Their first apartment, at 6 rue des Favorites, was in a fairly lively neighborhood. A tiny duplex, it had two small rooms, one above the other, the lower one sparsely furnished with just enough chairs for a few people to sit down, and a couple of paintings. There was a claustrophobic feeling to it, but at least the place was close to friendly restaurants and bars once you got outside. I never saw the upstairs bedroom, but cannot imagine it to have been particularly sybaritic. When Sam and Suzanne fled Paris to escape from the Nazis, the latter did them an accidental favor. Their apartment was locked up and left that way so that after the war they were able to reoccupy it without anything having been changed.

One night when they still lived there, Sam and I spent an evening together. I was driving and I remember that the dawn was just lighting the skies as we got to ue Frémicourt. Then something happened. All the streetlights went out, but not because dawn was breaking. An electricity strike had just started. In Paris, at least at that time, you got into your house by pushing a button, on the outside, to open your door. Without this *minuterie* functioning you could not enter or even warn somebody inside that you were there.

So Sam and I drove to my hotel, Le Pont Royal. There the front door was open but the elevator wasn't working. We trudged up seven floors to my isolated room at the top, briefly looked at the sun rising over Paris, and then climbed into bed, a nice big double one. Now I could say that I had been to bed with Samuel Beckett.

When Sam and Suzanne moved, it was to an even more appropriate setting for Beckett. It was right across from La Santé Prison, with a view down into the exercise yard. Sam had a deep identification with prisoners, so this flat was made to order. The neighborhood, near the outskirts of Paris where the Metro emerges from the underground to run down the middle of Boulevard St. Jacques (he lived at No. 38), was grim, impersonal, as bleak as any Beckett setting. It's hard to find a place like that in Paris, a *banlieu* where there are hardly any bars or restaurants or little shops or people in the streets. The building in which Beckett lived had several floors, a cramped entryway, and the usual tiny French elevator. On his landing, small in itself, were two doors leading to two separate apartments. To reach Sam's, you turned right, and he let you in. To the left you would find Suzanne. There were two rooms in Sam's part, a small study with a lot of books and papers very neatly arranged, and a bedroom with a skinny cot and an ordinary bureau. Then there was a narrow little kitchen placed horizontally in the rear, rather like a corridor that connected the two apartments. So the living spaces were connected but you could close them off with the doors placed at each end of the kitchen. Her friends could come and go to her place, and his friends could visit him, but they didn't have to see one another if they didn't feel like it. It was a unique, chilly arrangement, and I never saw Suzanne again after the move.

Of course, that might have been because I fell asleep at the Paris opening of *Endgame* sitting beside her. I'd just flown in from New York and was half-dead of jet lag—I heard she never forgave me for that. Later, as I understand it, she became ill and increasingly difficult and withdrawn, and perhaps saw no one.

Sam and she were in Tunisia when it was announced that he had won the Nobel Prize in Literature.

Beckett had at least one other close woman friend I know of during his time with Suzanne. She was an English woman, Barbara Bray, a translator who had worked for the BBC in London. Previously married, with two children, Barbara was nearly thirty years younger than Beckett. She moved to France in the early 1960s and lived there ever since. Slim and dark-haired, as I remember, she was pretty in an English way. She was highly intelligent and quite similar to Beckett: laid-back and concerned with accuracy in translation. Barbara was very close to him, and she may well have been one of his strongest attachments during the period I knew him. I recall several instances when he and I had been out drinking and it was late, but not so late for us—only about three in the morning. I'd offer to walk him home, and he would say something like: "No, I'm going to stop by and see Barbara."

During this period Beckett continued to live with Suzanne. When he finally married her in Folkestone, England, in 1961, he was 54, she 61.

Barbara's close friendship with Beckett continued. I remember one evening in particular in 1965 when Harold Pinter was in Paris for the opening of the French production of his plays *The Collection* and *The Lover*. Barbara, Harold, Sam, my girlfriend at the time Nicole Tessier, and I were at a bar right off Boulevard du Montparnasse where Beckett liked to go. It was called the Falstaff and featured beer. To me, except for the name, it was as French as anyplace else.

We occupied a narrow table that butted up against a wall, Barbara and Harold seated opposite each other, then Sam and my girlfriend next to each other, with me at the end. I began to notice that Barbara and Harold were discussing Sam very admiringly but sort of as if he were a sacred object they were having an academic chat about, not involving him in the conversation at all. I could see that he was getting increasingly irritated, and finally Sam took his stein and banged it on the table hard enough to spill some beer. Then he got up and walked across the room in the ungainly gait he had before his cataract operation, which gave people the impression that he was drunk when he was just having difficulty seeing. I watched him slowly climb the narrow stairs to the men's room and disappear. A hush fell over our table. When he reappeared and seemed to be making his way back to us, he stopped about twenty feet away and sat down at another table with two people whom I slowly realized were total strangers to him. He stared at us for a few minutes, then rejoined our party without comment or excuse. That was one of his rare shows of anger.

As I mentioned in *The Grove Press Reader*, similar moments of passion appear here and there in the emotional texture of Beckett's work, sudden oases of piercingly romantic fulfillment and loss in which the prose becomes suffused with sensuality and then with tears. I felt this most in *Krapp's Last Tape*, my favorite of Beckett's plays, a monologue written in English in 1958. In it, a ruined old man plays and replays tapes from his younger days, trying to find some meaning in his life. One passage is excruciatingly passionate. The affair between Krapp and his lover has now been destroyed beyond retrieval.

> We drifted in among the flags and stuck. The way they went down, sighing, before the stem! (Pause.) I lay down across her with my face in her breasts and my hand on her. We lay there without moving. But under us all moved, and moved us, gently, up and down, and from side to side . . .[20]

Then the previous tape is replayed.

Led to it by Beckett, I searched for the nineteenth-century German novelist Theodor Fontane's *Effi Briest* for clues to this passage. Finally Beckett revealed to me that it related to a summer with his cousin Peggy Sinclair in 1929 at a small resort on the Baltic Sea, where Peggy was engrossed in Fontane's novel about a young girl's calamitous life that ended with her death from tuberculosis. Although Beckett was only twenty-three at the time, his feeling for Peggy and the memory of their being together survived her engagement to another man and her death in 1933, coincidentally also of tuberculosis.

The story struck an incredibly strong chord in me. It reopened my suffering of the loss of a young love, my Nancy Ashenhurst. I still grieve for Nancy, and have dreams about her. This bond of early bereavement led me to find other references to Peggy Sinclair in Beckett's later works, particularly in *Ohio Impromptu*, a short play of extraordinary lyricism that was published by Grove in 1981 in a collection called *Rockaby and Other Short Pieces*. In *Ohio Impromptu* the protagonist seeks relief from the memory of "the dear face" by moving to an unfamiliar place, "back to where nothing ever shared." However, there is no relief until a man sent by "the dear name" comes to comfort him by reading and rereading a "sad tale" from a "worn volume." Finally the messenger says he has had word from "the dear name" that he (the messenger) shall not come again:

> So the sad tale a last time told they sat on as though turned to stone. . . .
> What thoughts who knows. Thoughts, no, not thoughts. Profounds of mind. Buried in who knows what profounds of mind.[21]

Beckett often sat "as though turned to stone" during his long silences. I remember him "buried in who knows what profounds of mind."

His friendship with Barbara Bray, I think, may well have given inspiration for a short, extremely bitter 1963 work called *Play* in which a husband, wife, and mistress, encased up to their necks in urns, are trapped in an eternal triangle, condemned endlessly to repeat the details of the husband and mistress's affair under the glare of a harsh, inquisitorial spotlight.

Shortly after completing *Play*, which Alan Schneider directed at the Cherry Lane Theatre in Greenwich Village, Beckett made his only trip to the United States. It was in the summer of 1964, and he came to be here for the shooting in New York of his motion picture *Film*, which I had commissioned him to write.

In 1962 I had started a new unit, Evergreen Theater, to produce films outside of Grove Press but with Grove people, specifically Fred Jordan and Dick Seaver, and one non-Grove person, Alan Schneider, a close friend I had come to know because of Sam.[22]

Very ambitiously, I made a list of writers—with the help of my associates—whom we asked to write scripts for us to produce. Those writers were, first and foremost, Samuel Beckett, as well as Harold Pinter, Eugène Ionesco, Marguerite Duras, and Alain Robbe-Grillet. They all said yes to our request and all of them wrote their scripts. Duras and Robbe-Grillet both wrote full-length scenarios for us. We envisaged the Beckett, Ionesco, and Pinter scripts as constituting a trilogy.

These five were all Grove Press authors. I invited three more to contribute, including another Grove author, Jean Genet. Fred Jordan and I went to London to make the request, but he said no. The last two authors we asked to write scripts for us were Ingeborg Bachmann and Günter Grass. I trailed Bachmann to Zurich (I think) to get her no, and I went to Berlin to see Grass. He lived in what I recall as being a sort of bombed-out area, in a precarious, small building. You reached its second floor, if he wanted you to, via a ladder that he extended down to you in lieu of a staircase. Grass was completely charming and friendly, but the outcome was the same as with Bachmann.

Out of the five scripts we did get, we were unfortunately able only to produce Samuel Beckett's *Film* because of financial constraints.

I set out to create a production team to turn Beckett's script into a motion picture. The most important member of that team was Sam himself. He wrote, he guided, and he kept the ship afloat. Alan Schneider had had no previous film experience but had done a great deal of successful theater directing, including plays by Pinter, Albee, and especially Beckett. There was no doubt in my mind that we could overcome that problem.

The other top two people on the production team were Sidney Meyers and Boris Kaufman. Sidney was an acclaimed veteran filmmaker who in 1960 had been awarded the BAFTA Flaherty Documentary Award for *The Savage Eye* (which he shared with Joseph Strick and Ben Maddow). Meyers was nominated for both the Venice Film Festival Golden Lion Award in 1949 and for an Academy Award for *The Quiet One* in 1950. He was also a consummate musician, a self-effacing, literate, and intelligent man, and he got along beautifully with Sam. And, not incidentally, he had helped me in a very important and selfless way at the end of the production work on my earlier film project, *Strange Victory*.

Boris Kaufman was our cinematographer, with Haskell Wexler and Helen Levitt. Boris was the brother of the famous Soviet directors Dziga Vertov and Mikhail Kaufman. Unbeknownst to me, he had won the Academy Award in 1955 for *On the Waterfront*, but very important for me was that he had been the cinematographer on Jean Vigo's great films *À Propos de Nice* (1930), *Zéro de Conduite* (1933), and *L'Atalante* (1934). These were perhaps my favorite films above all others. The filmmaker I had felt most akin to was Vigo. Our crew was now complete.

Judith Schmidt, my invaluable assistant, retyped the script after conferences held and audiotaped in East Hampton. We had flown Beckett in to stay there when he first arrived from Paris. He arrived at night at the little East Hampton airport where there was a very dramatic landing—they had thrown on some searchlights and it all reminded me of *Casablanca*. Several days later, we went back to New York City to shoot *Film*.

Alan Schneider had suggested Buster Keaton for the lead role in *Film* and Sam liked the idea. So Alan flew out to Hollywood to attempt to sign up Buster. There he found the great silent star living in extremely modest circumstances. On arrival, Alan had to wait in a separate room while Keaton finished up an imaginary (perhaps drunk) poker game with, among others, the legendary but long-dead Hollywood moguls Louis B. Mayer and Irving Thalberg. Keaton took the job.

Sometime after *Film* was finished and being shown, Kevin Brownlow, a Keaton/Chaplin scholar, interviewed Beckett about working with Keaton. Beckett said,

> Buster Keaton was inaccessible. He had a poker mind as well as a poker face. I doubt if he ever read the text—I don't think he approved of it or liked it. But he agreed to do it and he was very competent. He was not our first choice. . . . It was Schneider's idea to use Keaton, who was available. . . . He had great endurance, he was very tough, and, yes, reliable. And when you saw that face at the end—oh. At last.[23]

When Brownlow asked Beckett if he had ever told Keaton what the film was about, Sam said,

I never did, no. I had very little to do with him. He sat in his dressing room, playing cards . . . until he was needed. The only time he came alive was when he described what happened when they were making films in the old days. That was very enjoyable. I remember him saying that they started with a beginning and an end and improvised the rest as they went along. Of course, he tried to suggest gags of his own. . . . His movement was excellent—covering up the mirror, putting out the animals—all that was very well done. To cover the mirror, he took his big coat off and he asked me what he was wearing underneath. I hadn't thought of that. I said, "The same coat." He liked that. The only gag he approved of was the scene where he tries to get rid of the animals—he put out the cat and the dog comes back, and he puts out the dog and the cat comes back—that was really the only scene he enjoyed doing.

Brownlow asked Sam what the film meant, what it was about, and Sam replied, "It's about a man trying to escape from perception of all kinds—from all perceivers, even divine perceivers. There is a picture which he pulls down. But he can't escape from self-perception. It is an idea from Bishop Berkeley, the Irish philosopher and idealist, 'To be is to be perceived'—'*Esse est percipi.*' The man who desires to cease to be must cease to be perceived. If being is being perceived, to cease being is to cease to be perceived."

Beckett went on to say that distinguishing between the modes of being perceived was a major technical roadblock:

There was one big problem we couldn't solve—the two perceptions— the extraneous perception and his own acute perception. The eye that follows that sees him and his own hazy, reluctant perception of various objects. Boris Kaufman devised a way of distinguishing between them. The extraneous perception was all right, but we didn't solve his own. He tried to use a filter—his view being hazy and ill defined. This worked at a certain distance but for close-ups it was no good. Otherwise it was a good job.

Besides the problem of capturing the two perceptions there was another technical problem. It was when we attempted to use "deep focus" in the film. Originally, *Film* was meant to run nearly thirty minutes. Eight of those minutes were to have been used in one very long shot in which a number of actors would make their only appearance. The shot was based on a technique developed by Samuel Goldwyn and his great cameraman, Gregg Toland. (It had been used to stunning effect by Orson Welles, with Toland as cameraman, in *Citizen Kane*.) Even when panning their camera, "deep focus" allowed objects from as close as a few feet to as far as several hundred feet to be seen in the same shot with equal clarity. Toland's work was so important to Welles that he gave his cameraman equal billing. Sad to say, our "deep focus" work in *Film* was unsuccessful. Despite the abundant expertise of our group, the extremely difficult shot was ruined by a stroboscopic effect that caused the images to jump around.

We went on without that shot. Beckett averted this incipient disaster by removing the scene from the script.

In his book *Entrances* Alan Schneider recalls,

> Sidney [Meyers] proceeded to do a very quick, very rough cut for Sam to look at before taking off for Paris. And that first cut turned out to be not too far off from what we finally had. The editing was painstaking—and painful. Sidney always gently trying to break the mold we had set in the shooting, and Sam and I in our different ways always gently holding him to it. There was no question of sparring over who had the legal first cut or final cut or whatever. We talked, argued, tried various ways, from Moviola to screen and back again, to make it come out as much the film that Sam had first envisioned as we could.[24]

In New York, Sam and Alan stayed with me and my new wife, Cristina Agnini, in our house on Houston Street in Greenwich Village. When the shooting stopped, all Beckett wanted to do was get back to France as soon as possible so we booked an early morning flight, set our alarm, and I promised to wake him at 7:30, in time to get to the airport. At 9:00 a.m. Cristina and I woke up, horrified to find that we had overslept, and we were appalled to stumble over Beckett sitting outside our bedroom door, wearing his overcoat even though it was July. He had his packed bag on the floor next to him and was sound asleep. It never occurred to him to knock on our door. I made another airline reservation for 5:00 p.m., and the three of us spent the day at the New York World's Fair in Flushing Meadows, wandering among the exhibits. We somehow managed to lose our homesick writer along the way. After a frantic search we found him, on a bench, sound asleep again. We revived him enough for him to buy two knitted Greek purses—one for Cristina and one for Suzanne—whereupon we escorted him to an air-conditioned bar at what was then Idlewild Airport for drinks until departure time. "This is somehow not the right country for me," Sam told us at the bar. "The people are too strange." Then he said, "God bless," got on the plane, and was gone, never to return to the United States again.

Once Sam was back in Paris, things went on as before—I continued to visit him there. Since both he and I had been deeply involved in school athletic competition, I as co-captain of my high school football team and he the leader of his school cricket squad, sports provided us with another common ground. I tried my hand at Beckett's favorite pastimes, chess and billiards, but found them too maddeningly demanding of precision. Beckett, for his part, enjoyed playing my more slapdash table tennis. As a spectator sport we settled on tennis, which we both had once played, and now we often attended matches at Roland Garros stadium on the outskirts of Paris. I remember one time in particular, a match between the great American Pancho Gonzales and Lew Hoad, the Australian champion of the time. The referee was a Basque and an admirer of Beckett's. As he mounted his tall chair courtside, he waved enthusiastically at Sam. A couple of sets later, before a booing crowd, the referee was ejected at Gonzales' request after making a number of quite legitimate calls against him. Remarkably, he paused to chat for a moment in the midst of his forced exit.

Usually, however, Sam the writer and I the publisher just went out to eat and drink and talk. Beckett always had very set ideas about where to go and what to eat. At first his tastes were quite broad, but as the years went by they narrowed down, exactly like his writing, and the choices got fewer and fewer. In the beginning Beckett favored La Closerie des Lilas on Boulevard du Montparnasse, where Hemingway had liked to go, and where names of famous writers were embossed on the tables. There was also the grandiose La Coupole, a small bar called Rosebud, and the allegedly English pub Falstaff. But especially congenial was a seafood brasserie in a tough, nightlife neighborhood nearby, Ile des Marquises, where *le patron* revered Beckett and had a photograph of him on the wall along with huge glossies of Marcel Cerdan (the Algerian boxer and world middleweight champion killed in a transatlantic crash), the great American boxer Sugar Ray Robinson, and other assorted personalities. Beckett's photo hung between the two fighters.

One New Year's Eve, sometime in the early 1970s, Cristina, her mother, and our children—my daughter Tansey and son Beckett, Sam's namesake— were in Paris with me. Beckett was vacationing in Morocco with Suzanne. That night the phone rang in our hotel room. It was Marvin Josephson, the famed Hollywood agent, calling to say he was representing Steve McQueen, who desperately wanted to make a film of *Waiting for Godot*. Money was no object, Beckett could have complete control and any other actors he chose: Laurence Olivier, Peter O'Toole, and Marlon Brando were mentioned.

After I ascertained that the agent was very much for real and that the top price for a film property seemed to be $500,000, then a princely sum, I wrote to him and stipulated that amount. Josephson replied that the offer was $350,000, and it was absolutely firm and put in writing. The matter was dropped until I saw Beckett again on St. Patrick's Day for dinner at the Ile des Marquises. Anxious to secure some money for Sam, I told him of the offer for the proposed film, playing up Steve McQueen and, for some reason, Brando. Beckett asked what this McQueen looked like and I, grasping at straws, summoned up an image of James Garner. "He's a tall, husky, good-looking guy," I winged it. And Marlon Brando? "Even bigger, a huge, heavy-set fellow." Sam thought for a while and then said, "No. It will never work. My characters are shadows."

Near the end, Beckett refused to go to his old haunts, and it all narrowed down to an ersatz bistro called Le Petit Café in a monstrosity of a new hotel near his apartment. Originally the hotel was called the PLM, later changed to Pullman St. Jacques. It had a garish, undersized, Vegas-like marquee, and I thought of its lobby as resembling a souped-up railway station at rush hour with busloads of German and Japanese tourists swarming up and down its long escalators. All it needed was a bank of slot machines. Visiting athletes were also a specialty, and I remember the Scottish rugby team, brawny men in tams and kilts, all drunk as lords, horsing around in the lobby to the astonishment of a tour group of early-teenage Japanese girls. I also recall a boxing ring being set up in the lobby and a loudspeaker announcing: "Will the Australian trampoline team please report to the fourth floor." Beckett stayed oblivious to it, totally out of place and impassive in the midst of all this international action.

I, after intricate maneuvering, brought Beckett and photographer Richard Avedon together in April 1979 at Le Petit Café in one of the most awkward and enigmatic encounters of my life. The celebrated photographer said his technique of using a white sheet as a backdrop was philosophically derived from Beckett. He also had said to me that he had shot everybody he wanted to with the exception of Greta Garbo and Beckett. I made arrangements for Avedon and Beckett to meet, stressing to Avedon that there was no guarantee Beckett would actually agree to pose and it would not be an easy task to convince him.

Avedon came from Tokyo and I from New York with my fourth wife, Elisabeth Krug, known as Lisa, my daughter Tansey, and son Beckett who was then ten years old. Sam was his usual self, silent but listening. Lisa and my kids did the same, while Avedon, who seemed nervous, talked nonstop for about an hour until finally he said: "Okay, let's take the pictures." He asked both Samuel Beckett and my Beckett to go with him, and the three of them crossed the street and, for about half an hour, disappeared into a passageway through the Metro overpass. When they returned, nobody described what had happened, but I assumed the pictures had been taken.

I heard nothing further for a couple of months until one day I received two superb, very moving photos of my son with Samuel Beckett, beautifully mounted and framed and signed by Avedon. About a month later Sam himself, who had never before shown the slightest interest in such matters, asked what had happened to the photos. I wrote Avedon and received what I thought was a very peculiar response to the effect that Avedon had not taken any pictures of Samuel Beckett alone that day because the writer had seemed "unhappy," but that, because I had gone to so much trouble, he had taken a few shots of the two Becketts together.

My son Beckett said that after crossing under the Metro overpass they had come to a wall where a white sheet had been tacked up and an assistant waited for them in a car. There was a large camera fastened to a tripod. He described Avedon setting up the shot, focusing his camera with a black cloth over his head, then stepping out and squeezing the bulb a few times for the two Becketts and then for Sam by himself. The missing Beckett photos supposedly appeared in the French magazine *Egoïste*. I have never seen them, but a portrait of Sam alone was in Avedon's retrospective at the Metropolitan Museum of Art in New York in 2002.

A later, thornier encounter at Le Petit Café involved Beckett and Peter Getty, son of the famously wealthy Ann Getty, who, with Lord George Weidenfeld, had bought Grove, in a sad story to come, from me in 1985. (After Getty and Weidenfeld promised to keep me as CEO, they would wind up ousting me without ceremony the following year.) Smart and young, Peter Getty, who often borrowed subway fare from Grove employees to get uptown to his Fifth Avenue apartment, had learned I was meeting Beckett in Paris soon after my ouster, and asked to be introduced. I agreed, and Getty flew over, checked into a suite at the Ritz, and taxied out to Beckett's unlikely hangout, Le Petit Café, with a book he wanted autographed.

This was the only time Sam was not friendly to someone I introduced him to. It was a short, tense meeting. After autographing the book, he glared at Peter and asked, "How could you do this to Barney, and what do you plan to do about it?" Peter was very embarrassed, and mumbled something about consulting with his mother. Later, I heard that Beckett had told another suppliant from Grove, "You will get no more blood out of this stone," and he never allowed them to publish anything new of his again.

To me and a group of others assembled in his honor at La Coupole he said, "There is only one thing an author can do for his publisher and that is write something for him." And he did exactly that. It was the little book called *Stirrings Still*. It was to be his last prose work, and he dedicated it to me.

Stirrings Still is the meditations of an old man contemplating death. It brought back to me an ether dream I'd had as a little boy. I had an out-of-body experience, seeing myself as an object rocketing into space, zooming through a black void until I was transformed into a "knob of blackness." I knew I was experiencing the terror of my own death. Still, now, unable to sleep in a totally darkened room, I am hounded by that dream. When he wrote *Stirrings Still*, I don't know how much Sam was actually thinking of me, but I think I know why he wrote it. He was facing his own dream of death, which was fast approaching, and which, possibly, he finally made bearable by acceptance of that approaching darkness.

> Such and much more such the hubbub in his mind so-called till nothing left from deep within but only ever fainter oh to end. No matter how no matter where. Time and grief and self so-called. Oh all to end.[25]

In the mid-1980s, Beckett's health was clearly failing, although I couldn't admit this to myself. We now met exclusively at Le Petit Café, which had become his "club," and where he was totally ignored by outsiders. I took to staying at the

Pullman St. Jacques in order to be near him, and sometimes I ate meals alone in the fast-food café off the hotel's lobby. At breakfast they gave you a set of plastic-coated photographs, not unlike a deck of cards. One card had an egg on it, another card two eggs, another card a strip of bacon, and so on. To order, you went to the cashier and handed her the cards you'd selected.

In a funny way, it was pure Beckett. They had done away with the menu entirely, eliminating the need for words or translations of words; you could choose a meal in total silence. In the same vein, Beckett had made increasing use of the stage directions "pause" and "silence" in his work, and had pared down his vocabulary to fewer and fewer words.

At some point, Sam began having dizzy spells and falling in his apartment; apparently not enough blood was circulating to his brain. After brief stays in several hospitals he was moved to a nursing home only a few blocks from where he lived. The desire to go on had lessened even more. He was unsteady on his feet and even thinner, if that were possible, and therefore seemed taller and more and more like a figure done by his friend, the Italian artist Alberto Giacometti, who once had given Sam a drawing of a thin, striding man, a drawing Sam in turn gave to Cristina and me as a wedding present which we later used on the cover of Sam's *Worstward Ho*. Now he was just a ghost of even that drawing.

The nursing home was on a side street. It looked like the other small buildings on the block, with only a discreet plaque announcing its institutional function. You entered a sparsely furnished sitting room in which a number of old women, some with walkers, watched a couple of ancient TV sets. Then you went through a little dining room out into a tiny courtyard with a walkway and some grass. There were a few rooms looking out onto it. Beckett was in the first room, a cubicle with space enough only for a bed, a table, and two wooden chairs, with a small bath off it.

I visited Sam there a number of times. I found it cell-like and depressing and, together with his British publisher John Calder, tried to devise ways to move him to more comfortable quarters. But it was never easy to do Beckett a favor.

He also seemed to resist attempts to make his life more pleasant. In his perverse fashion he managed to get a phone on which he could not make overseas calls, declined to have a TV set or stereo equipment (although he loved music) or a bookcase or even a typewriter. He wrote things down in a little notebook in his small, intricate handwriting, kept his engagement records meticulously, and did always seem to have a bottle of Irish whiskey handy.

With Beckett it was a mistake to suppose that problems readily leant themselves to solutions, or that one thing necessarily led to another. Sam had started to go for walks, and sort of boasted to me—if you could ever say that Beckett boasted about anything—that he could walk farther than where his own apartment was, five blocks away. One day he told me he needed some papers from his apartment, so I asked why didn't he go home and pick them up and I would go with him?

Beckett threw up his hands. First roadblock: there was too much traffic on his boulevard; it made him dizzy. Well, let's go in a car, I said, pressing on. Beckett replied that he didn't have a car. Not to worry, I said, I'll get the car. Let's drive there. I was greeted with stony silence, and that was the end of that.

Perhaps a major factor was that Suzanne was still at the apartment and Beckett was ambivalent about the idea of seeing her. This was such an archetypical Beckett situation. It was *Endgame* again. Now they were Nagg and Nell in their garbage cans, unable to reach each other. She was ill, dying actually, although I didn't know that, and he, too, was ill. They were separated by only five blocks, yet they couldn't see each other. He needed papers from his apartment, yet he couldn't go there—all the entrances and exits were blocked.

The last time I visited Beckett I brought along an American TV set I had kept in Paris just for possible use with Sam, and a videotape of *Godot* being performed by the inmates of San Quentin State Prison. I had previously carted all this heavy equipment—the set, a transformer, and a VCR—in a huge shopping bag through customs to the Pullman St. Jacques, where Beckett used to come to my room. Now I lugged all the equipment to his nursing home.

Sam was visibly moved by the tape; the inmates had understood his play. So I thought, now I've got something going that he can enjoy in this arid place—we can have a correspondence utilizing videotapes. As I left, I casually asked Beckett if he would keep the set for future viewings. "Oh no, no, no," Sam answered, "I have no use for it." The subject was closed.

As I struggled out with my shopping bag, he said, "Oh Barney, that's too heavy for you. You shouldn't carry that." Then he walked over, lifted it, turned to me, and said, "No, it's all right. You can."

Again: You can't go on, you'll go on.

It was clear that the prospect of the introduction of ease or entertainment into his life distracted Beckett from the larger endgame already embarked on in his mind. A few months later he was *Not I*, as in the title of one of his plays. There was, at last, an *Act Without Words*.

Sam died on December 22, 1989. He was buried next to Suzanne, who died five months earlier, in the famous Cimetière du Montparnasse.

I was told that Barbara Bray was one of the few mourners at the secretive funeral. I received a letter from her that began: "Dear Barney, What can I say? We are all huddled together in our loss."

9

Grove Theater:
Harold Pinter and Other Playwrights

Once we had published Samuel Beckett, Grove continued to build a formidable list in the field of modern drama. We brought out most of the plays and other writings of Harold Pinter, Eugène Ionesco, Jean Genet, Joe Orton, Tom Stoppard, Friedrich Dürrenmatt, Brendan Behan, David Mamet, LeRoi Jones (Amiri Baraka), Antonin Artaud, Jack Gelber, Rolf Hochhuth, Ronald Harwood, Bernard Pomerance, William Inge, John Arden, Václav Havel, Alfred Jarry, Shelagh Delaney, and Slawomir Mrożek, and we republished Bertolt Brecht.

By the late 1950s, no other company was really competing with Grove in the publication of works for the theater. Many of the playwrights we published were not yet known widely in this country but their work would have a major impact on theater here and around the world.

What was more, we did something that many publishers didn't do—we kept an author's books in print and available. Grove had more than twenty-five volumes of Beckett in print and more than ten volumes of Pinter, Stoppard, and Ionesco, as well as many volumes of Mamet.

All was not smooth sailing, though. Brecht is an example. He had broken the US copyright laws in various ways, and we wanted to publish him in paperback. After being questioned by the House Un-American Activities Committee, Brecht decided to move to East Germany where he established the Berliner Ensemble theater company. Random House had been publishing his work in hardcover and Jason Epstein, who had come to Random House after making a tremendous success developing the Anchor Books trade paperback line at Doubleday, was adamantly opposed to Grove publishing Brecht in paperback. So Bennett Cerf took Jason and me to lunch and suggested that a compromise was possible. At a certain point during the meeting, Jason got up and said, "Why don't you give him Faulkner too!"—and left. Somehow we eventually reached an amiable solution to the problem without taking that drastic course.

When we signed up Pinter, I remember very well that we had not yet seen one of his plays performed, but his scripts clearly showed his writing was brilliant. The way he used silence was reminiscent, to me, of Beckett—but different. There was an all-pervading sense of menace. *The Dumb Waiter* was a good example. Pure menace, terrifying, brilliant theater charged with a silent danger.

Pinter's agent was Jimmy Wax. He and Harold were close friends. In New York they premiered *The Homecoming* on Broadway, but opening night was less than triumphant with many in the audience hating it. I remember asking Jimmy, "Who the hell did you invite to this opening?" I mean, at an opening when an author is already very well known, you can pick and choose who you're inviting—and you're giving away many tickets. At least you ought to get people who might like the play. But on that first night one woman in the audience stood up and shouted in the middle of the first act: "Let's get out of here, this is terrible!"

Pinter always talked and even acted as if he were a character in one of his plays. During the New York blackout of 1965, Cristina and I were in a Greenwich Village restaurant with Harold and my wife's sister. Initially, when the lights went out, we thought that the blackout was confined to the restaurant and its immediate vicinity. I got my car from our nearby house, parked it facing the restaurant, and turned on the headlights so we could see to eat. The restaurant staff did not object. We slowly realized there was a total blackout extending as far as we could see uptown. Harold sat there silently for a long time, then suddenly said, "Does this happen very often here?" I waited for about three minutes before answering, as if we were in one of his plays, and then said, "Not often. Every twenty years or so." Finally, Harold asked us to go back with him to his room at the luxurious, blacked-out Carlyle Hotel. We did and a city police officer carrying a flashlight escorted us up a back stairway. Back in his room, Harold read to us by candlelight a poem he had recently written. It was a memorable evening.

Pinter asked Beckett to critique everything he wrote, and Beckett liked Pinter both as a friend and as a writer, and paid him and his work close attention. The reverse was equally true.

On December 6 of that year I wrote to Pinter, saying, "I saw Sam and [he] seemed better than one might have hoped for. He told me that Barbara Bray had informed him that you had seen the New York *Godot* and liked it—but that you doubted that Sam would feel likewise. I am not so sure of that—No *Godot* can be all things to all people, but any given one—maybe this one especially could give a great deal of pleasure—and even insight—to many, including Sam. Why don't you tell him directly what you felt. I think that that would please him."

Harold was commissioned to do a screenplay of Proust's *Remembrance of Things Past* for a Rothschild family member, Nicole Stéphane. Barbara Bray and Joseph Losey worked with Pinter for a year to get it done. Then the Rothschild relative rejected it and, moreover, refused to let Harold produce it. She claimed all rights. Harold came with Wax to New York and called me. Pinter was very upset. He said he felt as if a part of him had been amputated. I assured him, "Well, at least Grove will publish it."

All this reminded me of growing up in Chicago, doing something when taking action was vital, no matter what the prospects of success might be, even if it was only symbolic. Bennett Cerf at Random, which had the American rights to all Proust publications, said they wouldn't stand in our way. The last Lafayette in France, an attorney in Paris on the Champs-Élysées who represented Proust's niece, also gave her approval for the publication of the screenplay. And so did Gallimard, the French publisher of Proust's work. So I cut the Gordian knot and we published Pinter's screenplay at Grove even if we could not make the film.

After all that, Harold later let me down with Beckett's play *Eleuthéria*, which Sam had initially told me I could publish in the wake of the disaster with Ann Getty and Lord Weidenfeld's acquisition of Grove. I asked Harold to write an introduction to our projected publication. He wrote back with two words, "I can't." I was crushed and felt betrayed. I took a passage out of Proust and sent it to him. It was where Swann says, "Good night, Albertine," and in the morning, he asks the maid, "Where is Albertine?" And the maid said, "Oh, didn't you know? She left last night."

Harold made me very sad. I hadn't thought we were that estranged and neither did he, or so I believed.

"Nothing will ever be the same." That was a phrase Beckett applied to *The Connection*, a play by a twenty-eight-year-old newcomer named Jack Gelber. It had opened in 1959 under the direction of Julian Beck's wife, Judith Malina, at the Living Theater, on the corner of Sixth Avenue and Fourteenth Street. Smashing the glass wall between actors and audience, *The Connection* brought the spectator—internally, not literally—right up into this pad where all these junkies, between riffs of onstage Charlie Parker–type jazz, were waiting for Cowboy to arrive with their fix. The reviewers from the daily papers would, in their hostility, have strangled it in its tracks if it were not for a rave in the *Village Voice* that kept the show going until other, equally affirmative, weekly appraisers could do their thing—and Grove could and did publish it. Beckett was right. Nothing in American playwriting has been quite the same since.

Grove also published Shelagh Delaney's *A Taste of Honey* in 1959. She was eighteen when she wrote the play, about a British working-class girl who becomes pregnant by a black sailor. Another playwright we put into print was Joe Orton, also from England. There was a Broadway opening of his first play, *Entertaining Mr. Sloane*, which also got a very similar reaction to *The Homecoming*. *Entertaining Mr. Sloane* had its premiere in London in May 1964. Orton went on to write a string of successful plays, including *Loot* and *What the Butler Saw*.

Quite a few other notable playwrights were featured in the pages of *Evergreen Review*. It was there that in 1960 Edward Albee's first play, *The Zoo Story*, first was published. I took Sam Beckett to Montauk see him, at Albee's strong request.

In 1967 we opened our own 154-seat off-Broadway playhouse, the Evergreen Theater, at 53 East Eleventh Street, just west of Broadway. The first performance there was Michael McClure's *The Beard*, a one-act fantasy about Billy the Kid and Jean Harlow, directed by Rip Torn. This wonderful and totally scandalous play had opened first in San Francisco at the Actor's Workshop in December 1965. Our October 1968 production featured a lightshow prelude performed with filmstrips and slide projections.

McClure had this to say about the play and our part in supporting it in *The Review of Contemporary Fiction*:

> As Goethe said, "You can expect me to be sincere, but not impartial."
> I can't be impartial where Barney is concerned. He is a terrific human being. Because of what he did—basically because of his generosity and his vision, his willingness to accept advice, his asking advice from the right people, his absolute bravery about taking his gamble, his politics, with which I generally agree, and his lack of fear. When I think of Barney I think of a man who defied the U.S. censorship system and he did it not once, but three or four times. . . . *The Beard* had been performed here in San Francisco—and we were busted—and it had been defended by the ACLU. It took a long time, but we finally won our case.[26]

The Beard became a favorite of mine. I published it in *Evergreen Review*, then as a book.

Another writer Grove championed was David Mamet, starting with his *American Buffalo*. To me, Mamet represented something extremely exciting. Of course, it didn't hurt that David and I had gone to the same Chicago school, Francis Parker, although not at the same time. But more than that, I saw a clear line of affinity from Beckett to Pinter to Mamet. Mamet was influenced by Pinter's work, just as Pinter was inspired by elements of Beckett's writing, especially his timing, and adapted it to his own work. Mamet's plays, like Pinter's, were charged with an air of menace, though Mamet's were altogether American. In *Glengarry Glen Ross* I thought Mamet had reached his highest level yet. All of that menace he'd really applied to his own language, his own view. Not a copy of Pinter, it is uniquely Mamet's own vision.

10

Into the Fray:
Lady Chatterley's Lover

In 1954, when Grove Press was still in its infancy, Mark Schorer, the distinguished literary scholar and professor of English at Berkeley, wrote to me suggesting that we publish an unexpurgated edition of *Lady Chatterley's Lover.* D. H. Lawrence's last major work had long been banned in England and put on the "proscribed" list by the United States Post Office Department. Now, Professor Schorer, whom I had never met in person, had placed the Lady on our doorstep. Here she was, waiting for her liberator. If we could prove to the satisfaction of the US courts our claims for the artistry of Lawrence as a writer and the specific merits of *Lady Chatterley's Lover* as literature, the victory for freedom of speech would be tremendous. It would be a savage kick in the face to Death and a lovely kiss to Life. What was more, it could afford me the opportunity to publish the novel I really had wanted to put out into the public sphere since my college days at Swarthmore: *Tropic of Cancer.*[27] This was clearly a Trojan horse for Grove. If I could get Lawrence through, then Henry Miller might surely follow.

Lawrence, with Italian publisher Giuseppe Orioli in Florence, had privately issued a 1,000-copy signed limited edition of the third and final manuscript version of *Lady Chatterley* in 1928, despite the disapproval of his British agent, Curtis Brown, and his publisher in English, Martin Secker. Orioli's efforts were largely in vain. Though a number of copies of this edition of the book, in mulberry-colored paper boards, got out, others were seized and banned in both England and the United States.

After Lawrence's death in 1930 at the age of forty-four, the truly obscene result for *Lady Chatterley's Lover* came in the form of the 1932 publication of an "expurgated" version by Secker in England and Alfred A. Knopf in the United States.

What was it that these publishers hoped to accomplish with this cleansing process? Were clean living and clean reading synonymous and equally meritorious? And who on earth did Knopf and his British equivalent choose to do the dirty work of purging our Lady of her dirty thoughts? How did these unnamed designated hitters choose which words, phrases, and paragraphs to swat out of the book? Any competent, "decent" publisher would have had a hand in choosing his home-team purifier. After all, it was his (in this case, read Knopf's) team. And what possibly did "expurgating" mean if not cutting out something already made illegal by our government, something supposedly dangerous, like absinthe. So, the Knopf "expurgated" *Chatterley* was deconstructed from the original to something along the lines of the de-sexed versions of Ovid given out to prep school Latin students, a kind of methadone before its time. It angers me to this day.

My thinking was, and is, that Knopf was effectively in collaboration with our Post Office in the evisceration of *Lady Chatterley*. They had left an attractive corpse, but her guts, her heart, her brain, and yes, her soul, were gone. Everything D. H. Lawrence had so wanted and worked to achieve with this particular and very special book had been thrown away.

Lawrence's widow, the now remarried Frieda Lawrence Ravagli, had always stood by him, including in his efforts to get *Lady Chatterley's Lover* published.

But after he died she seemed overwhelmed by the august weight of the fraternity of publishers and agents she had to deal with, and bowdlerized editions started to appear. Perhaps if her deceased cousin, the German fighter pilot Baron Manfred von Richthofen—the "Red Baron," probably the most famous ace of World War I—had still been around, the situation might have taken a different turn plus a barrel roll dive or two on the censors!

Alfred Knopf was not famed for his fighting propensities where censorship was concerned. However, he was right up there among the pretenders to the gentleman publisher's crown, so it was natural for him to follow the leadership of his English peers. For myself, I had no aristocratic pretensions to guard. I was ready if necessary to face being called a profiteer from smut. Henry Miller and his publisher, Jack Kahane of Obelisk Press in Paris, had already suffered through that, and Samuel Beckett had recently written to me, warning of what might lie ahead in the way of censorship in relation to his own work.

I was ready to fight if I thought I had the right books and authors to fight for, and now, thanks to Mark Schorer's suggestion, I did. It was time to challenge the Post Office to take us on. If necessary, we would take the fight to them. By shutting out *Lady Chatterley's Lover*, the censors would unwittingly create a weak point in the censorship wall. If companies with adequate funds and high literary pretensions could not step forward to exploit that exposed weakness, we would replace them.

Censors fell upon the unexpurgated version of *Lady Chatterley's Lover* because Lawrence, like lava flowing from a volcano, had inexorably gone on demanding a return to a more natural state—a lyrical one—in the relation between the sexes. He had set about trying to demolish the false restrictions on human relationships. He insisted on describing sexual episodes explicitly, and moreover, he was determined to give old Anglo-Saxon four-letter words their proper place in literature. When his book was banned in England, and dumped into the inventory of something called the US Collector for Restricted Merchandise Division, Alfred Knopf was not about to rescue it, and he found allies among some high-ranking academics who thought it fine for themselves to read *Lady Chatterley's Lover*, but dangerous for those less accredited.

The assumption was that most of us were susceptible to being corrupted, but a special few were not.

There was more to *Lady Chatterley* to offend the censors than its four-letter words and graphic lovemaking. The book, our self-appointed guardians felt, was written in a manner that was relatively easy to read. It was approachable. And they feared, rather than hoped, that it might be read by millions. They shuddered to think of all those lewd thoughts infecting the receptive souls of so many Americans, especially those impoverished by small incomes and miserable education.

As federal prosecutor S. Hazard Gillespie, Jr. would later state in a case against Grove, Mellors, the male protagonist in the novel was a gamekeeper and the heroine was an upper-class lady. This really upset the guardians of morals and class privileges. I felt from the outset that if it had been the reverse, a lord of the manor having sex with a pretty servant girl, it would have been all right. Also, the couple in Lawrence's novel had too much fun with sex. That would never do. It might be contagious.

To trigger the fight, I wrote to Joan Landis on March 31, 1954, who had worked for me at Grove in the early 1950s as a Bennington College intern, a most competent one and *muy simpático*. Originally directed to me by Wallace Fowlie, she was then living in Paris with her American husband. I asked Joan to buy four copies of the unexpurgated edition of *Lady Chatterley's Lover* and send them to me in New York. They were mailed on April 22. And then to guarantee that the books would not slip by some careless customs agent, I wrote to the New York Customs Service (now known as US Customs and Border Protection) notifying them that the books were en route. If you are intent on having a duel you have to notify your opposite number.

A month went by with no word. We were told that a delay of a month or so was not unusual for overseas parcels. But after a while when we hadn't received the books, I assumed they had been seized, though I had no official word one way or the other. So I asked Joan to airmail me an additional copy.

When I received the airmailed copy, I again wrote the Customs Service informing them that they had let *Lady Chatterley's Lover* slip through. Shame on them, I added. I then promptly redelivered it to their New York office to make sure they knew that this dangerous book had indeed arrived on our shores.

New York Customs did not want to be responsible for making a gaffe. Probably they did not want to risk a lawsuit from Grove Press or somehow being made to look like fools. This bureaucracy, even at the crest of its self-appreciation, decided that sending it up to another level was the prudent thing to do. So they dispatched the book to Washington, where the Collector for Restricted Merchandise—one of the more arcane departmental heads of our government—was to act as judge. I envisioned him ensconced in the deepest basement of the US Post Office building, the American equivalent of the Vatican's subterranean library of proscribed literature and art.

It wasn't until August 11 that Irving Fishman, Deputy Collector for Restricted Merchandise, offered an official position:

> The book in question is obscene within the meaning of Section 305 of the Tariff Act of 1930. This book will therefore be seized and forfeited in due course as provided by law.

The Mikado was in residence! His Lord High Executioner was ready to perform! It had taken months to get our gallant Lady Chatterley into trouble with the law, but now I had a basis for a suit against the federal government challenging its right to ban her. The gauntlet had been thrown down. It soon became apparent the Post Office was not about to be outdone by Gilbert and Sullivan.

Our case against the banning of the book—one that would later come into play during our battle to publish *Tropic of Cancer*—was based from the beginning on the concept of "literary merit." For me, there was a little taint of convenience attached to that concept. Nonetheless, it was the best ammunition at hand. It was also our law.

Next, I asked Mark Schorer to write an introduction for our edition to further this concept of literary value. To me, what he wrote still stands as one of the preeminent studies of D. H. Lawrence's book. At our request, Schorer visited

Frieda in Taos, New Mexico, where she gave him access to all three manuscript versions of *Lady Chatterley's Lover*. His account of the development of the final, unexpurgated draft demonstrated how vigorously Lawrence had struggled to perfect his novel as a work of art. The scholarly apparatus Schorer provided for our edition would later be of great help in the courtroom. If there was ever any desire on Schorer's part for profit, I never knew about it. The only fault I ever noticed in Mark was his affection for the Harvard Club. At the time, its bar was for men only. To me that condemned it before I ever entered, but to accommodate him and my attorney, Charles "Cy" Rembar, who was to be so crucial to the Miller lawsuits, I went to this blasphemous den more than once. (For the record, my lawyer in the initial stages was Ephraim London.)

I wrote to many critics, scholars, and attorneys seeking support for our claim that the book was of significant literary value and by no means obscene. Not all responded favorably, but many did, helping to build our basic defense.

Bennett Cerf, co-founder of Random House, who had won the landmark obscenity case against James Joyce's *Ulysses*, took me by surprise. He was one of the publishing gentry, but was nevertheless approachable and somehow, to my mind, vulnerable. But on *Lady Chatterley's Lover* he almost derailed us. In reply to my plea for support he wrote, "I can't think of any good reason for bringing out an unexpurgated version of *Lady Chatterley's Lover* at this late date. In my opinion the book was always a very silly story, far below Lawrence's usual standard, and seemingly deliberately pornographic. . . . I can't help feeling that anybody fighting to do a *Lady Chatterley's Lover* in 1954 is placing more than a little of his bet on getting some sensational publicity from the sale of a dirty book."[28] Still, I liked Cerf and more or less ignored his nasty response. Despite his initial reaction, ultimately he would become a good and valuable friend in the battle for *Lady Chatterley*.

Bennett Cerf aside, I received more than enough favorable support to proceed. Jacques Barzun, the cultural historian, wrote:

I have no hesitation in saying I do not consider Lawrence's novel pornographic. Its aim is that of all his work: artistic, moral and indeed inspired by a passion to reform our culture in ways that he thought would produce greater harmony, happiness, and decency.

And Archibald MacLeish responded:

Only those to whom words can be impure per se or those to whom "certain subjects" cannot be mentioned in print though they are constantly mentioned in life, or those to whom the fundamental and moving facts of human existence are "nasty" could conclude on the evidence of the text itself that *Lady Chatterley's Lover*, as Lawrence wrote it, is obscene.[29]

Lawrence's original edition of *Chatterley* was not in copyright. When he and Orioli brought it out, the book immediately became public property as far as publishing rights in the United States were concerned. Indeed, as I recall, when Knopf published the expurgated version in the United States in 1932, he did not even bother to register copyright. That further hardened the fact that anyone who wanted to publish it could do so without interference from the copyright office or any other publisher. Only the threat of arrest for publishing obscenity would remain.

I wanted to present the book in the best way possible. Although Ephraim London assured me *Chatterley* was in the public domain, that is, unprotected by copyright and publishable by anyone, with no strings attached, I wanted, emotionally and pragmatically, to have a signed agreement with Frieda Lawrence. I asked Mark Schorer to speak to her, and through him I offered her a ten percent royalty on all copies sold, although I was not obligated to do so.

Frieda, understandably, was quite confused about the legal technicalities. "I have the copyright," she wrote, "but Knopf has the publishing right. . . ."

I wrote to her explaining that legally there was no copyright, but that I would much prefer to have her "agreement and enthusiastic support."

All she could bring herself to do was wish me good luck. God bless her for that.

In England, Frieda was represented by Laurence Pollinger, a literary agent who had worked for Curtis Brown. Unlike Brown, he had supported Lawrence's decision to publish the private, limited edition. Pollinger had by this time formed his own firm and became a dominant influence on Frieda, controlling Lawrence's literary property, not to mention Frieda's income. When he learned that Grove was considering an American edition of the unexpurgated *Lady Chatterley's Lover*, although he knew that on legal grounds no one could stop us, he was adamantly against it. Could it have been that some sort of social snobbery and class loyalty was intruding again? I think so.

There were other obstacles. A Knopf executive, William Koshland, whom until then I had considered a friend, wrote to the American agent Allan Collins with instructions concerning Grove. Collins telephoned me and reported that Knopf considered himself the only authorized publisher of the US edition of *Lady Chatterley's Lover*, and that version was now under license to the paperback house New American Library. Further, Collins went on, if Grove succeeded in winning a positive court decision in our censorship case, Knopf would expect to be the publisher. Thus, Alfred Knopf used a literary agent to let us know his stand. On the one hand he didn't think an unexpurgated version could be published here. And on the other, if it could be, he intended to do it himself, thus benefiting from our expensive court actions, leaving Grove—which had far less clout than Knopf—in serious, precarious financial difficulties. Ultimately, he did not do that, but New American Library and others would take advantage of Grove's legal battle on behalf of the book. His stance was a preview of things to come. He couldn't prevent Grove from going ahead but, ultimately, to his credit, he did not carry out his threat. Still, it was hardly a gentle kind of coercion.

Most of the negotiations on the rights for *Lady Chatterley's Lover* were conducted in the spring and summer of 1954. At the time I had little money to work with. My father had helped me out until his death in September 1954, but the sums he contributed were relatively small, in line with the $3,000 paid for the original Grove Press and its inventory of perhaps a thousand paperbacks, which I had stored in the third floor apartment of the brownstone I lived in on West Ninth Street in Greenwich Village. I could not ask him to finance such an open-ended gamble as a long court case for a book whose rights I didn't even own. After his death, although my mother was willing to help, I found myself embroiled in a hands-on fight with the bank that had been named co-executor of my father's estate with me—the Continental Bank. The money was to be put in a trust for my mother for as long as she lived, and the remaining funds would go to me. Obviously, the situation was not conducive to freeing up money for the *Lady Chatterley* battle against censorship.

I was co-executor, with the biggest bank in Chicago, of my father's estate. What I did was rather incredible—I can now see this in hindsight. I took my father's bank, Metropolitan Trust Co., and merged it with Grove Press. Practically overnight Grove consisted of paperback and hardcover books and 90-day US government bonds! Both were confected from paper, but that was the only similarity. Predictably, the Continental Bank, my co-executor, objected.

Suddenly I was involved in a two-front war—the kind of war I had been taught by Karl Marx to most assiduously avoid. Some people might have considered the Continental Bank tougher and more dangerous than even the US Post Office. It had to be settled by a mixture of court action and guerilla warfare. And it was.

I did not lose, but I emerged from the battle with a significantly diminished inheritance for my mother and ultimately myself. However, my insightful, wonderful mother, to whom the estate had been left, and who stood to lose the most if merging Grove and the Trust Co. proved to be a disaster, enthusiastically endorsed my most unusual request to the court to dismiss my co-executor, the Continental Bank.

Time passed. We were publishing other books, meanwhile. But *Lady Chatterley* was not getting any closer to going to the printer. Frustrated, in 1955 I decided to offer, once more, a compromise to Alfred Knopf. Although Grove had already incurred considerable expenditures to bring things this far, I would turn the entire matter over to Knopf on the conditions that they publish the book with the text unadulterated and that, if a legal action ensued, they would pursue the case to its conclusion. Also, alternatively, I offered to work together with them. In the event we won in court, I suggested, we would publish the book under either a Knopf or Grove imprint and share costs and any profit.

Frieda Lawrence was enthusiastic. "It's very exciting," she wrote. "I think it is an important fight not only for this book, but others in the future. I shall be most interested in what Knopf answers."

Alfred A. Knopf, whom I never got to know, or even had the opportunity to discuss this terribly important publishing matter with, bowed out, but, predictably, on his own terms. He had his colleague William Koshland write me that they would "leave the matter for resolution between you and Laurence Pollinger." Pollinger was dead set against Grove publishing the book and we were stymied in our efforts to reach some amicable solution. Again Ephraim London reaffirmed our legal position:

> The fact that Pollinger, Collins and Frere [of Heinemann & Co., a British publisher interested in doing its own edition] are opposed to a Grove Press edition is immaterial, for none has any right in the United States to the third version of the work; in fact, no one has, for the book is in the public domain, that is unprotected by copyright and publishable by anyone, with no strings attached.

But I was still in a tough spot. Without a heavy bankroll, how could I publish the book and risk an immediate competing edition from Knopf? When I did not hear from Pollinger, I reluctantly decided to shelve the project for the time being. That was in March 1955. Frieda died in August 1956. It turned out that our decision to publish *Lady Chatterley's Lover* could not be carried out until 1959.

While my fight against the censors was on hold, I was not idle as a publisher. I was rapidly building our catalogue. In the same year that we laid the groundwork for a test of the obscenity laws, we published the first English-language edition of Samuel Beckett's *Waiting for Godot*, the most important single book we were ever to publish. Other books and people we published during that time included

Jean Genet's plays *The Maids* and *Deathwatch*, and two novels by the delightful Nigerian author Amos Tutuola, *The Palm-Wine Drinkard* and *My Life in the Bush of Ghosts*. We also distributed twenty titles on world art with National Gallery London Publications. They had none of Pollinger's animus against us, nor did the eminent British firms Chatto & Windus or Faber and Faber, T. S. Eliot's publisher. In 1955 we published Donald Keene's beautifully edited and translated *Anthology of Japanese Literature*, supported by UNESCO, as well as Beckett's novel *Molloy*, and many out-of-print classics, including books by Jane Austen, the Brontë sisters, and Mark Twain. Meantime, I had the stupendous stupidity to turn down J. R. R. Tolkien's *The Hobbit* and Lawrence Durrell's *Justine*, both offered to me by Faber.

In 1955, a French film version of *Lady Chatterley* was released and became immediately banned in New York. Ephraim London, who by now was a Lawrence expert, took a case against this banning all the way to the US Supreme Court. The case was scheduled to be heard in January 1959. London told me he was absolutely sure he would win. Such a precedent, of course, would be a big help in any lawsuit that was sure to arise when Grove published the book—if we could get it published. It seemed to me an auspicious time to proceed.

In December 1958, I told Mark Schorer that Grove was going ahead with the publication of *Lady Chatterley's Lover*, and requested that he get the manuscript of the unexpurgated version in shape for the printer. Much work had to be done, checking Lawrence's notes and corrections, and making sure that our version would be as authentic as possible. I asked Archibald MacLeish for permission to use his brilliant 1954 letter in defense of *Chatterley* as a preface to the book. He readily agreed, rewrote the letter, and changed the date to 1959. Our jacket copy featured statements on Lawrence by Edmund Wilson and Jacques Barzun—the auspices could not have been more impressive. Schorer added a bibliographical note to frame the edition with proper literary and historical material. Our presentation of *Lady Chatterley's Lover* was as good as we could make it. At least I was satisfied I had been true to Lawrence.

I sent a book announcement to the *New York Times,* which it published on March 19, 1959, stating that Grove Press was preparing to publish *Lady Chatterley's Lover* in the unexpurgated version. We wrote:

> There is no reason, literary or legal, that this modern masterpiece should be withheld from the American public any longer. The book is a beautiful and tender love story, with a prominent place in modern English literature.

Our advertising was done in the same understated but somehow historical style as our initial announcement. It was handled by "our" advertising agency, Sussman and Sugar. We also organized a carefully orchestrated publicity campaign, designed to keep a representative selection of daily newspapers and weekly periodicals fully and promptly updated about our fight to circulate the book freely.

It was a big help when we contracted with Readers' Subscription, perhaps the most literary book club of its day, to offer the novel to its members. The club was headed by Arthur J. Rosenthal, who later became the director of Harvard University Press. Not only did its distribution to members add to the overall sales figures, but its law firm helped with our legal defense. Arthur was a perfect partner. He had great integrity and he was no snob: Arthur was the kind of guy who wouldn't ride in his father-in-law's large private plane because of the appearance of accepting the gift of a free ride. (I, on the other hand, never hesitated to replace him if the seat was made available to me to go in comfort from East Hampton to New York!)

Orders began to pour in after the *New York Times* announcement. But some booksellers were nervous, and they had a right to be. We assured them that Grove Press would pay legal fees in the event they got into trouble with local law enforcement—a rather innovative offer for its day, or any day for that matter.

The media was very receptive to our publicity about *Lady Chatterley's Lover.* Most magazines accepted our advertising. *Newsweek* and *Time* gave us nice feature stories in their May 4, 1959 issues, which coincided with our announced publication date. The *New York Times*, having at first turned down our advertisements, published a very favorable review by Harry T. Moore, an important literary critic and an expert in Lawrence and censorship. Ben Grauer, a prominent TV newsman, interviewed Archibald MacLeish about the book, while Mike Wallace, in his pre–*60 Minutes* CBS career, interviewed Ephraim London about his litigation on behalf of the film version. The media showed real excitement about all this. There was a very real sense that the roadblocks to free expression were being seriously challenged and perhaps even broken down.

Then came a small explosion. I fired Ephraim London. What happened was this. Ephraim had gone with a group of us—Schorer, Harry T. Moore, my third wife Cristina, her sister Luisa, and perhaps several others—to Boston for the opening of a Harold Pinter play I had published, *The Birthday Party*. We were all seated together in a hotel dining room in Cambridge, and Ephraim began to describe how he was planning to conduct the *Chatterley* case. I disagreed with him on some now-forgotten point. He immediately put me down, brusquely stating, "We're going to do it my way, or not at all." My knee-jerk reaction was to tell him that he was finished on the case. I remember thinking that this was probably inevitable. I was not going to be muzzled by my own attorney while I was engaged in a fight for freedom of expression. Ephraim, who had defended Alger Hiss and Lenny Bruce, and who was responsible for removing the ban on Rossellini's film *The Miracle,* was admittedly a great attorney. And he had been deeply involved with me on settling my father's estate. But my whole publishing effort—even my own freedom—was involved. I wanted a voice in the defense.

In need of fresh legal counsel, I hired Cy Rembar, a neighbor in East Hampton, to represent us in the case we knew was coming. Once all was said and done, I don't think Cy approached the case much differently from how Ephraim would have done it. But he at least let me think I was involved in the decision-making process each step of the way. Fortunately, he was also a highly intelligent and capable lawyer. Ultimately, he also became an authority on First Amendment cases.

By March 2 we had a 7,000-copy advance sale. *Lady Chatterley's Lover* would go through fourteen printings—161,000—between the first order on March 17 and the last on July 22, the day after Judge Bryan cleared the book of obscenity charges.

The US Post Office took official steps to ban the novel from the mail on April 30, 1959, when Robert K. Christenberry, Postmaster of New York City, ordered 164 copies detained. On May 6 he sent official notice that the book was "nonmailable pursuant to 18 U.S. Code 1461 . . . in that it is obscene, lewd, lascivious, indecent, and filthy in content and character. The dominant effect of the book appeals to prurient interest"—the legal standard the Post Office intended to uphold.

Grove complied with the Post Office order to not mail any more books until the issue had been settled, and we agreed to a May 14 hearing date in New York. The Post Office ban was more the statement of a censor than a police action, but if it withstood legal challenge, it would suppress the edition. The ban itself, however, did not seriously interrupt Grove's distribution of *Lady Chatterley's Lover*. We had already mailed about 30,000 copies before the ban took effect, and continued to ship books by truck to wholesalers. For small orders, Grove shipped by railway express and shared the cost with the bookstores. We continued to advertise, distribute, and defend the book, and we kept the issue alive through the press. Stories were carried regularly by UPI, AP, the *New York Times*, *Time*, *Newsweek*, and *Publishers Weekly*, to name a few. I might add that the press was extremely important and had a significant role to play in putting pressure on the Post Office and informing the public.

As Cy wrote in his book, *The End of Obscenity*, "The Post Office and other government agencies are part of the executive branch, but they also have legislative and judicial powers. Their legislative powers are exercised when they issue regulations, their judicial powers when they decide how the regulations apply to disputed situations."[30] Our Post Office hearing on May 14 certainly seemed to me like a trial. The presiding judicial officer, Charles D. Ablard, acted very much like a judge. Postmaster General Arthur E. Summerfield, who had instigated the proceedings and appointed the judicial officer and prosecutors, himself held a "theoretically judicial posture."[31] We were asked to present evidence that *Lady Chatterley's Lover* was not obscene. Grove Press, Readers' Subscription, and the US Post Office were all represented by legal counsel.

The Post Office official, using the language of the most recent Supreme Court ruling on obscenity, the Roth decision of 1957, found that the literary merit of *Lady Chatterley's Lover* was "outweighed by the obscenity; that the dominant effect of the book, taken as a whole, is one which appeals to prurient interests."[32] He based this opinion on Lawrence having chosen sex as a central theme, and believed it was compounded by the author's frank discussion of sexual intercourse and his use of four-letter words. The Post Office's position was that the book was obscene "to the average person, applying contemporary community standards."[33] They rebutted our claim that they were acting as censor, saying they were merely executing the law and that they had exercised no prior restraint but had waited for the publication date to take action.

I had chosen to publish *Lady Chatterley's Lover* as a challenge to the censors. Rembar and I did not simply want the book made available for sale, to defeat the Post Office. No, we wanted to "shrink the scope of anti-obscenity laws"[34] by establishing our right to publish the book, arguing that such resided within the guarantees of the First Amendment. Rembar's opening argument was that the Post Office was indeed functioning as a censor despite its denials. No fool, he knew that the best chance to win the case would be in a higher court, outside the jusrisdiction of the Post Office, and he accordingly built his argument for the record.

Rembar, with eloquent authority, argued that Grove Press was a legitimate publisher that had delivered a literary masterpiece to the public in an appropriate manner. He presented Grove's promotional materials to show that the company "was no fly-by-night trying to cash in on one big dirty book."[35] Introducing published advertisements, news articles and editorials, and book reviews, Rembar focused upon the concept that public opinion had already established a "community standard" approving *Chatterley* as a "major literary event."[36] Then he turned to experts to defend the novel's artistry. The great critic Malcolm Cowley, who had earlier revived the reputation and career of William Faulkner, spoke to the "literary and hortative ends toward which Lawrence aimed his novel, and the increasing frankness of current literature."[37] Alfred Kazin, another towering critical figure of the time, was called upon to discuss, in Rembar's words, "a change in the range of tolerance in the general reading public over the past thirty years."[38] In my own concluding testimony I stated that my objective "as a publisher in a free marketplace [was to look for] stimulating, challenging, possibly profitable opportunities to publish good books" and that the public had grown beyond the legislation that now governed it:

> It occurred to me, and I am sure it occurred to many other publishers, that since the book was written in 1928 the emotional maturity of the American people has undergone a great change. . . . It occurred to me that it would be incomprehensible if this book were published today that the public would be shocked, offended, or would raise any outcry against it; but rather they would welcome it as the republishing, the bringing back to life, of one of our great masterpieces, and therefore I went ahead and published it. Thus far, all of my anticipated feelings have been rewarded with what I expected to happen as having happened, with the exception of this hearing.[39]

The entire proceeding was conducted in one long day. Rembar requested that the ban be lifted while a decision was being written, but Ablard decided that this was not within his jurisdiction.

Two weeks later, on my thirty-seventh birthday, May 28, 1959, Ablard came to his so-called decision—which was that there was no decision. Apparently sympathetic to our case, he had passed the ball to Postmaster General Summerfield, stating that overturning the ban on *Lady Chatterley* would "cast a doubt on the rulings of a coordinate executive department."[40] We again asked that the ban be lifted but received no reply. On June 10, 1959 I sued the Postmaster of

New York City, Robert K. Christenberry, who was in possession of the books, but Postmaster General Summerfield's decision came the following day.

Based on standing law, *Lady Chatterley's Lover* was found to be obscene despite Grove's testimony:

> The book is replete with descriptions in minute detail of sexual acts engaged in or discussed by the book's principal characters. These descriptions utilize filthy, offensive and degrading words and terms. Any literary merit the book may have is far outweighed by the pornographic and smutty passages and words, so that the book, taken as a whole, is an obscene and filthy work.[41]

Oddly, I had already formed a great deal of sympathy for Charles Ablard. We had no choice but to go to the press and inform them that the Post Office, despite professional literary opinion and the guarantees of the First Amendment, had made this outrageous decision. The ensuing editorials and stories provided further evidence for Rembar to use in court to rebut the argument that the book offended "community standards of prurience."

Our day in court came on June 30, 1959, before Frederick van Pelt Bryan. The court read the record of the prior hearing, there were no additional witnesses. S. Hazard Gillespie, Jr., US Attorney for the Southern District of New York, represented the Post Office. Grove Press argued that the publication of *Lady Chatterley's Lover* was guaranteed by the US Constitution; that the book was not obscene, and even if it were found to be so within the limits of the statute, it was nonetheless protected under a larger constitutional umbrella. It was a new tactic, and one that would be advanced in later trials. Rembar recalled, "I would ask the court to pay little attention to what had been said to be obscene or not obscene under the various statutes. No matter what Congress or the state legislature had meant to do, the First Amendment necessarily confined their enactment in narrow straits."[42]

The Post Office, outside its own territory this time, reminded the court of its power to ban mailed books and postulated that they knew obscenity when they saw it, even if a publisher did not. They conceded that Lawrence's writing was good, with the caveat that "the excellence of Lawrence's descriptions make it all the more necessary to ban the book." It was a stunning statement. The better the writing, the worse the crime? Gillespie read one of the novel's sexual interludes aloud, and turned to the court: "I say to you where you find passages of that type spread throughout a book which literally describes the decline of a woman of this nature, your Honor is faced with a very serious problem."[43]

He further attempted to bind the court to the earlier Summerfield ruling with the judicial powers of the Post Office, claiming that "the determination by the Postmaster General is conclusive upon the court unless it is found to be unsupported by substantial evidence and is clearly wrong." Fortunately, Judge Bryan rejected this argument, ruling on July 21 that "The Postmaster General has no special competence or technical knowledge on this subject which qualifies him to render an informed judgment entitled to special weight in the courts." The Post Office had operated outside its jurisdiction, and "discretion" in obscenity cases was beyond its powers. Bryan dismissed Summerfield's ruling and would decide "whether *Lady Chatterley's Lover* is obscene within the meaning of the statute and thus excludable from constitutional protection."

He found in our favor based upon the merits of the book itself and the concept of community standards:

It is not the effect upon the irresponsible, the immature, or the sensually minded which is controlling. The material must be judged in terms of its effect on those it is likely to reach who are conceived of as the average man of normal sensual impulses. . . .

The material must also exceed the limits of tolerance imposed by current standards of the community with respect to freedom of expression on matters concerning sex and sex relations.

Bryan concluded that *Lady Chatterley's Lover* was not an obscene work and was therefore protected by the First Amendment. The Post Office had to deliver the books without further interference. Its powers had been fundamentally redefined. Our victory was overwhelming. The right of "serious publishers to issue books without threats of confiscation and prosecution" had been upheld.

The Post Office appealed on December 2, 1959, and lost again on March 25, 1960. The Bryan decision would stand as a landmark precedent in deciding all future obscenity cases. We had succeeded in removing the legal risk for the bookstores, and press coverage of the obscenity proceedings, combined with our advertising campaign, had resulted in massive public interest in buying the book. But of course we had no copyright on *Lady Chatterley*. Pollinger refused to deal with us, so I said therefore we had no further obligations to the estate.

Grove had sold 110,000 copies of Lady Chatterley's Lover by the time Bryan's decision was announced on July 21, 1959. The book was second on the *New York Times* bestseller list on September 6, and then sales declined steadily. There was still great interest in the book but our market exclusive had disappeared. Pirate paperbacks were killing the sales of our hardcover edition.

New American Library (NAL) had been licensed in 1946 by Knopf to publish an expurgated paperbound edition in 1946. It was revealed that, during the trial, NAL had made a separate agreement with Pollinger to publish a censored paperback edition, which was ready for sale when Bryan's decision was made public. Based on the contracts with Pollinger and Knopf, NAL proclaimed their edition to be the legitimate one in an advertising campaign. Knopf issued a statement clarifying that he had licensed only the expurgated edition to NAL. He had not been party to the Pollinger contract with NAL and, to his credit, withdrew his support from both.

Pocket Books also emerged as a competitor. I had negotiated paperback reprint rights with them in May of 1959. A contract was drawn up that we had agreed upon, but when Pocket returned their copy for my signature, they had made changes that were unacceptable and the deal was dead. I then signed with Dell Publishing for them to distribute a paperback reprint. Pocket Books had been developing their own edition and simply went ahead without an agreement with Grove.

By September 10, 1959 there were five paperbound editions of *Lady Chatterley's Lover* on the market. Grove had a distribution agreement with only one, Dell, and 1,750,000 copies of the Grove paperback were by then in print. We also had a contract with Random House for a Modern Library edition. We were forced to run a special on the hardcover to get rid of them: one free with ten. *Publishers Weekly* noted that "the public image of the whole book trade has been cheapened by the '*Chatterley*' sweepstakes." At the end of the day, we may have saved *Lady Chatterley* from the censors, but we still had to fight the pirates just like D. H. Lawrence.

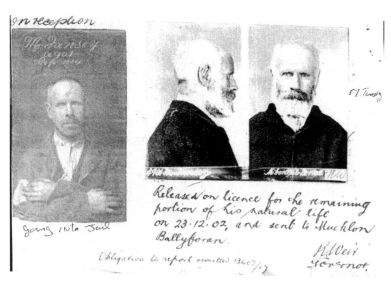

Mugshots of Michael Tansey, Barney Rosset's maternal great-grandfather, 1884 and 1902.

Barney Lee Rosset, Jr., 1923.

Barney Rosset, Chicago, c. 1928, Lake Michigan in background.

Mary Tansey Rosset and Barnet Rosset, Sr., aboard *S. S. Lurline*, trip to Hawaii, 1935.

THE SENIOR

NANCY ASHENHURST

Ever since the days when Nancy sat on the front steps writing plays and reading fairy stories, she has been giving Parker the benefits of her fine literary and dramatic talents. It was Nancy who was behind the scenes of the A. S. U. plays, Journey's End, Bury the Dead, and X Equals 0; and it was Nancy who created The Purple Cow and many other such stories and poems will see her name at the top of the Dramatis Personae of many successful plays—her ambition. Her remarkable performance as Trelawny of the "Wells" is ample basis for our conviction. Although Nancy appears fragile and ethereal, she is really resolute and strong-willed, and will leave a striking impression wherever she goes, as she has done at Parker.

BARNEY ROSSET

Barney is one of those unusual personalities who is outstanding in many fields. He has always stood foremost among Parker athletes, having helped win the Track Championship twice and having been co-captain of the football team as a senior. Equally outstanding is he in the classroom, where he has been a great asset by dint of his bountiful factual knowledge and definite ideas on almost every social issue. His acute social-consciencenets has made him an aggressive member of the A. S. U. and an ardent worker in all it's projects. He has appeared in all A.S.U. productions and will long be remembered as Raleigh in Journey's End. Also among his dramatic successes is his performance in Trelawny as Ferdinand Gadd. The two Trivia which will ever call him to our minds are flashy automobiles and a hilarious laugh.

HASKELL WEXLER

"Wex" is one of the intellectual leaders of the school and is respected by everyone for his mental ability and courage of his convictions, whether one agrees or disagrees with what he says. Haskell's radical social philosophy has found expression in all his classes—classes which he has enriched with his numerous reports, for he is a chronic report giver. He has been the guiding light and mainstay of the A. S. U. and has appeared in all their productions from the Captain in Bury the Dead to Stanhope in Journey's End. He also appeared on the stage as Sir William Gower in the second Senior play. His interests also extend to the athletic field and to the columns of the Weekly, for he was co-captain of the Football Team and Editorialist and Sports Editor of the Weekly.

Parker School, senior class yearbook, 1940.

In his senior year at Parker School, Rosset appeared in a production of R.C. Sherriff's play *Journey's End*. Rosset standing on left, Haskell Wexler extreme right.

Mary Tansey Rosset and son Barney, Chicago–New York trip, April 1941.

Nancy Ashenhurst and Haskell Wexler, at home shortly after their marriage, c. 1943.

Barney Rosset at a Camp Kanchapara, India, awaiting assignment, Fall 1944.

Barney Rosset with his Rolleiflex camera.

A duck is presented for approval to Barney Rosset and other US soldiers, China, 1944.

Barney Rosset and his "Foto Moto" weapons carrier, Chinese/Japanese front, January 1945.

Chinese refugee in liberated Liuchow, the day after the departure of the Japanese, July 1945. Photo by Barney Rosset.

Barney Rosset and Meredith "Muddy" Rhule on pillbox, May 1945.

Joan Mitchell, Fulton Street apartment, Brooklyn, 1947. Photo by Barney Rosset.

Joan Mitchell and Barney Rosset in front of their apartment, 1 Fulton Street, Brooklyn, NY, 1947.

Barney Rosset, c. 1948.

Joan Mitchell and Barney Rosset in the one-room Paris
apartment they shared at 73, rue Galande, 1948.

Barney Rosset plays chess, 267 ½ West Eleventh Street, Greenwich Village, New York City, 1948. Photo by Haskell Wexler.

Barney's cat Minoulouche during chess, 267 ½ West Eleventh St., 1948. Photo by Haskell Wexler.

Barney Rosset and Cuban dancer Nora Penalver with proprietors of La Cabane Cubaine, 42, rue Fontaine, Paris, early 1950s.

Barney and second wife Hannelore "Loly" Eckert Rosset, honeymoon aboard *SS Flandre*, September 1953.

Grove Press front window with view of Grace Church, 795 Broadway, New York City, Summer 1954.

Barney Rosset, Grove Press office, 795 Broadway, New York City, Summer 1954.

The Evergreen Books/Grove Press first English edition of Beckett's *Waiting for Godot*, 1953.

Robert Motherwell's East Hampton Quonset hut, designed by Pierre Chareau, was sold to Rosset in 1954. Beckett stayed here when he came to the U.S. in 1964.

Barney and son Peter, 1955.

Barney Rosset and Grove Press' First Amendment attorney Charles Rembar.

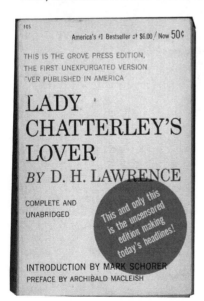

First Grove Press paperback edition of *Lady Chatterley's Lover* (1959).

Richard Seaver and Barney Rosset, Living Theater event, 1960. Photo © Estate of Fred W. McDarrah.

Allen Ginsberg, Gregory Corso, and Barney Rosset, Washington Square Park, New York City, 1957. Photo by Burt Glinn/Magnum Photos.

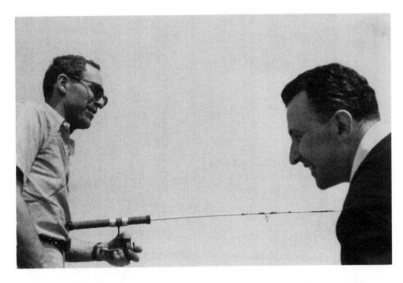

Barney Rosset and Maurice Girodias, East Hampton, NY, 1960.

Book party, Robert Gover's *One Hundred Dollar Misunderstanding*, 1962. Photo ©
Estate of Fred W. McDarrah.

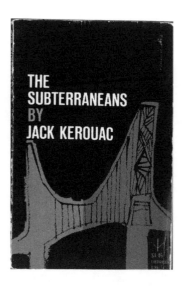

Jack Kerouac's *The Subterraneans*, 1958.

Henry Miller's *Tropic of Cancer*, 1961.

Hubert Selby Jr.'s *Last Exit to Brooklyn*, 1964.

The Autobiography of Malcolm X, 1965.

Samuel Beckett and Barney Rosset on the set of *Film*, 1964.

EVERGREEN REVIEW VOL.**1** NO.**1**

SARTRE   BECKETT   SCHORER   MICHAUX
DODDS   HAMBURGER   PURDY   FEINSTEIN

$1.00

No. 2
$1.00

EVERGREEN REVIEW

SAN FRANCISCO SCENE

MILLER   REXROTH   GINSBERG   KEROUAC
DUNCAN   FERLINGHETTI   MILES   RUMAKER

evergreen

EVERGREEN REVIEW NO. 51   FEBRUARY 1968 / ONE DOLLAR

The Spirit of Che: Castro / Debray / Guevara / Karol
Roth / Bosquet / Plus: Kerouac / Rukeyser / Blackburn

evergreen

DECEMBER 1971 / ONE DOLLAR

THE SEQUEL TO
"STORY OF O"
BY PAULINE REAGE

EYEWITNESS ACCOUNT
FROM THE GUERRILLAS
IN ETHIOPIA

NEW FICTION FROM
WILLIAM S. BURROUGHS

COLOR PORTFOLIO BY
JEAN-PAUL MERZAGORA

Drawing by Gregory Corso for Barney Rosset, c. 1965.

Rosset together with Norman Mailer, late 1960s, at a Grove party. Photo courtesy Astrid Myers Rosset.

Barney Rosset and Fred Jordan, Grove Press offices, c. 1970. Photo by Bob Adelman.

Fred Jordan, Lord George Weidenfeld, and Barney Rosset, American Booksellers Association convention, New Orleans, May 1985. Photo by Arne Svenson.

<u>PETITION</u>

We the undersigned strongly endorse Barney Rosset's continued leadership
of Grove Press. Together, Grove and Rosset are major forces in American
publishing. In the second half of this century, there has been no one
and no company as daring, as controversial, as imaginative in publishing
and we are all the better for it.

Now we learn that, despite assurances to the contrary, outside intersts
are coming between Barney Rosset and Grove Press, intent on separating
them. We object. And we ask Ann Getty and the Wheatland Corporation,
owners of Grove Press, to either give Grove a chance to exist autonomously,
under Rosset's leadership, or to allow the company to be bought by more
sympathetic owners.

Petition on behalf of Barney Rosset, signed by Samuel Beckett, 1986.

Samuel Beckett and Barney Rosset, Paris, 1986. Photo by Bob Adelman.

Samuel Beckett watches a production of *Waiting for Godot* staged by inmates at San Quentin State Prison on a television brought to him by Barney Rosset. Paris nursing home room, 1988. Photo by Barney Rosset.

Portrait of Barney Rosset by Allen Ginsberg. Inscribed by Ginsberg:
Publisher-hero Barney Rossett [sic] *whose Grove Press legal battles liberated
U.S. literature & film—at Tower Books, N.Y. symposium on new 90's
Censorship Politics, June 20, 1991.* © 2010 The Allen Ginsberg LLC.

Astrid Myers Rosset and Barney Rosset at Kenzaburō Ōe's Nobel Prize award ceremony, Stockholm, Sweden, 1994. Photo by Vilgot Sjoman.

Kenzaburō Ōe is made a foreign honorary member of the American Academy of Arts and Letters, New York City, May 21, 1997. Photo by Astrid Myers Rosset.

Return to China, Kunming Airport, 1996. Photo by Astrid Myers Rosset.

11

A Return to Film:
Film, I Am Curious (Yellow) and Other Celluloid Adventures[14]

In 1963 I decided to make another try at film production. Evergreen Theater, Inc., was to exist as a separate unit, and it would originate and produce motion pictures. The Evergreen Theater team was to consist of Grove editors Richard Seaver, Fred Jordan, myself, and theater director Alan Schneider, who had directed both stage and television versions of *Waiting for Godot* and had a Broadway hit with *Who's Afraid of Virginia Woolf?*

I described the goals of the Evergreen Theater as "a logical extension of our activity as publisher of many of the leading contemporary playwrights and novelists." In the wake of Hollywood's postwar decline, there was a growing audience for films of a higher intellectual quality, more in line with the literature Grove was publishing.

Foreign films led the way. By the early 1960s, foreign releases outnumbered domestic productions by nearly four to one. And more than a few recent imports were from directors who had formerly worked as writers, playwrights, and journalists, including Jean-Luc Godard's *Breathless*, Grove author Alain Robbe-Grillet's *Last Year at Marienbad*, Michelangelo Antonioni's *L'Avventura*, Federico Fellini's *La Dolce Vita*, and François Truffaut's *Jules and Jim* and *Shoot the Piano Player*. The link between literary and cinematic art was underscored by the newly popularized notion of the *auteur*, which came into fashion in this country along with the French New Wave directors who fostered it.

This was the context in which we created Evergreen Theater. Greatly helped by Random House's Jason Epstein, we entered into an agreement with Four Star Television to produce original scripts provided by Grove and *Evergreen Review* authors.

In the fall of 1963, as I have mentioned, we asked for and secured film scripts from five writers: Beckett, Ionesco, Pinter, Robbe-Grillet, and Duras. Requests were also made to others, including Jean Genet, who declined. He was then and later a Grove author, but that did not keep him from angrily, though with a wonderfully comic affect, dismissing the proposal from Fred Jordan and me. Using the London hotel room's TV set as a prop, Genet explained to us—or at least to himself—that the little people on the screen were not really there. He proved this by walking to the back of the set. Where were they? He wanted "real actors." Later, though, we would distribute the only film Genet ever directed, *Un Chant d'Amour*, a black-and-white twenty-six-minute film he had made in 1950. It was beautiful, incredibly emotional.

A September 1963 article in the *New York Times* gave hints about the nature of some of these commissioned scripts. Pinter described his piece as one that "might be described as a triangle set in an English basement." He went on to portray Ionesco's work, like his *Rhinoceros*, as satirizing "conformity by combining spy-thriller and comedy effects into one adventure." Under a misspelled attribution as "Barney Grosset," I characterized Duras's love story as being "set in a rural French town that uses the stream-of-consciousness effects of *Hiroshima, Mon Amour*" while Robbe-Grillet's *Frank's Return* was "an unusual adventure set in a Caribbean locale." Actually, Robbe-Grillet's was meant to be done in collaboration with my friend Haskell Wexler as cinematographer and co-director and set in Portuguese-speaking Brazil.[45]

We planned to combine short films by Beckett, Ionesco, and Pinter into one feature-length production, with someone different directing each segment. Beckett's *Film*, as I mentioned earlier, was the first—and ultimately the only one of the five—to be made by Evergreen Theater. It premiered at the 1965 Venice Film Festival, and made its US debut at the New York Film Festival that fall. It then toured numerous international festivals, and won awards at films festivals in Venice, Oberhausen, and a number of others. But it did not succeed at the box office.

Duras, Robbe-Grillet, Pinter, and Ionesco also completed their screenplays. The BBC eventually produced Pinter's, and Ionesco's *The Hard-Boiled Egg* was finally made by James Fotopolous and shown at the Museum of Modern Art in 2006. Duras' script, which we could not finance, evolved into her novel *The Ravishing of Lol Stein*, published by Grove in 1966.

In 1967 we announced the acquisition of the Cinema 16 Film Library, Amos Vogel's film society, which had ceased regular programming in 1963 but continued as a nontheatrical distributor, mainly to universities. Purchased for around $50,000, the library consisted of 200 shorts and experimental works, including films by Georges Franju, Stan Brakhage, Carmen D'Avino, Peter Weiss, Agnès Varda, Kenneth Anger, and Michelangelo Antonioni. We now had the distinction of distributing many of the finest works from the cinematic avant-garde to complement our growing list of books.

That same year we took out a ten-year lease on an empty theater on East Eleventh Street, as mentioned before. We rebuilt this space, installed good film facilities, and reopened it as the Evergreen Theater, a venue for plays and films. We also opened a 1930s-style bar in the front, which we called the Black Circle, and moved our growing offices into the floor above the theater.

Around this time we also began buying features to run in other commercial theaters. The first slate included a handful of literary-related titles (Alain Robbe-Grillet's *L'Immortelle*, Norman Mailer's *Beyond the Law*, Mary Ellen Bute's *Passages from Finnegans Wake*), documentaries (Allen King's *Warrendale*,

Frank Simon's *The Queen*, and Frederick Wiseman's *Titicut Follies*), and international cinema (Jean-Luc Godard's *Weekend*).

When two of these features—*Beyond the Law* and *Weekend*—screened at the New York Film Festival in 1968, we received a lot of attention for a party we gave at the event. We had rented a large nightclub, and Amos Vogel sent out the invitations. You couldn't get inside unless you were on his list. Three very tough guys arrived and said, "We're coming in." Amos said no, and they came charging into the party. I was standing at the door, and the next thing I knew I was on the floor with my glasses rolling around. But somehow it had a comic aspect. I asked them what they were doing and they said, "Oh, you guys are all conservatives." And I said, "Look at the walls!" I had hung Brecht posters all over the place. They looked around, apologized, and left. Mailer had a violent argument with his wife at the party, and Godard never showed up. *Life* magazine ran photos, and the *New York Times* noted that people like François Truffaut and Jeanne Moreau were left standing on the sidewalk because the party was so overcrowded, unlike the box offices for these films when they were released.

Earlier I mentioned Norman Mailer's film *Maidstone*, which we did in the Hamptons. It had a very promising premise. Supposedly there are two teams of CIA people, one of which thinks it's a good idea to assassinate the character Mailer plays, a would-be presidential aspirant, and another that wants him to get elected and not killed. The actors were each given a chip indicating which team they were on, information they could not share with anyone else. At some point the good ones were supposed to save Norman and the bad ones were supposed to try and kill him.

One of the actors was Hervé Villechaize, who became quite famous later when he appeared on the TV show *Fantasy Island*. One night, after the film crew had left my house, my mother-in-law stepped outside and came back screaming, "There's a midget in the pool!" And there was Hervé floating on his back, unconscious. My wife Cristina and I fished him out, placed him on the side, and raced to Bridgehampton, where Norman was, and said, "Go get your midget!" And he did, and took Hervé to get his stomach pumped.

The next night Hervé, who was also a pianist, gave a concert during a party sequence that was part of the film. The actor who was supposed to play the lead in this scene was drunk, and Norman ordered him out of the huge room. I found myself next to him, outside on a stone terrace with his girlfriend; I was sitting next to them and overheard the actor say, "I'm going to kill Norman when he comes out." When Norman appeared, the actor jumped on him from behind. Norman turned around, slugged him, knocked him into the bushes, and then ignored him. The guy slowly got up, tackled Norman, and started to hit his head against the stone terrace. At that point José Torres, a former world champion light-heavyweight boxer and a close friend of Norman's, walked by, and Cristina said, "José, you've gotta save Norman!" José said he couldn't do it because he'd get arrested, being a prizefighter. So I jumped on top of the actor and put my hands around his throat. I pulled him off Norman, and Cristina and I were still holding him, although by now he was standing, when some guys came over, Black Panthers, I think, one with a bottle of whiskey with which to hit the actor over the head. Cristina slipped around behind and took it from the guy's hand. The actor ran off, fell off some large stones and wound up in the hospital. That was one night! I'd gotten all these people in East Hampton to lend Norman their houses as settings for the film. After that evening, I was persona non grata to them all.

The next day actor Rip Torn, who was supposed to have been the assistant director of the film but, with reason, felt thwarted, said to Michael McClure, "Come with me. We're gonna kill Norman today out on Gardiners Island." Michael decided he didn't feel like going, and Cristina and I didn't feel like going either. Rip took a little hammer to the island. In the film we saw him hit Norman with it but the wound looked a lot worse than it was. Nobody came to help. Norman's wife started screaming, "He's killing Norman!" Then Norman bit Torn so badly on the ear that Torn ended up in the hospital and Norman went home. This whole five minutes or so of film looks staged when viewed. However, it was real.[46]

Norman must have edited the film himself because he's all that's left in most of it. All those mad acts—throwing the midget into the pool and the attempted killing of the actor—aren't in it.

One feature film brought far more attention—and income—to the Grove film division than I ever could have hoped for. While attending the Frankfurt Book Fair in September 1968, I read a report in the *Guardian* about a Swedish film called *I Am Curious (Yellow)*. I instinctively knew the film was perfect for us and contacted the head of Bonnier, the premier publishing company of Sweden. They put us in touch with the foundation that produced the film, and I sent two of our authors, Phyllis and Eberhard Kronhausen, to Sweden, to see it. They liked it and I went to Sweden to purchase the US rights for $100,000, a generous sum at the time. Directed by Vilgot Sjöman, a protégé of Ingmar Bergman's, and produced by a nonprofit fund led by Göran Lindgren of the Sandrews Film and Theater Co., *I Am Curious (Yellow)* centers on Lena, a sincere young would-be female journalist on a journey of awakening. Incorporating documentary footage and street interviews, the film analyzes, through Lena's eyes, class struggle and women's rights in Sweden. It also contains some brief sex scenes, linking sexual liberation with political liberation.

Though hardly explicit sex by today's standards, *I Am Curious (Yellow)* was a scandal the minute it hit this country; at the airport it was seized by US Customs officials on charges of obscenity. The parallel between this and the battles I had fought over censorship in print was immediately apparent. I declared at the time that *Curious* might win for the film industry the same freedom afforded literature in the *Lady Chatterley's Lover* case. My prediction did come true, but it took more than a year's worth of local and federal court cases. As we had done with the legal cases for the books, we brought in notable witnesses for our defense, including Norman Mailer and film critics Stanley Kauffmann, John Simon, and Hollis Alpert. The jury found the film obscene but, in an almost unprecedented move, the ruling was later reversed by the US Court of Appeals, which declared *I Am Curious (Yellow)* was not obscene under the Supreme Court's definition of the term.

When *Curious* was finally able to open in New York on March 10, 1969, at our Evergreen Theater and the Cinema Rendezvous on Fifty-seventh Street, it was greeted with massive local and national attention. Virtually every critic felt obligated to weigh in on *Curious*, but many journalists and op-ed pieces claimed incorrectly that the film showed a great deal of "hardcore sex." (In the *New York Times*, Vincent Canby noted that *Curious* didn't show anything more explicit than many of Andy Warhol's recent films, which played without any uproar. The difference was, however, that Warhol's films did not have to get through US Customs.) We downplayed *Curious'* sex appeal with text-heavy print ads and it quickly became a phenomenon, with lines wrapped around Cinema Rendezvous for many weeks.

One thing that helped enormously was an argument between Jacqueline and Aristotle Onassis that occurred when they went to see *Curious*. She hated it and insisted on leaving; he insisted on staying and kept his bodyguards with him. Jackie went out on the street to hail a cab, and a photographer followed her. She knocked the guy over and received a summons, and that was the start of the paparazzi thing in the US. The film was already winding down in New York, but this gave it new life—not only in the city but all around the country.

We were careful about booking the film outside New York; it was the first major national release we had attempted. In some places the film was booked on a standard percentage deal. In others, we rented the theaters ourselves. In Minneapolis we actually purchased a theater just to show the film and sold it when the run was over! Since state and city governments could still block screenings, our lawyer, Ed de Grazia, developed an innovative strategy of hiring well-known local civil rights lawyers in each market, paying them a percentage of the box-office receipts from the area in question. We won most of the dozens of cases that arose, while avoiding the enormous legal costs that had almost crushed us during the *Chatterley* and *Tropic of Cancer* battles. *I Am Curious (Yellow)* went on to pull in $6 million as our share, coming only about a million and a half away from toppling *La Dolce Vita* as the highest grossing foreign release of its day.

Aided by the massive attention from *Curious*, film was now in full swing at Grove. By the end of 1969, our film division was handling more than 400 titles, mostly shorts. *Evergreen Review* had switched to a monthly format in 1968, and much of the increased content focused on cinema. Beginning in early 1969,

Evergreen began running translations from France's prestigious film magazine, *Cahiers du Cinéma*, including interviews with Ingmar Bergman, John Cassavetes, Jacques Demy, Roman Polanski, Glauber Rocha, and Miklós Jancsó. Regular reports on film were filed by future Hollywood screenwriter L. M. Kit Carson, critic Nat Hentoff, and journalist Dotson Rader. In our book division, too, film became a new focus, as we published a series of photo-illustrated screenplays by Bergman, Antonioni, Beckett, Godard, Kurosawa, and Truffaut (which we marketed to the growing number of college film courses), as well as Parker Tyler's *Underground Film: A Critical History*.

Amos Vogel, long allied with us because of the Cinema 16 acquisition, joined the company in 1969 as a very special "film consultant" and film editor of *Evergreen Review*, where he was in charge of the expanded film section. In our press release, Amos stated what he planned to do in his new job:

> I have joined Grove because I believe it has the potential to become a major force for modern cinema in America. This movement—encompassing Godard as well as Brakhage, the avant-garde, and the independents, the young political filmmakers as well as the explorers of a new aesthetic—requires new patterns of distribution, exhibition, production, and publicity, a willingness to utilize new technological tools and an openness to the "subversion" of established, already ossified norms and techniques. Grove's resources and well-known predilection for modernity, unorthodoxy, and artistic freedom provide this possibility. I should like to help realize it.[47]

We sent Amos to international festivals to scout new films, bankrolling the acquisitions with the money we made from *Curious*. In Czechoslovakia, Amos and Grove editor Fred Jordan were tracked by both the FBI and the Czech secret police. In spite of this, Amos managed to acquire films by young Eastern European directors, such as Jaromil Jireš.

The overwhelming response to *Curious* allowed a speculative plan that was years ahead of its time—a home video version of *Evergreen Review*. Companies like Motorola, Sony, and CBS were then busy developing separate home video systems for the consumer market. I saw a new opportunity and compiled a 16mm prototype of "Evergreen Cinema," which I screened on college campuses. In a front-page article in *Variety*, "Evergreen Vidmag for Cassettes Piloted, With All the No-Nos for TV," the magazine saw the idea as revolutionary:

> Nielsenless, sponsorless, networkless, stationless and blipless programming for the home bijou is in the works. Such massive unburdening of the tube portends limitless horizons. Adult TV. Polemic TV. Obscene TV. Unpatriotic TV . . . try to imagine CBS News' *60 Minutes* or NBC News' *First Tuesday* [with] the radical lib of Godard instead of the double-think of Stan Stunning on the nightly news.[48]

Unfortunately, nothing concrete resulted from all this, again because of financial constraints.

Another major project for us was the Grove Press International Film Festival, which screened twelve Grove-distributed features at three New York venues in March 1970, accompanied with a program guide that took the form of an issue of *Evergreen*. The event included Ousmane Sembène's *Mandabi*, Nagisa Oshima's *Boy*, Glauber Rocha's *Antonio Das Mortes*, and Marguerite Duras's *Destroy, She Said*. The festival kicked off an innovative distribution plan: all titles would be available simultaneously for theatrical release at art houses as well as nontheatrical distribution to universities and secondary schools. (*Mandabi*, for example, was distributed to New York public high schools as a classroom tool for teaching students about modern Africa.) The event garnered a great deal of attention. In the March 29, 1970 *New York Times* Vincent Canby wrote:

> Conceivably, if New Line, Grove (with its current Grove Press International Film Festival of 12 films), Janus and other distributors can succeed in finding a public for films that would probably collapse in regular theaters, it will provide further impetus for the production of the kind of films that the major producers simply are not geared to handle.[49]

Though this festival was considered a critical success, its subsequent booking strategy achieved mixed results. We did not, however, shy away from our vision of socially leftist films. Only days after a women's liberation group occupied our offices in 1970, Jean-Luc Godard and Jean-Pierre Gorin arrived at Grove. As the "Dziga-Vertov Group," the two had made *Pravda* and *See You at Mao*, two experimental features that we were distributing. With money we provided, Godard and Gorin were working on two other Dziga-Vertov films. Along with Grove staffer Kent Carroll, the two filmmakers embarked on a US college tour. Unsurprisingly, their highly theoretical works failed to attract favorable reactions or large audiences.

Around this time one of the ongoing *Curious* cases went to the Supreme Court. In a case against Maryland (the only state which then still had its own censorship board), the Supreme Court issued a deadlocked 4–4 verdict in the spring of 1971, thereby upholding the lower court's ban due to Justice William O. Douglas' abstention from voting because, he said, his publisher had sold an excerpt from his book, *Points of Rebellion*, to *Evergreen Review*. (The excerpt had appeared in issue No. 77, April 1970). Despite the Supreme Court's non-ruling, the many legal actions around *Curious* seriously eroded the reach of film censorship. Our legal counsel, Ed de Grazia, later wrote that the film's case "was widely considered to have broken the grip of governmental interference with the depiction of sexual lovemaking on the screen."[50]

By this time, the early 1970s, Grove was falling into financial decline, partially as a result of our fight against censorship and despite the great success of *I Am Curious (Yellow)*. Because we had made a substantial amount of money, I bought a lot of foreign films—which were no longer really viable because many of the art theaters had closed down, overnight, in 1970. They had started showing X-rated porno films instead. There had been a big market for foreign films in this country, and suddenly it was gone. We had helped kill our own market.

Despite waning financial prospects, our film division had by then gained a reputation as one of the most important collections of cinema in existence. In 1972, the Kennedy Center's American Film Institute in Washington, DC, honored Grove by presenting a retrospective of our films from January 19 through the end of the month. In 1973, the newly formed Pacific Film Archive at Berkeley ran an even more comprehensive retrospective, citing our achievements "in the most challenging areas of independent filmmaking—the American underground, the political cinema of Europe and the Third World, and the cinema of personal expression in Eastern Europe."

One of the films on view at the PFA's retrospective was a "collaboration" with Godard that to my knowledge has not been screened since. In 1971, Godard and Gorin delivered one of their Dziga-Vertov features, *Vladimir and Rosa*, into which Grove had invested some $25,000. Godard had told us the film would be a political fantasy about Lenin meeting Rosa Luxemburg during the 1968 Paris student rebellions. It turned out to be a fictionalized rendering of the Chicago Seven trial, with French actors playing characters based on Bobby Seale, William Kunstler, Jerry Rubin, and Abbie Hoffman. The film was a travesty. When I invited Rubin and Hoffman to watch *Vladimir and Rosa* at our offices they ranted and insulted it from the first frame on. As it happened, my old friend Haskell Wexler stopped by. He had an amateur crew shoot footage of Rubin, Hoffman, and me mocking the film, and later we spliced excerpts into the print of the original film. We called this new film *Vladimir and Rosa and Jerry and Abbie* and screened it in New York. No reaction from Godard. Then the print disappeared.

By 1971, with our theatrical booking basically dead, we became almost exclusively an educational distributor, creating extensive catalogs with film/book packages for college courses. A number of unique political films had become part of our catalog by this time, including rare shorts from the People's Republic of China and *The Funeral of Jan Palach*, a bit of footage depicting a Czech student's self-immolation as protest against the Russian invasion of Prague. It arrived anonymously and gratis. The FBI raided the apartment of a Grove employee because of this film, although it was hardly pro-Communist. We had also amassed a large number of African American films, including William Klein's Muhammad Ali documentary, *Float Like a Butterfly, Sting Like a Bee*; Agnès Varda's *Black Panthers*; Thomas Reichman's *Mingus*; and Lionel Rogosin's anti-apartheid feature, *Come Back, Africa*, which was set in South Africa's Sophiatown and launched the career of Miriam Makeba.

Evergreen Review ceased publication in 1973 (although a single further issue was produced in 1984). That last issue of 1973, No. 97, was devoted exclusively to Bernardo Bertolucci's *Last Tango in Paris*. Although the film had not yet been released in this country, it was already causing a ruckus for its reportedly explicit sexual content. I asked Grove editor Kent Carroll to put together a special issue on the film that featured essays by contributors such as Norman Mailer, Alberto Moravia, and John Simon. When *Last Tango*'s distributor, United Artists, refused to issue press photos prior to the film's release, Kent asked a projectionist he knew in Paris to clip frames from a print of the film still playing there. Then Kent's girlfriend at the time, an airline stewardess, smuggled the stolen images back to us, where they were used in this special *Last Tango* issue. Published in a newspaper format, it is one of the more elusive of all *Evergreen Reviews* today.

12

Profiles in Censorship:
Henry Miller and *Tropic of Cancer*

It is January 1962. A battle is being waged on multiple fronts. Twenty-one lawyers around the country are fighting in nearly 60 separate legal actions. In New Jersey alone, one attorney is concurrently juggling twenty-six criminal cases as well as a federal action. In Illinois, a single lawyer will eventually bring sixteen separate actions together to the state supreme court. The highest courts in four more states—Massachusetts, New York, California, and Wisconsin—will weigh in before the final showdown on the floor of the United States Supreme Court.[51] As the head of Grove Press, which published Henry Miller's *Tropic of Cancer*, the book at the heart of these lawsuits, I will wind up testifying in only two of these actions, but key to my testimony is a paper I wrote about Miller's *Cancer* more than twenty years earlier in which I asserted, "writers must have a liberal society—or they are stifled."

My whole life has brought me to this point: my Irish family's outrage at British brutality; my years at Francis Parker, the progressive school I attended in

Chicago; my fervent support for the loyalists during the Spanish Civil War—all of this history is being played out right here at home in the censorship wars. But the enemy has advanced as far as they can. They will not get through.

The first time I met Henry Miller was in 1959, when I flew to California to visit him in Big Sur, an unlikely, strange, but beautiful place clinging to the sides of rugged mountains poised on precipitous descents to the Pacific Ocean below. I brought a new friend with me, Valerie Desmore, whom I had met not long before in London, where one night I'd visited a wax museum with Samuel Beckett's British publisher, John Calder, who was in many ways my English counterpart. His press shared an avant-garde aesthetic with Grove, and we had many authors in common. John brought Valerie with him that evening. She was a young painter who had been studying with Oskar Kokoschka in Italy. When I saw her, I was struck by her beauty and radiant energy. She reminded me of Merle Oberon in *Wuthering Heights,* and like Oberon, Valerie had some sort of Asian, Indian, South African background. What was more, I gathered that she was quite familiar with Henry Miller's writing.

After our trip to the wax museum, in the cab on the way to drop Valerie off, she sat on my lap. Having gotten her phone number from John, I called her a couple of days later from New York and invited her to go with me to California. She happily agreed. I met her at Idlewild Airport, fetched her luggage, and the two of us raced to catch our plane to San Francisco. We really were still total strangers, essentially sharing one thing only: a deep admiration for Henry Miller.

In San Francisco I rented a car and we headed straight for Big Sur, although one could hardly call the road straight, as it wound toward Henry's strange half–Okie hut, half-citadel perched on the edge of a mountain, all of which gave me vertigo. To get to it you first came to a rather primitive shack, sort of a combined guard station and souvenir shop, replete with items celebrating the author's career. Our arrival was telephoned ahead from the shack at the bottom of the hill, and we entered Henry Miller land.

As it happened, Henry himself was off seeing a daughter from a previous marriage, who was in a mental institution. His recent and very lovely wife, Eve McClure, was alone at home, and was warm and receptive in greeting us. I explained to her that we had come all this distance because I was interested in publishing an unexpurgated edition of Henry's controversial novel, *Tropic of Cancer*, in the United States. Eve warned me, "When he gets here, he's not going to be very happy about this. I think you should publish it, but I will pretend I'm against it, because anything I say, he disagrees with."

When Henry finally arrived, he was cool and noncommittal. It was pretty clear to me that he had little interest in dealing with the problems that would inevitably arise if I brought out this challenging, uncompromising novel, originally published in Paris in 1934. I did my best to persuade him to consider my offer, but it was hard to break through his almost hostile reserve. Eve spoke up as she had promised, but even her strategy didn't work as she had hoped. Henry was much more interested in discussing a book he was working on at that time, *The Smile at the Foot of the Ladder*, with the American painter Abraham Rattner, who coincidentally resided in East Hampton, where I was living at the time. It was certainly not a very successful meeting. Valerie and I left, subdued.

At the bottom of the hill, we had to find a night's lodgings. Big Sur was decidedly not a place of bright lights. I located what seemed to be a cross between an abandoned motel, or perhaps one which had never opened, and a semi-abandoned truck stop. Picture Humphrey Bogart and Lauren Bacall's *Petrified Forest*, but without the bar. Our room of bare-board walls, with a single swinging yellow light bulb, was unfriendly, even sinister.

There was nothing for us to do but go to bed. That night, a storm of historic proportions hit the cliffs of Big Sur. Little did I know it was a sign of things to come. Valerie and I, who before had retreated to opposite sides of the double bed, now madly held onto each other, our arms and legs entwined. At dawn, we drove down the precarious highway along the coast, en route to Los Angeles, from which we would head our separate directions. I was defeated, but only temporarily.

From the first time I encountered his work I believed that Henry Miller was a great American writer who said, in his own unique way, exactly what he felt. He expressed himself in an original American idiom and became famous in part because he was considered to be a forbidden author. But to me, he was the contemporary embodiment of Walt Whitman—the open voice, deeply loving of the society in which he lived, yet fiercely critical of it. His free, wildly provocative, and poetic attitude would later be absorbed by Jack Kerouac, Allen Ginsberg, and Lawrence Ferlinghetti, among others. They were the first to say so, though Henry never quite believed them. These strange new writers sharing their creative powers were truly fresh blood in the vein of American literature that coursed from Whitman to Miller and flooded the heads and hands and hearts of those who became known as the Beat Generation.

As mentioned earlier, I had originally read *Tropic of Cancer* while at Swarthmore in 1940, having obtained a contraband copy at the Gotham Book Mart after reading about it in Miller's own book, *The Cosmological Eye*, published by James Laughlin's New Directions in 1939. One reason I enjoyed *Cancer* so much, aside from its ripping-open kind of honesty, was the uncanny way in which it combined the comic cleverness of French surrealism with the crude originality of our own psyches. In his novel, Miller discussed Proust and D. H. Lawrence's *Lady Chatterley's Lover*, and he liked them for the same reasons I did. Lawrence's text was very elemental, and in a way ugly and stupid in its early chapters, but then there arose from it an almost mystical feeling, a sense of the numinous, which grew stronger as the story went along. Henry was doing something similar. Both Miller and Lawrence developed and communicated an intense, freeing belief that we should live the kind of life we desire—and they inspired each of us to believe and do the same.

As for censorship, Henry himself was sort of proud that *Tropic of Cancer* was a banned book. He claimed he didn't want too many readers, once writing me,

> Frankly, I am beginning to doubt that I ever want to see an American edition of these banned books. *The notoriety, the unpleasantness involved, seem hardly worth the price.* I have always felt deep down that no great change can be expected in America—either on the part of our legislators or our judges. As for the public—it is indifferent, it seems to me. The vast majority, I mean. I am in no hurry to make myself a scapegoat for what seems like a lost cause.

To me this seemed terribly defeatist. But by the time I was trying to convince him to allow Grove Press to publish his novel, Grove had already overcome many censorship laws with our publication of *Lady Chatterley*. We had shown that with determination, real change could be accomplished. I knew Grove Press was the natural choice for Miller and *Tropic of Cancer*, and simply didn't want to take no for an answer, so I wrote back to him, coaxing, "I must say that I very much disagree with your idea that there would be notoriety and unpleasantness involved . . ."

In the summer of 1960, Henry responded as follows:

> Part of my reluctance to wage open combat with our American authorities arises from the fact that I see no evidence of genuine revolt in the people themselves. We have no real radicals, no body of men and women who have the desire, the courage, or the power to initiate a fundamental change in our outlook or in our way of life. . . . It is not enough . . . to win the privilege of reading anything one pleases—usually more trash— but to obtain the right to read books which are distasteful, obnoxious, insidious and dangerous not only to public taste but to those in power. How can the people wrest such rights and privileges from their appointed representatives when they do not even suspect that they are living in a state of subjugation? When they imagine themselves to be a "free people"? To

win a legal battle here or there, even if sensationally, means nothing. One does not acquire real liberty through these operatic victories. . . . What I mean to say is that to be hailed and accepted by an unthinking public as the Petronius of our time would afford me no satisfaction. . . . I would triumph as the King of Smut. I would be given the liberty to thrill, to amuse, to shock, but not to edify or instruct, not to inspire revolt.

A strong statement. Yet at the same time, he confessed he was terrified that his books would morph into college textbooks, tolerated and dismissed by blasé students, much as he felt *The Communist Manifesto* had.

I assured him, "Don't worry, it'll never happen." What I did not tell him was that I had long ago determined to publish *Tropic of Cancer* and had taken step after strategic step toward that goal. I could not let even Henry himself deter me.

After that trip to Big Sur nothing very positive happened until I got a telegram from Maurice Girodias and Heinrich Ledig-Rowohlt in Hamburg in early 1961. Maurice wired me, "Come, Henry Miller is here!"

Girodias was the publisher of the Olympia Press in Paris, a house whose list, like John Calder's, was very much in the same spirit as Grove. Girodias was the son of Jack Kahane, whose Obelisk Press had first published *Tropic of Cancer* with Anaïs Nin's help. Maurice, as a child, had drawn the now-classic cover illustration for the original Obelisk edition. Rowohlt was Miller's German publisher; he published both *Tropic* books. They had spoken to Miller on my behalf and were instrumental in getting his approval to meet with me again.

Immediately, I boarded a plane, but just as it had that night in Big Sur, bad weather once again intervened, causing our flight to be diverted to Scotland. I had to take a train from Glasgow to London, and it wound up taking me about three days to get to Hamburg—but there Henry was.

He was in a very different mood. A much better mood. We played ping-pong, talked about life, became very friendly. Henry really liked Rowohlt, and Rowohlt had great influence on him. So did Girodias, and with encouragement from the two of them after a few Hamburg days and nights, he finally signed a contract with Grove. We paid him an advance of $50,000, which was a lot of money at that time. Michael Hoffman, his agent, was also there. He was not overly amicable, but at least he carried out his function, and our deal was struck.

Now I could get to work. Publication would be the easy part. Grove's larger and immediate task was to challenge the censors back home. We needed a strategy to take on both the US Customs Service, which banned the book from being imported, and the US Post Office, which banned its distribution through the mail.

Henry, it soon became apparent, for all the fearlessness of his writing, was fearful of the courts, and was not such a great crusader. By the time we were ready to publish, he was spending time in Switzerland, nervous as hell, even from a distance.

The booksellers were equally nervous. In order to encourage them to stock *Cancer*, I insisted that Grove guarantee to indemnify them for any legal costs arising from prosecutions over selling the book. All this was going to cost us heavily but the stores needed that reassurance while the ban was still in force.

The first assault came from the Post Office, which seized hardcover copies of *Cancer* from us on June 12, 1961, launching the initial legal challenge to the book. The date for a hearing was set, but the assistant general counsel of the Post Office's Fraud and Mailability Division didn't wait, and quickly charged the novel with being "obscene, lewd, lascivious, indecent and filthy in content." We fought right back, releasing the following statement:

We assume that the Post Office, having once made a serious error which the courts corrected, will not make the same mistake again. The assumption seems particularly justifiable in view of the fact that the Post Office decision in the *Lady Chatterley* case was the work of one man— the former Postmaster General. We trust that the present Postmaster General is fully aware of the fact that serious and respected works of literature cannot constitutionally be excluded from the mails.[52]

The legal machinations that soon developed seemed to overwhelm Henry, so it was better all round that he stayed away. However, he was called to testify at a Post Office hearing in New York scheduled for June 26, 1961. I cabled him in Paris, adding that the government "GUARANTEES NO PROSECUTION AGAINST YOU STOP EXPECT YOU WILL SAY NO BUT WOULD LOVE TO HAVE YOU."[53]

Before he could decide whether or not to take my advice, the Post Office abruptly backed down, canceling the hearing on legal advice from the Justice Department. Later the *Washington Post* revealed that Postal Department lawyers felt that "many people found Miller's writings . . . disgusting and shocking but not sexually exciting. For this and other reasons, there was remarkable agreement that the Government could not win if it charged that Miller's work is obscene."[54] And the *New York Times* wrote,

> Officials termed this a tactical step. They explained that suits testing whether the novel was obscene by legal definition were pending, and that it would be wise to await their outcome. However, it was learned that the Justice Department had advised the Post Office to drop the case for another reason—that it was likely to lose in the courts.[55]

It appeared that half the battle had been won with hardly a shot fired, but we were still left with one adversary, US Customs. A complete lack of coordination between Customs and the Post Office created a laughable anomaly. As Earl Hutchison put it, in *Tropic of Cancer on Trial*, "From June 13 until August 10, 1961 . . . a person could have had his copy of *Cancer* seized at the port of entry, then walked into the terminal and picked up an American edition at the bookstore there."[56]

By August 10, following legal advice, the government announced it was lifting the Customs ban on *Tropic of Cancer*. At that stage we had 130,000 copies in print and we were ready to roll.

On the face of things, we were in the clear. However, our lawyer, Cy Rembar, treated the victory with deep caution. Though the Post Office had backed down, Cy felt that since the case had never been decided by the federal courts, the issue of censorship would be litigated in the lower courts throughout the country.

Meanwhile, Dell Distributing, Inc., which had previously distributed a number of Grove paperbacks, including *Lady Chatterley's Lover*, and was terribly important to us, got the jitters. William F. Callahan Jr., Dell's executive vice president, notified me on May 17, 1961, that "We are exercising our prerogative of refusing to handle any title of Grove Press we deem inadvisable. Accordingly, we hereby disclaim any responsibility for the sale or distribution of the Grove Press edition of *Cancer*."

That came as a blow. What disappointed and mystified me was that Dell pulled out long before both cases were due to be heard. Macfadden Publishing took over from Dell, and although both companies would later distribute *Cancer*, Dell's nervousness was a sign of things to come. Local pressure began to build everywhere, like those storm clouds over Big Sur—with two major battles behind us, the worst lay ahead.

●◡

Tropic of Cancer sold more than 68,000 hardcover copies in the first week of publication. By the third week it was on bestseller lists all over the country, including those of the *New York Times* and the *New York Herald Tribune*. And by the end of 1961, *Publishers Weekly* listed *Cancer* sixth in Bookstore Bestsellers (non-paperback) with 100,000 in sales, right behind *The Carpetbaggers* by Harold Robbins.

Despite such healthy sales, more trouble was brewing. One month before our June 24, 1961 publication date, the executive vice president of Brentano's, a major bookstore chain in New York City, had warned Aaron Sussman, the gifted head of our advertising agency, a man who was fiercely loyal to us, "Our counsel has very strong feelings about the inherent danger in the sale of this book and continues to advise us against it. . . . I am very unhappy about this situation and want you to know it."[57]

Soon enough, Doubleday, Scribner's, and Macy's refused to carry *Tropic of Cancer*, and in August the *Chicago Tribune* announced it would no longer list "filthy" books—namely *Cancer*—on its bestseller list.

These lists were influential but inherently flawed in the way they were generated. Writing in July to Belle Rosenbaum of the *New York Herald Tribune* book review staff, I pointed out,

> I am most happy that you are interested in our rather unique problem. I can't recall such a situation in the history of publishing. We have contacted many of the stores on your list of 43 best-sellers reporting for your bestsellers' list, "What People Are Reading" of last week (July 9) and found some astounding and, I might add, disheartening facts: at least 11 of these 43 are not even selling *Tropic of Cancer*. Another six are selling it under the counter. I'm sure you can see what this does to the accuracy of the best-seller lists. . . .
>
> An interesting sidelight to the whole problem is that, although the above figures show that 26 percent of the bookstores reporting to you do not carry *Tropic of Cancer*, our sales reports indicate that nationally only 10 per cent are not. This apparently means that the "little" stores are handling the book. Why this is true, I don't know. Unfortunately, the small stores, where the book is selling marvelously, don't report to the best-seller lists and consequently don't help to solve this inequitable situation.[58]

By then most reviews were in. Many critics treated the book as a serious work, finding parts repulsive but still holding that *Cancer* as a whole was not obscene. *Time*, however, referred to *Cancer* as "a very dirty book indeed," one of many such books "sewer-written by dirty-fingered authors for dirty-minded readers," while *Life* suggested "*Tropic* will be defended by critics as an explosive corrosive Whitmanesque masterpiece (which it is) and attacked as an unbridled obscenity (which it is). It will probably sell a million. On *Tropic*'s literary merit? Guess again."[59]

Meantime, Massachusetts Attorney General Edward J. McCormack, Jr. was less ambiguous. He found the book "positively repulsive" and "an affront to human decency," adding, "I have never in my life read anything that was so degrading and demoralizing and so brazenly animalistic." He asked for a rec-ommendation from the state's Obscene Literature Control Commission on the "filthy . . . rotten" book.[60]

I fired back at him, "It appears that Massachusetts, with the one-track mind of the rhinoceros, is again about to assault the Constitution and its amendments which the forefathers of her citizens fought so hard to obtain. If the Commission supports the Attorney General, we are prepared to fight the case in court with all our resources."

This was our chosen course, even if the obstacles were mounting. On July 20 the Commission unanimously recommended that the Attorney General take legal steps to ban *Tropic of Cancer* in the state of Massachusetts. The book was also banned in Texas on August 15, with the chief of police in Dallas con-demning its "crude, vile, indecent language."[61]

The expanding legal situation in itself was sapping our resources at Grove, but we faced even more pressing problems. The $7.50 hardcover edition was doing well, but we knew *Cancer* would really find its market in paperback. Our most immediate danger was that the book was effectively out of copyright, in that the US government would not grant copyright to materials that were considered obscene, and other publishers were lining up to cash in on ground Grove had painstakingly broken.

I discovered in September that the Hall Printing Company in Chicago, one of the country's biggest printers, had already printed a 75-cent edition of

Cancer for Universal Publishing, a company with a name suggesting its desires, but not its real dimensions. Their copies would be ready for sale by October, so the pressure was on to stop them.

We realized we had a serious headache with copyright and took every legal action we could think of—along with some extra-legal ones to boot—to stall both Hall and Universal. We did the same with Kable News Company, another distributor, and also circulated this letter to retail stores:

Dear Bookseller:

Word has just reached us of a turn of events that must fill all responsible members of the book trade with a sense of outrage: In defiance of the specific protests of Henry Miller, an unauthorized paperback edition of *Tropic of Cancer* is at this moment being prepared by another publisher for distribution.

Henry Miller has informed all parties concerned that Grove Press is the only authorized publisher of *Tropic of Cancer*. Yet despite this warning, preparations for the unlicensed edition are going ahead.

Naturally, we would have preferred to continue with the sale of the hardcover edition. But the turn of events has left us no choice. We are rushing through our own AUTHORIZED paperback edition of *Tropic of Cancer*, and we will get it into your hands as quickly as possible. . . . This edition will be:

1. The ONLY paperback edition authorized by Henry Miller;
2. The ONLY paperback edition on which Henry Miller is being paid royalties (the advance and royalties have been substantial);
3. The ONLY paperback reprint of the famous hardcover edition which has risked prosecution and costly legal battles to fight for the admission of . . . *Cancer* in the United States;
4. The ONLY paperback reprint of the famous Grove Press edition which, as a result of substantial sums spent in advertising and promotion, has become one of the nation's leading bestsellers.

Any unlicensed and unauthorized edition is evidently trying to hitch a free ride on the coattails of Grove Press and the efforts we have made on behalf of *Tropic of Cancer*. An unauthorized edition also exploits the courage of booksellers throughout the country without whose help the fight for admission of the book could never have been won.

This turn of events is reminiscent of that of two years ago when a number of publishers sought to take advantage of your and our efforts for *Lady Chatterley's Lover*. We appealed for your help then, and you responded magnificently. We are asking for your help again now. You can help by ordering and displaying prominently the AUTHORIZED paperback edition of *Tropic of Cancer*.

Cordially,

Barney Rosset[62]

Our discussions with Universal were tense and fractious but in the end we agreed to buy the 400,000 copies of the book they had already printed in Chicago and pay $30,000 in cash immediately. We stripped and discarded the covers and reprinted the first thirty-two pages to include a passionate and thoughtful introduction by Karl Shapiro, entitled "The Greatest Living Author." Universal accepted our claim to copyright and promised not to pirate the book again. Our erstwhile enemy was now our Exhibit A that the book should be considered in copyright.

Grove's paperback edition of *Tropic of Cancer* was printed by Western Printing Company, based in Wisconsin. They too were feeling anxious about what lay ahead. I received—and signed—a request from Mark Morse at Western to the effect that Grove Press agreed to indemnify and hold Western harmless against any and all claims, demands, suits, actions, proceedings, or judgments arising from their printing of *Cancer*.

And of course Macfadden Publications, Inc., which had taken over from Dell, also required full indemnity before taking on the book. The contract included the following clause (which we accepted):

If any suit is brought, or prosecution instituted, against you or one of your officers, for selling or distributing *Tropic of Cancer* by Henry Miller, published by us, on the ground that the book is obscene, we shall undertake the defense at our own cost, provided we shall have the right to designate the attorney and (provided that the books shall have been paid for). If copies of the book are seized and confiscated by government authority because the book is alleged to be obscene, you will be credited with the price paid by you or charged to you for such copies seized and confiscated.

Since taking off in 1939, paperbacks had become a huge market. In 1960 Americans bought a million paperbacks a day from more than 5,000 newsstands, cigar stores, supermarkets, drugstores, bookstores, colleges, and schools. Sales volumes like this gave a vital boost to the publishing industry and were a key part of Grove's future, if it was to have one.

We issued a 95-cent paperback edition of *Cancer* on October 10, 1961. It helped launch our Black Cat line, our "pocketbook" paperback-size imprint. We were prepared for adverse reaction but the sheer scale of acrimony still caught us all by surprise. Nothing like it had ever been seen before. Lawsuits sprang up all over the country with Cy Rembar providing a standard defense and Grove financing legal costs locally for each case.

Our general briefs always began as follows:

The case before the court involves the resolution of an issue of constitutional law. The First Amendment to the United States Constitution, with its guaranties of freedom of speech and press, protects the publication and sale of Henry Miller's *Tropic of Cancer* unless the book can be shown to be utterly worthless trash that lies outside the protection of the First Amendment. . . .

It is submitted that this book, being a recognized work of literature, cannot be found to be worthless, and that therefore its publication and sale may not, under the Constitution, be suppressed or impeded.

We based our free speech argument on the Supreme Court's declaration that the First Amendment protects speech or writing of the "slightest redeeming social importance."

We felt we were ready, but nothing could stop lawsuits against us from multiplying all across the country. The American Civil Liberties Union stated in their November 27, 1961 *Weekly Bulletin* that "The current censorship drive against *Cancer* is being conducted entirely at the state and local level."[63] We could surrender or we could fight back. *No pasarán!* I thought, recalling the Spanish Civil War. Our Madrid would not fall easily.

Fred Jordan, one of my most trusted and talented editors at Grove, sent a letter to *Harper's* magazine stating:

In the past few weeks police intimidation, whether through threats or actual arrests, has resulted in *Tropic of Cancer* being taken off sale in a major part of the United States. . . .

If all this had been accomplished by orderly legal procedure, it would have been bad enough, especially in view of the fact that the Department of Justice cleared the book and officially allowed it to go through customs and the mails. But we have seen very little semblance of orderly procedure.

In Amarillo, Texas, the sheriff seized several thousand copies from an interstate carrier after the thoroughly terrorized wholesalers had returned (or were returning) the books. The local paper there states the sheriff wants to burn the books. Perhaps he has.

In New Jersey the Attorney General of the state said the book could not be legally prosecuted. The day after his statement three of his county prosecutors secured a number of criminal indictments and books were seized all over the state. . . .

In suburban Chicago some eleven communities confiscated books through police action and with no due process of law whatsoever. We can point out many, many other such instances.

To our knowledge there have been over fifty arrests. In Chicago itself a detective went into the Greyhound Bus Terminal and asked if the book was on sale. He was told no, but that the store would like to sell it if the detective did not object. He said he had no objection. A clerk sold a copy, the detective arrested him, and the clerk not only is now awaiting trial, but has also been ejected from the YMCA where he lived because the arrest made him undesirable.

Of course, we are defending him and the others. As of now we have some fourteen court actions pending. In most instances we have been hiring legal firms in each area and putting them to work. In three cases (Chicago, Cleveland, and New Jersey) we ourselves have started actions against the police. Of course, when we decided to publish *Tropic of Cancer*, we anticipated trouble, and were prepared to meet it. Our case on a Federal level was disposed of with a victory on our part. Then we were banned in Massachusetts. After the trial the judge pondered for six weeks to produce a negative decision which charged the book with being indecent and impure and, moreover, with not having a plot.

Since then the roof has fallen in. . . .[64]

There were some bright spots amid all this legal warfare. I found it hugely encouraging that some booksellers refused to bow to intimidation. In Rhode Island, Brown University brought action against the state's Attorney General. A law firm in Cleveland volunteered to fight police censorship there, as well.

Even so, as *Publishers Weekly* pointed out in January 1962, Grove was facing "brush-fire censorship, most of it taken in hasty disregard for the due process but most of it highly effective." Rembar remarked at the time that it was "like being in the middle of a battle. We know we're being shot at, but we're not always sure about the direction the shots are coming from."[65]

Fear in the book trade was widespread. Our sales reports revealed at that point that *Cancer* was banned across America in at least 57 cities, while the book was being sold openly in only New York, Minneapolis, San Francisco, and Washington, DC. We estimated that 75 percent of the nation's dealers either refused to handle copies or returned them after shipment because of local police action, actual or threatened.

The tiny tyrants were having their day.

"*Tropic of Cancer* has run into more massive opposition from censors across the United States than any other serious publishing venture in memory," reported Anthony Lewis in the *New York Times* in January 1962. "Though 2,500,000 copies are in print, it is impossible to buy the book in most parts of the country. It is not on sale in Massachusetts, Rhode Island, and these among many cities: Los Angeles, Chicago, Philadelphia, Cleveland, Atlanta, Miami, Dallas, Houston, Seattle, Hartford, Wilmington (Del.), Indianapolis, Des Moines, St. Louis, Trenton, Buffalo, Phoenix, Oklahoma City, Birmingham."[66]

Remarkably, through 1962 and 1963, *Cancer* would remain on the best-seller paperback list. But while more than two million copies were sold, a further 750,000 copies were returned by bookstores and distributors fearing prosecution.

Though the controversy raged on—*Cancer* was now targeted by Citizens for Decent Literature (CDL), a national organization founded in Cincinnati, and local pressure groups discouraged public libraries from stocking the book—sales kept us going. The revenue stream financed legal fees and numerous extra costs that snowballed with the controversy. Looking back, I have no doubt Grove would have taken a catastrophic hit had Universal run its pirated edition of *Cancer* in 1961. But it did not. Obviously our protecting spirit, our numen, was guiding us at each decisive moment.

While all of this was going on, we were preparing to publish *Tropic of Capricorn*, Henry Miller's sequel to *Cancer*, in September of 1962. November of that year would see the sixteen actions in Illinois, which were being handled by Elmer Gertz, transferred to the State Supreme Court, so another protracted siege seemed to be on the horizon. But much to my surprise—not to mention relief—there was no big fuss with *Capricorn*, though it too had been banned by the Customs Service. Some 25,000 hardcover copies were sold in the first three months after we brought it out.

Meanwhile, litigation with *Cancer* continued apace. Each case took about four weeks to resolve, with, as Earl Hutchison put it, "verdicts as varied as the judges and juries in the cases." *Publishers Weekly* commented on March 5, 1962,

"The most censored book in American publishing history has neither been universally exonerated by the law nor universally condemned."[67]

I was more determined than ever to continue the fight. Obscenity cases with *Cancer* reached the highest court of five states. Decisions were generally tight but we won in Massachusetts, California, Wisconsin, and Illinois (where an "obscene" ruling was later withdrawn). Surprisingly, we lost in New York.

As far as I was concerned, the Skokie, Illinois, case was the turning point. Illinois, my home state, would be all my previous battles pulled together, made personal, and then settled. I was deeply troubled by the degree of intimidation which the police in Chicago suburbs used to discourage the selling of *Cancer*. The great journalist Hoke Norris, who covered the trial for the *Chicago Sun-Times*, wrote a detailed article about it for *Evergreen Review*, No. 25 (July–August 1962).

The Chicago story seems to begin . . . in Montreal, Canada, at the annual conference of the International Association of Chiefs of Police. . . . One of the chiefs in attendance was George E. Whittenberg of Mount Prospect, a suburb of Chicago. Whittenberg . . . had never heard of *Tropic of Cancer* before he fell into conversation with a chief of police from a city in the East. "This gentleman asked me if I had ever seen the book or read it, and I said no, I had never heard of it," Chief Whittenberg said later in a deposition before the trial. "Then he said they had had trouble with it in the East, and he said he understood it was back on the market again."

On October 9, a Mount Prospect police sergeant, Fred Hedlund, informed Whittenberg that a driver for the Charles Levy Circulating Co., which distributes most of the paperbacks in this area, had informed him "of a book entitled Tropic of Cancer, which he [the driver] thought was an obscene book."

Whittenberg continued by saying that he had gone with the sergeant to "1 North Main Street and he [the sergeant] pointed out the book to me. . . . He pulled the book out, and I stood there for four or five minutes and thumbed through the book from page to page."

He was asked by Elmer Gertz, attorney for Grove Press: "And you looked at page 5? . . . And a few other places?"

"Yes, sir."[68]

Page five (along with much of six), again and again seems to have been the police's fixation. "O Tania, where now is that warm cunt of yours, those fat, heavy garters, those soft, bulging thighs?" it reads in part. "There is a bone in my prick six inches long. I will ream out every wrinkle in your cunt, Tania, big with seed. . . . After me you can take on stallions, bulls, rams, drakes, St. Bernards."[69]

This sort of instantaneous literary and judicial judgment was to be found throughout the case, not only among police officials but also newspaper columnists, clergymen, and the writers of wrathful letters. Chief Whittenberg went to six drugstores and found *Tropic of Cancer* stocked in five of them. At the first store where he discovered copies, he pointed it out to the manager, one Max Ullrich. "I asked Mr. Ullrich," the chief said, "to please check the book entitled *Tropic of Cancer* before he put it out on the racks. . . . He took one of the books out of the package . . . and . . . thumbed through it. He thanked me for stopping in, and he said he would not put it out for sale."

Our attorney asked, "Did you call his attention to any particular pages?"

"Page five, yes."

Whittenberg followed up his personal persecution of the book by calling his fellow chiefs, including the police chief in Des Plaines, the Niles police chief, and others to alert them to the danger. One of these chiefs, in turn, called the village of Skokie to tell their acting chief of police, Robert Morris, about *Cancer*. "Captain Morris later showed page five to the Skokie juvenile officer, the assistant village manager, and the corporation counsel; it was agreed that the book was 'obscene and vulgar.'"

As Norris further noted in *Evergreen*:

Oddly enough, there was only one arrest in the suburbs during all this activity. It was made in Maywood [by an officer who said] . . . "Well, when we walked into the store I showed [a copy to the owner] Mr.

Penney, I scanned through the book and I happened to look at page 5 and showed Mr. Penney page 5 and I asked him, I said, 'This isn't the sort of thing, the sort of book, that we would like to see get into the hands of the children around town here,' and he says, 'So what?' I said, 'So I think that you ought to not display it here where the kids can come in and buy it.' 'Make me,' he said. I said, 'Well, listen, either you cooperate or we are going to go over and see the judge and let him make a decision as to whether you can. . . .' He said, 'You wouldn't dare.' So I said, 'Well, I just would dare, and you will have to come along,' and we took the books off the shelf and locked up the store for him and went over there [to a judge].

Norris continues, "The first legal action against the suburban policemen was taken by Mrs. Isabel Condit, a housewife from Morton Grove, and Franklyn S. Haiman, professor of group communication at Northwestern University, chairman of the North Shore chapter of the American Civil Liberties Union, and president of the Northwestern chapter of the Association of University Professors. They asked for a restraining order against the police chiefs." Attorneys were supplied by the ACLU. Condit and Haiman "charged that the chiefs had abridged their rights by interfering with the sale of *Tropic of Cancer.*"

Things then further heated up. Grove Press and Henry Miller, represented by Elmer Gertz and his associate, Sidney Z. Karasik, joined the case. Known as *Haiman v. Morris, Acting Police Chief of Village of Skokie*, the case was heard in January 1962 by Judge Samuel B. Epstein in Chicago. Apart from appearing before the grand jury in Brooklyn, it was the only occasion during the whole controversy when I was called upon to testify.

Hoke Norris's *Evergreen Review* piece summarized the city's state of mind and the issues in the trial:

In this most Puritan, most evil, most enlightened, most bedeviled, most entertaining, most dingy and corrupt city, where snow turns black overnight and you can hear the best music you ever listened to—here there was never any doubt from the start that it was the book that was on trial.

The complaint did state that the defense lay elsewhere. Certain police officials of Chicago and some of its suburbs had interfered with the sale of the book, and its publisher and others were asking for an injunction that would keep their hands off it. But before they could be restrained, or go unrestrained, we had to know whether this was a good book or an evil book—whether it was a work of literature, or a work of pornography. . . .

Mr. Mabley, who used to work for the Chicago *Daily News*, said *Tropic of Cancer* was "like a slut walking down a neighborhood street, half undressed and spewing filth to those near her," and that it "deals heavily with carnal experiences, with perversion, with human filth and excrement."

That set the tone for much of the debate in court.

The first witness was Dr. Richard Ellmann, professor of English at Northwestern University, a PhD from Yale, and the author of several books, including a monumental biography of James Joyce which won the National Book Award for nonfiction in 1960. Ellmann characterized *Tropic of Cancer* as "a criticism of life in Paris at that time and, by extension, a criticism of life throughout the world at that time," proclaiming the book "a work of literary merit and literary importance."

Kilgallon then asked about "the method of masturbation employed by one of the characters where he cores out the center of the apple and smears it with cold cream and uses it in that fashion."

Ellmann answered, "I should say it was slightly disgusting but that it's an essential element in the disgusting picture of the *Tropic of Cancer* which is a diseased civilization. You must represent disease as disease."

Mr. Kilgallon next asked Dr. Ellmann about Miller's description of a painting of "a nude woman being half raised from the sofa in a position so that she could fart," and the description of a female artist who was "painting a nude and had difficulty painting the cunt in that the brush slipped in and she couldn't get it out again." Weren't these passages pornographic?

"No," Dr. Ellmann replied, the passages were not pornographic when considered in their context.

Later Kilgallon inquired, "Would you recommend this book, *Tropic of Cancer*, to your students whom I put in the adolescent category?"

"Well," Ellmann said, "when I informed them I was going to testify here there were suppressed cheers. . . . The answer is that I would recommend this book for good reading to students, yes."

The judge then stepped in. "Would you recommend that this portion [the notorious page five] and perhaps other abridgements be made in the book without seriously affecting the literary merit of the book?"

"No," Ellmann responded. "I feel that the whole literary merit of the book depends upon its bluntness and honesty in this kind of representation of somewhat exaggerated feelings. . . ."

I was the next witness, called to the stand on Friday, January 12. Gertz later wrote that I was "a scrappy one who sometimes found it difficult to be patient with his interrogators." Probably true.

What really agitated the guardians of public virtue was the book's coming out in paperback. It had been quite a test getting this far, but when *Cancer* hit the market in paperback the gloves really came off. As I say, we never expected the legal battle to escalate the way it did, but it quickly became clear that paperback books were treated very differently from hardbacks. Reasons for targeting paperbacks were neatly summarized by William B. Lockhart and Robert C. McClure in "Literature, The Law of Obscenity, and the Constitution," published in the *Minnesota Law Review* in 1954:

> The volume of their sales, the manner of their distribution, their modest price and ready accessibility to the public, the provocative nature of some of their jackets and blurbs, and the existence of a national organization that had already sharpened its teeth on comic books and magazines [the National Organization for Decent Literature]—all these contributed to the outbreak of censorship aimed at literature in this form.[70]

In other words, the less affluent were not as well-equipped with the intellect necessary to withstand sexual temptation when presented in book form as the affluent and educated. The wrongheadedness and elitism of this assumption infuriated me. This was not the way I believed a democratic society should function.

Paul Molloy, TV and radio critic for the *Chicago Sun-Times*, wrote on March 16, 1962:

> This book, we are told, was published for the edification of adults willing to pay $7.50 for a wallow in Miller's sewer. Sure it was—except that shortly after the $7.50 hardcover was published, out came the paperback version. Judge Epstein can find it in many drugstores right near the soda counter—where teen-agers can buy it for the price of two banana splits.[71]

As I pointed out in my testimony, "We, naturally, thought that at some much later date, we would bring out a softcover edition," but the attempt of a rival house to bring out an unauthorized edition prompted Grove to rush a paperback version into print "in order to protect our very, very substantial interest in this book." I further told the court, "I would imagine that I would be perfectly content to have my child read this book whenever he or she wished to do so. If another parent felt differently, I wouldn't argue with him." Furthermore, I did not "believe in the idea of second-class citizenship," especially concerning the right to read books.

The district attorney set out to prove that my motive in publishing *Cancer* was purely to make money. He wanted to portray me as an illiterate money-grubber peddling a "literary" sex item. That was when I pulled out of my jacket pocket the school paper I had written at Swarthmore in 1940, titled, "Henry Miller Versus 'Our Way of Life'" and started to read it aloud. How could he argue that I had no commitment to the novel's literary value when I had been making a case for it since before I'd even graduated from college? He hastily stopped me and removed me from the witness stand, not to be called back.

Marvin Glink, attorney for Robert Morris, asked whether *Tropic of Cancer* was autobiographical and attempted to ascertain the novel's facts. Cross-examining Dr. Ellmann on January 11, 1962, Glink said, "Doctor, let me read to you from page one: 'Last night, Boris discovered that he was lousy. I had to shave his armpits and even then the itching did not stop . . .' Is that believable and truthful?" Told that it was, Glink asked, "When you were in Paris in '37 or '38, did you encounter people who would become infested with lice?"

The judge broke in to indicate that the truth or falsity of a particular statement might not be relevant. But Glink explained, "I am going to point out a fact that shows that this is absolutely unbelievable, judge."

"Well, let's find out what parts are truthful and what are fiction."

Mr. Gertz interrupted, "I could show you places in Chicago where you see vermin."

Glink asked his next question: "Doctor, . . . isn't it a fact that at this time, lice control was not exercised by means of shaving but by ointments?"

"That's beyond my competence. I am not an expert on lice."

Judge Epstein sustained the objection to this preposterous line of questioning and struck it from the record. Under further questioning Dr. Ellmann also disqualified himself as a medical expert on whether argyrol was used at the time in the treatment of gonorrhea or silver nitrate was used for the protection of the eyes of newborn infants. Asked later about the subject of the lectures delivered in Dijon by the hero of the novel, Ellmann replied that the subject was the love life of animals.

"Elephants' fornication, isn't that right?" Glink asked.

"I don't think elephants fornicate . . ." Dr. Ellmann said. "They have sexual relations."

It was all utterly absurd.

In the midst of this, a highly poignant and unexpected intervention occurred outside the spotlight. One day, a young man came up to me and introduced himself as the judge's son. I had never met him or his father previously. This young man quietly told me that his dad had said that if we slightly adjusted a legal tactic, and he told me specifically what it was, everything would *probably* work out just fine. It involved some minute point of legal procedure and I cannot remember it. He had spoken to me, perhaps, thinking I had known that my father and Judge Epstein had been friends.

I passed the word on to Gertz and Rembar, we shifted to whatever it was I had been told to do for a defense strategy, and the rest is history.

Judge Epstein announced his decision on February 21, 1962. He wrote, "It is a book of social significance, a literary work acclaimed by many eminent critics. Its effect on children is irrelevant."

This was the climactic moment of the entire Miller crusade for me. The police were instantly enjoined from interfering with the sale of *Tropic of Cancer*. My father had died some years before, but that episode with the judge's son made it feel as if he, or his spirit, was personally involved in the case. Along with my testimony, it made the whole thing all the more special. Needless to say, I was elated.

The day the judge handed down his decision, I sensed we were in the home stretch. No matter what came next, I knew *Tropic of Cancer* had been set free from the philistines. Indeed, of all the opinions handed down, Judge Epstein's was the one that tapped into something deeper than mere questions of obscenity when he observed that

> taste in literature is a matter of education. Those who object to the book are free to condemn and even to urge others to reject it. . . . Voluntary discrimination is a far cry from censorship established by law whereby all readers are geared to the taste of the relatively few. . . . Let the parents control the reading matter of their children; let the tastes of the readers determine what they may or may not read; let each reader be his own censor; but let not the government or the courts dictate the reading matter of a free people. The constitutional right to freedom of speech and press should be jealously guarded by the courts.[72]

A statement supporting Epstein's decision and calling for an end to the ban on *Cancer* was signed by 198 leading American writers, critics, and the heads of 64 publishing companies. We printed the decision and the list of people supporting it on the cover and in the first two inside pages of *Evergreen Review*, No. 25. That cover and those two pages brought alive to me my own sense of the numinous.

Judge Epstein endured condemnation for his decision, and the Illinois Supreme Court reversed it, but by then it little mattered. Shortly after, the US Supreme Court ruled in our favor.

◗ ◗

The other time I testified was when Henry Miller became, as Earl Hutchison put it, "a wanted man in his old hometown of Brooklyn." Before the Supreme Court ruling, a grand jury accused him, me, and Grove Press of "conspiring to produce an obscene book." The charge was outrageous, as anyone except the Kings County district attorney could see, but we *had* to defend ourselves. Was there ever a better chance for a counterpunch?

Henry was named as defendant, along with me, Grove Press, and three distributors. The Brooklyn grand jury first considered the case in the fall of 1961 and decided the following summer to consider indicting under Penal Law 1141, which stated that "A person who sells . . . or has in his possession with intent to sell . . . any obscene, lewd, lascivious, filthy, indecent, or disgusting book . . . is guilty of a misdemeanor."

We had assumed we would be arrested when we appeared in the courtroom. Beforehand, Miller and I had lunch at the Albert Restaurant on Sixth Avenue with Cy Rembar and several others. We planned to head over to court for our expected arrest, but when lunch was over, Henry wouldn't go. Cy and I went without him.

They arrested and fingerprinted me, and Cy convinced them to let me go without bail. The charge was that I had *commissioned* Henry Miller to write *Tropic of Cancer* in Brooklyn. But in 1934, when *Cancer* was originally published, I had never been in Brooklyn *and* I was twelve years old! I mean, how worried can you get with charges like that? Besides, Miller obviously wrote the book in France!

The hearing proceeded. When I was brought before a grand jury, I thought they looked like nice, ordinary people—possibly sympathetic.

The district attorney, Edward Silver, asked me, "Do you know that these people [on the grand jury] have children who go to school here in Brooklyn and right near the school is a book stand selling *Tropic of Cancer*? Do you know how terrible that is?"

My reply was swift and simple. "If those children are buying that book and they actually read it all the way through then their parents are to be *congratulated*."

The jurors seemed very amused. The district attorney asked me to read page five of the book aloud, and so I did. And that's when the jury really started laughing and ultimately refused to indict me.

The DA, determined to the end, then had to go it alone. He produced what is known as an "information," a charge a district attorney can make when he fails to persuade the grand jury to find cause for further court procedure. The charge against us, once again, was for violating the state anti-obscenity law. It ranked as a misdemeanor, not a felony, but it carried a maximum penalty of three years of imprisonment. To me it felt more like a scare tactic than anything else, but as far as Henry was concerned it had the desired effect. The rest of us saw it as the farce it was, but because it could still hurt us we had to take it seriously.

The information was made on two counts—conspiracy to commit a crime as well as actually committing it. And, lest we forgot, our crime related to "the said obscene, lewd, lascivious, filthy, disgusting and indecent book."

Rembar pleaded not guilty on my behalf. The district attorney asked to set my bail at $500 but I was released on my own recognizance. It was decided that Henry would be treated separately. The Criminal Court issued a warrant for his arrest but the Brooklyn DA never pursued Henry's extradition from California. Maybe he lost heart after seeing California's highest court rule *Cancer* was not obscene. Statements were prepared for a hearing in early 1964 but it was impossible to insulate the Brooklyn case from legal developments elsewhere.

The Illinois Supreme Court reversed Judge Epstein's decision on June 18, 1964. Gertz and Rembar felt the Illinois ruling finally gave us an opportunity to reach the US Supreme Court. Our strategy was to petition for certiorari, a ruling by which the Supreme Court can review a lower court decision on the basis of certifying constitutional rights or the constitutionality of a state statute. But the battle took an unexpected turn when an intermediate court in Florida also ruled against the book. The Florida court's opinion was based on a local statute that also provided us with a reasonable chance to apply for certiorari. Even though we rated our chances very good with the Illinois case, a 5–4 majority of US Supreme Court Justices agreed to review Florida's *Grove Press, Inc. v. State, Gerstein* on a certiorari basis, and all five reversed it. No papers were filed or arguments presented, but in announcing the judgment on June 22, 1964, the Supreme Court referred to another obscenity case judged earlier that same day (*Jacobellis v. Ohio*, Jacobellis being the owner of a movie theater, arrested for "possessing and exhibiting an obscene film," Louis Malle's *The Lovers*), which had the same verdict—Not Guilty.

Justice William J. Brennan's ruling on the case was widely publicized, and followed the defense strategy we had taken all along.

> It follows that material dealing with sex in a manner that advocates ideas, or that has literary or scientific or artistic value or any other form of social importance, may not be branded as obscenity and denied the constitutional protection. Nor may the constitutional status of the material be made to turn on a "weighing" of its social importance against its prurient appeal, for a work cannot be proscribed unless it is 'utterly' without social importance.[73]

We were finally in the clear. It took a few months after the Supreme Court decision before everything else fell into place. On October 2, 1964, the Brooklyn Criminal Court granted a motion by the Kings County district attorney to dismiss the information against us. The warrant against Henry was also withdrawn. At last Henry Miller and his books did not have to hide. The pivotal moment in the American travails of *Tropic of Cancer* had ended in victory for all of us: Henry, me, Grove Press, our attorneys, the laws of our land, our people, and our Constitution. My determination to publish *Tropic of Cancer* was consistent with my long-held conviction that an author should be free to write whatever he or she pleased, freedom of the reader to read anything, and a publisher free to publish anything. *Anything.*

13

Maurice Girodias

In many ways Maurice Girodias of Olympia Press was my French counterpart. We shared similar tastes and worked with many of the same authors. Our first contact came by way of the Scottish writer Alexander Trocchi, a friend of Henry Miller's, who was then the editor of the Paris-based literary magazine *Merlin*. In a letter of May 13, 1953, Girodias wrote me:

> Dear Sir,
>
> Mr. Alexander Trocchi has already informed you of our venture. Our firm is bringing out several books by Henry Miller, D.A.F. de Sade, and Guillaume Apollinaire, and of which you will find a description on the enclosed list.
>
> I am also sending to you, under separate cover, one sample of each of the first two volumes which have just been brought out, PLEXUS

by Henry Miller, and an English unexpurgated version of LA PHILOSOPHIE DANS LE BOUDOIR by the Marquis de Sade.

We thought that you might be interested in the distribution of those works in the U.S., [although] this would involve problems of a special kind which you might perhaps not want to tackle.

In any case, I would be very pleased indeed to know what your impression is regarding those books, and I look forward to hearing from you.

My firm is also publishing jointly with "MERLIN" the English version of Samuel Beckett's WATT, for which we would also like to find a distributor in the U.S. This is an altogether different problem, and I would like to know whether you would be interested in that title, which will be out in the first days of June, and will sell at 800 to 1,000 francs.

Yours very sincerely,
Maurice Girodias

I replied on May 21st:

Dear Monsieur Girodias,

Thank you for your letter of the 13th May. Mr. Trocchi had already informed me of your venture.

As you say in your letter, your books might present problems which we would not be equipped to handle, but I can only ascertain that after looking at them. Again, this might pertain to some but not to others. As soon as I have seen the books, I will be able to let you know.

We would be [most] interested in seeing WATT, and if you will send me a copy by airmail I will be very happy to give you a quick reply as to the possibilities of our handling it in this country.

Our catalogue is coming to you under separate cover. As you will see, we have an anthology of the works of de Sade, accompanied by an essay of Simone de Beauvoir. Thus, we have more knowledge of the field for de Sade in this country in the moment than perhaps other people.

Grove soon became closely involved not only with Girodias in France, but also with John Calder in England, another progressive publisher whose tastes I shared. I recommended to Beckett in a letter of February 17, 1958 that he work with John: "I would urge you and Lindon to take Calder as English publisher whenever possible. He is a bit odd, but I like him, we are doing many things together, he likes your work very much, and although he may be a risk he may also end up a much better publisher for you than someone like Faber."

The three companies—Grove Press, Olympia Press, and John Calder Books—shared a certain spirit. In an interview published in *The Review of Contemporary Fiction*, Calder himself noted how our association with each other had grown:

> The three publishing companies that were in constant touch with each other, exchanging rights, contracts, and information, were Grove Press, Olympia Press, and my own English company, John Calder (Publishers) Ltd. Barney had introduced the "egghead" paperback with Evergreen Books . . . I agreed to import them into Britain and sell them in the British and Commonwealth markets. . . . Our payments to Grove became slower and Barney with his own cash problems began to look for a different solution. . . . In spite of many years of frustration and sometimes trying to dislike him, I always found myself drawn back to a new cooperation when the chance offered. Our collaborations were often abortive, destructive, and frustrating, but never boring.[74]

John Calder once owed us some money, and we settled the debt while we were at the Frankfurt Book Fair by playing a game we had seen in *Last Year at Marienbad*. You played with matches laid out in a pyramid form on a table. If you were stuck with one at the end, you lost the game. John won and the debt was cancelled. We were playing this game at a nightclub, much, I think, to the discomfort of everyone else because we were not looking at the girls. Dick Seaver was with us and he kept telling me that I would lose. I did not care; I just wanted to get rid of the debt.

Since I have given you Calder's opinion of me, let me also note what Girodias had to say in the second volume of his autobiography, *Une journée sur la terre*:[75]

I saw Barney . . . at the Frankfurt Book Fair, which I attended every fall. His personality was curiously out of place in this ultra-professional milieu and, with his incredible mood swings and aggressive behavior toward anyone unlucky enough to offend him, he soon became unbearable. I had previously seen only his charm and humor, and these sudden changes from Dr. Jekyll into Mr. Hyde astounded me: he became diabolical, exhibiting a totally gratuitous spitefulness toward innocent people unable to stand up to him. Then, abruptly, just when the tension was becoming unbearable, the frightful mask of Mr. Hyde would vanish and the good Dr. Jekyll would reappear, full of kindness and friendly mischief. There was a rather unpleasant air of mystery to all this that detracted not at all from his powers of seduction.

Our relationship had taken a curious turn since Barney met my old flame, Liline Duhême. The model for Zazie [the young protagonist of Raymond Queneau's novel *Zazie dans le metro*, which Louis Malle adapted for film] had already allowed herself to be seduced by the offer of a trip to New York and—who knows?—the mirage of an American marriage. Their liaison seemed strange to me, but it created a kind of added bond between us, almost a blood tie, rather on the order of a marriage between Mafia families. . . .

I invited Maurice to come to New York, and he arrived in April 1959:

I realized very quickly that New York was not just a city of escaped convicts; luxury existed cheek by jowl with squalor, as the sumptuous dinner that reunited us a little later in a pseudo-French restaurant would prove. Liline was there, deeply moved to see her old pals again, one of them an ex-fiancé [i.e., Maurice himself]. . . . Her presence was particularly ironic. I was surprised to find her still on the trail of Prince Charming, even if it did take us back a ways, but seeing Barney in the role I had once played really was too much. . . . Along with my authors, did I also have to make a gift of my memories?

These few days in New York flew by at an insane pace, eight to twelve meetings a day, cocktails, interviews, dinners, lunches, not to mention breakfast meetings. George Plimpton at his club, an excruciating interview with a guy from the *Village Voice* who was unaware that Europe existed. . . . During a visit to the Grove Press offices on University Place, which is in fact not a "Place" but a mere street, I was introduced to Fred Jordan. There was also Barney's secret, Judith Schmidt, with whom I'd been carrying on an intense correspondence for a long time, and thanks to whom my dealings with Grove had been relatively smooth, at least on the administrative level. It was a pleasure to meet a forthright, loyal person in a house where everyone talked while looking out the window.

Now Girodias, in the above reminiscence, mentions that I had been going out with Jacqueline, whom he called Liline and had once almost married. When Jacqueline and I became estranged, he tried to mediate, writing on October 3, 1959:

I just had a very heartbreaking interview with my distressed little friend, Jacqueline. I hope you won't take it too badly if I say a word or two in her favour. She is a rare human being, even if she is not quite what she should be; and I like her very much. I was very happy that the two of you got along so well. Now I realize that she is taking it very badly. I know she is not over-dramatizing. So, forgive me for this maudlin discourse; whatever you do will be all right, but you should not leave her too long in this sort of uncertain situation. She may be hardboiled and everything—but I haven't seen her like this until now.

Part of the problem was, with her in Paris and me in New York, it was hard for me to ignore the women who were within reach. She warned me against this in a letter of July 29, 1960: "Don't prove Sam [not Beckett] right by going about as a skirt-chaser. You're much better than that. You know it, and I do, too. Think of us, think of your life. I want so much for you to be happy and for you to give me the pleasure of trusting me to help you to be so and not to waste the genius that you have. Little velvet ears, don't suggest to me that 'you're always prepared to help me if you can.' The only way is to be together, truly."[76]

Earlier, though, she had pinpointed the ineradicable problem that made a long-term commitment from either of us difficult. She loved Paris and I loved New York. On December 6, 1960, she wrote: "I miss you so much. New York is where my heart should be, with you. Why are you American? I didn't like America enough to want to live there, but it taught me a lot. What are you thinking in your dear little head, how do you feel about things? With you everything's so fast, so inventive and rushed, one never knows."

A few days later she continued with that theme: "I wish you could see everything, that you were here with me. But I don't like the rhythm of American life. Like your friend Beckett, I like living in Paris. I wish I were Joan and that we'd live together here as you did. . . . Try to come skiing in February. Then you'll come back in May and then I can go to East Hampton. If you want, I'll take care of our two children. A year goes by quickly, and I know that, like me, you don't want to be unhappy anymore. We don't have to get married right away. We really should get to know each other, be sure of ourselves and that we can adapt. It's harder at our age, we're neither young nor old but in between. But I love you. I don't want to love anyone else at all."

This was a doomed affair if ever there was one.

To return to my literary dealings with Girodias, let me take up the topic of our different tastes. *Tropic of Cancer* was first published by Maurice's father,

Jack Kahane, at Obelisk Press, and Maurice, as a child, had done the abstract illustration for the cover of the international edition. Maurice and I had many things in common, but not what most people would think. What he thought was erotic was very different from what I thought was erotic. I don't know of any book we agreed upon, except for *The Black Diaries* of Roger Casement, the Irish revolutionary.[77] Maurice did a wonderful book on him and wrote about half of it himself. And there we were totally in sync. Our hero was a homosexual Irishman.

Casement worked as a consul for the British State Department and became well known for his humanitarian efforts in the Congo and Peru. But by 1913 he had quit, and he denounced the British by saying he wasn't British but Irish. When World War I broke out he went to Germany to ask for support for an independent Ireland and to try to obtain the release of Irish prisoners. The Germans cooperated with the British and delivered him back to Ireland in a submarine, where he was arrested on April 24, 1916, the same time as the Easter Uprising. Only four months later, on August 3, Casement was hanged by the British.

The British said he was homosexual and the Irish said he wasn't. But he was. He had written diaries while he was in the Congo, mostly about the treatment of people there, but he also wrote about his love affairs. The British brought out the diaries and the Irish said they were forgeries. What ultimately happened is the British came to the United States and got the Catholic Church to stop Irish Catholics from supporting Casement because they were raising all kinds of money for his defense. Maurice obtained the original diaries and published part of them and made him seem very sympathetic. I published the book here and received marvelous comments from Paul O'Dwyer, who said Casement was not homosexual. He understood immediately Casement's importance. If you don't get somebody mad, no one is ever going to hear about it. This was all due to Maurice, who wanted the world to know that Casement was a political renegade who was fighting for the rights of people in the Amazon and the Congo, who also happened to be gay.

Grove had its share of financial problems, but only Maurice could pull off the trick of going bankrupt in Paris under the Nazis—when you could sell anything. There was a paper shortage, and if you printed something, it sold. The only real question was how many books could you get printed. But Girodias managed to go broke. He was a Jew who lived under the Nazis; he went bankrupt, but did not go to jail. I still don't understand how he managed that.

He had feuds with a number of his authors, who thought, rightly or wrongly, that he was cheating them out of their royalties. Vladimir Nabokov was one of those who considered Girodias less than admirable. On November 25, 1959, Girodias wrote to me:

Incidentally, did I tell you that Nabokov was in Paris recently? Gallimard gave a cocktail party in his honour, and the board of directors had a heated argument before the invitations were sent out: Should I be invited or not? Should they be brave and risk a public scandal or not? Finally they decided not to invite me; but the girl in charge of the invitations sent me one in spite of the instructions she had received. I wondered what I should do when I received the invitation, then I decided that even if it were a humiliation for me to be slapped before 200 scandal-loving people, at least it should help to increase the sales; so I decided to go. . . . When I arrived there, there was an unmistakable commotion, cameramen got into position, etc. Good Madame Ergaz, Nabokov's agent in Paris, offered to introduce me to "Le Maître"—with obvious misgivings. We waited a good twenty minutes in the queue of people waiting to be introduced to the urbane grand homme; then we shook hands with surprising hypocritical smiles on our faces, he asked me whether I expected him to speak in French or English, that he could speak both, and that he thought my English was quite as good as my brother's, and that perhaps we could speak in Russian, hee hee; and then he ducked, sort of whirled around and floated away after a few seconds, pretending that he was being summoned by his wife who was standing nearby. . . . Well, there had been no exchange of insults or blows. On the following day, Mme Ergaz called me on the phone and told me that she had met Nabokov again later on, and had asked him in front of several people what he thought of our meeting. "Girodias?" he said, "was he there? But I never met him!" Tough, eh? The genuine Nabokovian touch . . .

I wrote back to him about this encounter on November 30, 1959:

Your description of your meeting with Nabokov is hilarious. I would have given a great deal to see the famous encounter. Perhaps I could have tripped him as you advanced toward each other and have created one of the great incidents in literary history. Too bad you French have no imagination in such affairs. When he asked you whether he should speak French or English, you should have said that you were happy to know that he could speak at all.

After his bankruptcy under the Nazis and when the war had ended, Girodias restarted his company, but he faced fresh legal problems in the 1960s with censorship. He wrote me on April 11, 1963: "The situation here is really most awful and disgusting. I am being sentenced once a week, or nearly, and for the most ludicrous reasons. It seems difficult to continue publishing books in France, and I am now trying to start a branch abroad—perhaps several branches."

I brought up the idea of doing an anthology, culling excerpts from some of his books which had not been published here. Girodias agreed and wrote me on May 20, 1964, about what would become *The Olympia Reader*: "I would be enchanted to be able to work out this wonderful, conclusive, exhilarating, soul-saving and hair-raising project with you, my old crony." He did the book and we published it.

But nothing could avert his downfall. By the end of the year, Maurice was once again declared bankrupt. He lost a prosecution against him for publishing obscenity and was sentenced to jail, given a $20,000 fine, and banned from publishing for twenty years.

I wrote to Lawrence Ferlinghetti about the situation: "Maurice informs us that his prison term has been decreased to two years, the suspension of publishing decreased to three years, and fines decreased to $5,000; and all of that is also [being] appealed. This comes from Maurice himself, in a very optimistic note. You might also note that we are doing an OLYMPIA READER made up of excerpts from the books published by The Olympia Press."

Aside from both doing battle against censorship, Maurice and I shared quite another sort of problem. Her name was Valerie Solanas.

Maurice, who had published her *The SCUM Manifesto* (an acronym for Society for Cutting Up Men), had been her first target the day she shot Andy Warhol on June 3, 1968. Maurice was not at his office so instead she went to Warhol's place and shot him. After the shooting Maurice visited Solanas in the hospital and gave her money. When she was released from prison in 1971, Solanas began a harassment campaign against Grove Press.

In early August in 1971, Solanas was calling the Grove offices all the time. Fred Jordan wrote in an interoffice memo after she called on August 4: "She asked if Barney would be interested if she were kidnapped. I said Barney is not interested in you at all, period. She asked who he is interested in. I said Barney is interested in the people he deals with, he doesn't even know you. Finally I said her constant telephone calls are beginning to annoy us, and that we have nothing to do with her."

She was arrested September 11, 1971, on a charge of aggravated harassment after sending letters and placing telephone calls in which she threatened my family. Having been released on her own recognizance and after missing the court date for her hearing, she showed up outside the Grove offices with a bench warrant out for her arrest and an ice pick in her pocket. She was taken into custody later that day. As my lawyer, Shad Polier, wrote Dr. Naomi Goldstein who was assigned to evaluate Solanas's psychiatric condition,

"While there is every reason to believe that she intended to assault Mr. Rosset with the ice pick, the District Attorney concluded that there was not sufficient evidence of specific intent to provide the basis for an arrest on the charge of possession of a dangerous weapon. Apparently there will not be sufficient evidence for such a charge until such a time as Miss Solanas attempts to make an actual assault."

One night Paul Morrissey, film director and Warhol associate, and I followed her. Our theory was that if we followed her, she couldn't kill us. We had a lookout. A guy saw her coming down the street and we could not get the two police detectives who were assigned to shadowing her. They were caught in traffic. She had announced prior to this that she was going to kill me. There she came, so we ran around the block, onto University Place and found a cop who, discovering the ice pick she was carrying, disarmed her.

On January 5, 1972, Solanas was certified as mentally ill. She escaped from prison nearly a year later and Maurice and I were immediately alerted. The following day we hired Pinkerton guards to work at the Grove offices. Solanas called Grove on February 23 to ask if the police had been notified and to request that we send a letter to her doctor stating that a job awaited her at Grove. She sent many letters, one dated March 5, 1973, where she said, "By the way, when I was in front of Grove with the ice pick I wasn't going to hurt anyone," and "You're also trying to get me to think you, Rosset, are afraid of me. Surely you must know, if I really wanted to get you, I wouldn't warn you or subject myself to trouble over the letters before I had a chance to get you."

By March she was back in the House of Detention in East Elmhurst, New York. She continued to write to us: "How can I be prosecuted for a letter I wrote while a mental patient?" She sent "demands" on April 17 that included this requirement: "The correct edition of the *SCUM Manifesto* printed on the front pages of the ten largest Sunday papers in the English-speaking world. . . . My royalties from past editions of the *Manifesto* I estimate the work has sold several million copies (exactly how many millions I haven't decided yet) and I want 10% of the gross" as well as "a public confession, written jointly by me and one of you."

From there she ended up in obscurity, in and out of asylums. She died in 1988 in a welfare hotel in San Francisco.

There are and there always will be contradictions about Girodias's life because he was a very contradictory, enigmatic person. I think Maurice was extraordinary, a serious publisher of great importance. He had a unique sensibility that was hard to pin down. He was also a dandy. I would say his tastes were *arcane.* If he had been on the road with Kerouac, he would have kept his tie on. He had a streak of mysticism, just like Henry Miller, who was a sort of mentor to him. At least once he traveled to India, to the French enclave of Pondicherry by way of the southern tip of India, two days by taxi from the last train tracks, where there was a guru, a Frenchwoman known as The Mother.[78]

And Maurice and I shared another odd bit of fate: we were both of Jewish and Catholic ancestry and neither of us ever heard the other say a good word about any established religion. Beyond that, we had both cherished and loved Jacqueline without allowing any feelings of jealousy to interfere.

In 1959 André Malraux, who had written the book I treasured the most of any, *Man's Fate,* condemned Maurice for publishing books that were forbidden in their countries of origin, although not in France, a strange crime indeed and a charge especially peculiar in terms of who made it. At that moment he was the minister of culture for France, serving under Charles de Gaulle. How could this great writer, this great activist who worked his heart out helping the Spanish Loyalist Air Force during the Civil War in Spain, how could he, this man who had been imprisoned for robbing a temple in Indochina, a non-crime as far as he and Maurice were considered, put Maurice in jail for publishing some great books in France, including those of Henry Miller, because they had been illegal in the United States?

I wrote Malraux a letter, asking him to let Maurice out of jail. He actually answered me, very cursorily, I thought. However, shortly thereafter Maurice was released. I would like to think I had at least a little bit of influence in the matter.

14

The Beats and *Naked Lunch*

Grove Press published the Beat Generation writers, ultimately including William Burroughs, almost from the beginning. For me personally it all started with Henry Miller in 1940 and went into high gear when Donald Allen joined Grove in the early 1950s.

As I have described, Don and I first met as slightly aging, post–GI Bill classmates in a Columbia University publishing course. I admired Don very much, and respected his judgment and his knowledge. After we started *Evergreen Review,* Don immersed himself in this special group of writers who had formed a loose alliance with each other and were mostly living in San Francisco. Our descriptive phrase for the Beat phenomenon was the "San Francisco Scene," and their work formed the basis of *Evergreen Review,* No. 2, in 1957, which played an important role in attracting poets and writers whom Grove subsequently published.

Why San Francisco? Well, as Kenneth Rexroth wrote in the issue, taking a potshot at the East Coast establishment, "It is easy to understand why all this has centered in San Francisco. It is a long way from Astor Place . . ." (At the time, Grove's office happened to be only three and a half blocks away, at 59 West Ninth Street.) The issue, which Don and I edited, included such writers as Brother Antoninus (William Everson), Robert Duncan, Lawrence Ferlinghetti, Jack Kerouac, Michael McClure, Josephine Miles, Jack Spicer, Gary Snyder, and Philip Whalen, along with Allen Ginsberg and his epochal *Howl*. And finally, we included Henry Miller, to me the pioneer Beat spirit and readily accepted as such by his younger colleagues. Our "San Francisco Scene" became a landmark of its own and was the only *Evergreen* issue we ever reprinted—and more than once.

Lawrence Ferlinghetti rightly described the issue as "mainly Donald Allen's baby" but, he continued, Don "went heavily by what Allen Ginsberg told him to publish. Allen suggested who should be in there."

So these San Francisco writers, along with Ferlinghetti's oh-so-bright City Lights, were illuminated permanently by *Evergreen*. We went on to publish many of them in book form—Kerouac, McClure, and others, and later, of course, Don Allen placed them very prominently in his landmark Grove anthology, *The New American Poetry*.

There were strong political overtones in all of this. I think a truly important, catalytic moment was the 1968 Democratic National Convention in Chicago. That "happening"—tumultuous protests in the streets—took on the aspects of a battlefield. One photograph, which we published in *Evergreen Review*, was literally taken in the war zone. William Burroughs, Jean Genet, Dick Seaver, and Allen Ginsberg marched together, a likely crew indeed. To me, the Beat Generation writers, even if they didn't always see it that way, were also of necessity a courageous political movement and a proud icon for freedom of expression. It was what it was, and it was also a part of me.

I think now of Allen Ginsberg as the organizer of the Beat Generation, the conceptual person who guided the others. Wherever there was a moral battlefield somewhere or other on this planet, say Czechoslovakia or India or Cuba, more often than not Allen Ginsberg showed up, ready to shed light into the darkness, chant Om, bring a sense of beatitude and peace to the scene. William Burroughs was the brain of the Beat Generation; Jack Kerouac, the Beats' shining star, was its heart, and Allen was its soul. This in no way dims the luster of Lawrence Ferlinghetti or Michael McClure or Gregory Corso or Gary Snyder or many others. But Allen and Jack have always held a special place for me. My relationship with Allen lasted some forty years. The two of us felt we shared in the battle to liberate literature, and with it American consciousness. At the time of his death in 1997, I wrote a letter to a newspaper affirming his importance, "Ten years or so after World War II, Allen Ginsberg took strength and inspiration from the same place which had so buoyed up Walt Whitman. There were cries of madness and suicide from Brooklyn and other areas, but those same cries once again brought compassion and love." My final words applied simply to the great Beat poet. "His generation was the 'beat generation.'"

One thing Grove shared in common with the Beats was a passion for standing against censorship. Ferlinghetti had fought for *Howl* and McClure went through all sorts of indignities and troubles with his play *The Beard* in Los Angeles. They did their own part nobly and well. Our Grove tribe was closely allied to the Beats, and fighting censorship came with membership in Grove.

Much as I respected the Beats, things did not always go smoothly. I must confess to making a mistake in allowing Don Allen to edit Kerouac's *The Subterraneans*, which infuriated Jack. Don, who later became a close friend of Kerouac's, "straightened out" Jack's very different kind of language and sentence structure. Kerouac responded, "What the hell, what do you think you're doing? I did it that way on purpose." Don put it all back together the way it had been. *The Subterraneans* was the most successful Kerouac book Grove ever published, but we did many more, including *Doctor Sax* and *Mexico City Blues* (both 1959), and *Satori in Paris* (1966).

Kerouac wrote me a letter on May 15, 1958:

Dear Barney:—

Sorry I haven't seen you except a minute since New Year's Eve. Glad *Subterraneans* doing well.

I'm very happy to hear you're ready to do *Doctor Sax* next. It's a work of great prestige. It's an autobiographical Gothic myth set in New England. Rexroth + Ginsberg both agree it's great. The subject matter will take us off the "hipster" trail awhile.

Let me know what you think, + I can then get busy + type up a nice clean new ms. of *Doctor Sax* for the printer on my new typewriter.

Drop a line anyhow.

Your friend,

Jack

In 1961 I went to Milan to testify in a trial in support of the Italian publisher Giangiacomo Feltrinelli, who was being sued for publishing Kerouac's *The Subterraneans*, which the public prosecutor claimed was a work of pornography. I was the sole witness for the defense.

I met Feltrinelli in New York in 1959 when I was asked to interview him for a radio program we were producing at Grove. Already expressing his admiration for the Beats, he said they were "a new generation of hard authors and writers who tell the facts of life as they see it, in a harsh way, telling them in a crude way." He believed such writing was salutary. "In every country there are problems and there is good and bad, and the only way to deal with that is to write about it or speak about it in direct terms."[79]

Feltrinelli was to have his own hands full with censorship battles for translations of other Grove books, including Selby's *Last Exit to Brooklyn* and Henry Miller's Tropics, but Kerouac's *Subterraneans* really hit a nerve. One aspect of the book that set the judges off may have been its interracial romance between a white man and a black woman.

Ann Charters, in *Beat Down to Your Soul*, perceptively noted the attraction many of the Beats felt for black people, saying that "[John Clellon] Holmes and

Kerouac romanticized the lives of drifters and [black] jazz musicians." She goes on, "James Baldwin understood that these contemporary white writers were appropriating what they imagined as the specially soulful quality of black experience to empower themselves," and then quotes Baldwin himself, "I had tried to convey something [to the Beats] of what it felt like to be a Negro and no one had been able to listen: They wanted their romance."[80]

"The words of Beat slang are always violent, incisive, compact, and chosen from monosyllabic words," *Subterraneans* translator Fernanda Pivano wrote in the preface to the Italian edition. In Kerouac's case, Pivano stated, such language is put into patterns borrowed from the methods of jazz improvisation "with its diversions and return to a central theme." Kerouac was particularly inspired by bop, she continued: "Bop was characterized by its detachment from conventional melody, which proceeds according to pre-established syntactic rules, to follow a form of improvisation which was an end in itself, so as to absorb existing melodies."[81]

Another sympathetic portrayal of Kerouac's artistic intentions in *The Subterraneans* came from none other than Henry Miller. In his preface, he wrote,

> We say that the poet, or genius, is always ahead of his time. True, but only because he's so thoroughly of his time. "Keep moving!" he urges. . . . But the stick-in-the-muds don't follow this kind of talk. . . . So what do they do? They pull him down off his perch, they starve him, they kick his teeth down his throat.[82]

It was almost as if Miller foresaw what would happen to the book in Italy, where the "stick-in-the-muds" attempted to stop the book's distribution. The courts put Feltrinelli's company on trial, citing *The Subterraneans* as pornographic. In June 1961, the Milan prosecutor's office seized all copies of the book and sued the publisher.

Kerouac wrote a letter to the Italian judge presiding over the case, which we published in *Evergreen Review*, No. 31. He presented a surprising and highly literate analogy between his writing style and his Catholic upbringing, describing his form as "strictly confessional in accordance with the confessional form of . . . *Notes from the Underground*. The idea is to tell all about a recently concluded event in all its complexity, at least tell all that can be told without attempting to offend certain basic sensibilities in polite society." Responding to the question of how he arrived at creating a novel with such a purpose in mind, Kerouac answered, "The practice of my narrative art, frankly, Gentlemen, has its roots in my experience inside the confessionals of a Catholic childhood. It was my belief then that to withhold any reasonably and decently explainable detail from the Father was a sin."[83] Thus, Kerouac disarmingly presented a Catholic side to his art that was sure to please the tribunal, which was bound to be influenced by the church. I myself, alone in the court with the judge, had tried my best to underscore the religious origins of Kerouac's art.

At a hearing in October, the court acquitted the publisher and rescinded the seizure. It was reported to me that the conclusion of the judges was as follows: "*The Subterraneans* isn't pornography because the book as a whole is not simply a vehicle for sexual description, the fragments of the book in question are not merely titillating unless they are removed from the context of the rest of the book. The book is therefore not obscene under Article 528 of the law."

As I recounted in my winter 1997 *Paris Review* interview with Ken Jordan,[84] one of my less stellar moments with the Beats happened with Allen Ginsberg present during an adventure I had with Timothy Leary in late 1960. I had never met Leary before, or really even heard of him, when Allen and Peter Orlovsky brought him to my place on Eleventh Street. Leary gave my girlfriend Ann Holt and me a big handful of pills—LSD—which we had never heard of. I suppose we didn't have to take the pills, but Leary was from Harvard and seemed kind of respectable. The drug had an effect, I'll tell you. My apartment was on two floors, and the three of them went upstairs and turned on African music and danced while Ann and I stayed downstairs and became paranoid. We backed into the corner of the room we were in. Joan Mitchell's paintings kept coming out of the wall and I'd go and push them back in! Then Allen came down and taught me something I have never forgotten: how to throw up. It was fantastic. I had an absolute phobia about throwing up until that point but never since. Allen taught me to relax, that throwing up is not a bad thing. He coaxed and coaxed me to get rid of some of the LSD. And it worked.

The next day I went to the office but when I returned to the apartment Ann was lying unconscious in a big pool of blood in the living room. She had tried to commit suicide, slitting her wrist with a razor. Thank god she was still breathing. Fred Praeger, a publisher and friend, as well as an acknowledged CIA agent, was my tenant living on the other two floors of the building. He gave me a handkerchief and I made a tourniquet. St. Vincent's Hospital was one block away. It took them three hours to save Ann, but, bless them, they did.

Afterward, Leary said the whole thing was my fault because I hadn't guarded Ann for 72 hours. Then he took her to Massachusetts and tried to get her to marry him. I received a letter from him with all these questions about the LSD: "After you took the LSD did you feel a) 10 percent better or b) 20 percent better" and so on. I was so infuriated I gave it to somebody I knew from Francis Parker who was at Harvard Medical School, a psychiatrist. He said, "After reading this I am ashamed to be associated with Harvard." Shortly after that, Harvard threw Leary out.

On January 5, 1961, Leary wrote me:

I do feel that you were somewhat deprived. The dosage you took was too moderate to produce a real visionary state. I expect that Ann's experience was deeper because she took an estimated equivalent of 20 mushrooms—i.e., three times your dosage.

. . . I am very interested, naturally, in your reactions—during and after. As well as those of Ann. I'm going to be in New York January 13–16. Can we get together for lunch to exchange notes?

I wrote back on January 24:

> Many thanks for sending me the curandero questionnaire. I find it
> very interesting, although I confess I am not able to answer it. For
> example, I never have been able to decide whether or not I find it
> easy to get intoxicated or whether there is some difficulty involved.
> However, good luck with it.

William S. Burroughs, as I also mentioned in *The Paris Review*, was so special by
himself, very special in a literary sense. One day Ginsberg brought Burroughs's
manuscript, *Naked Lunch,* to the Grove office. I believed it was a work of genius,
especially the Dr. Benway character. Now when you read the book it sounds
almost coherent, but back then, it was like looking at an abstract painting. We
had never seen anything like it before. Burroughs turned language and concepts
all around, and he used a good figure, a doctor, to send up the whole society. And
of course he had strong concepts about all kinds of drugs, whether they were good
or bad and how to break your habit.

Ginsberg had taken it upon himself to market the *Naked Lunch* manuscript
and had met rejection for two years, even from such venerable champions of free
expression as Olympia Press and City Lights. Maurice Girodias's first response
to *Naked Lunch*, which had been brought to him by Terry Southern and Mason
Hoffenberg, was negative, a "no go." Allen next showed the manuscript to City
Lights, but Ferlinghetti wasn't interested in the mixture of sexuality, violence,
and psychopathology.

The next stop was the office of *Chicago Review*, the literary magazine of
the University of Chicago. Ginsberg sent *Naked Lunch* to what he thought—
correctly, as it turned out—would be sympathetic student editors. Both Paul
Carroll and Irving Rosenthal were drawn to Burroughs' iconoclastic satire.
The first excerpt from the book was published in the Spring 1958 issue of

Chicago Review. Although a faculty member, Richard Stern, groused about the journal becoming "a magazine of San Francisco rejects," since it had also published such California writers as Robert Duncan and Michael McClure, the storm had not yet broken. The lack of outcry emboldened Rosenthal and Carroll to publish an even larger chunk from the novel in the Winter 1958 issue, which included Kerouac, Burroughs, and Edward Dahlberg.

Then, of course, the press caught wind of what had been going on at the magazine. A front-page column by Jack Mabley appeared in the *Chicago Daily News* in which the "vulgarity and courseness" being purveyed by the *Chicago Review* was excoriated. No actual authors were cited in Mabley's piece. When the University of Chicago chancellor, Robert Maynard Hutchins, was alerted to this controversy, he banned Burroughs and other Beats from appearing in the *Review*. Hutchins had previously made a name as being a liberal leader, but now he radically changed his position by clamping down on free literary expression. Rosenthal, Carroll, and others resigned in protest and decided to start their own independent magazine, *Big Table*. It was financed with private donations and ads, but now faced a new hurdle when an issue with another excerpt from *Naked Lunch* was seized by the Post Office as obscene.

The poet John Ciardi wrote a June 27, 1959 editorial in the *Saturday Review* castigating the Chicago Post Office, pointing out "it is not interested in the law, but only its own kind of harassment." He also offered a reading of *Naked Lunch*: "Only after the first shock does one realize that what Burroughs is writing about is not only the destruction of depraved men by their drug lust, but the destruction of all men by their consuming addictions."[85]

The work was put on trial in Chicago in front of Judge Julius Hoffman, who would later try the Yippies for their alleged disruption of the Chicago convention and, in a less historically significant moment, presided over my divorce from Joan Mitchell. His verdict was "not guilty." In his judicial opinion he wrote, "*Naked Lunch*, while not exactly a wild prose picnic in the style of Kerouac, is, taken as a whole, similarly unappealing to the prurient interest. The exacerbated, morbid and perverted sex related by the author could not arouse a corresponding interest in the average reader."[86]

Meanwhile, the hullabaloo and national press coverage—along with the steady sales of *Big Table*—convinced the publishers that had earlier ignored Burroughs' novel to rethink their positions. While still involved with Carroll and the Chicago people, Rosenthal, who had meticulously edited the excerpts from *Naked Lunch* that had appeared, moved to New York. We gave him a job at Grove Press. He began editing the manuscript with Burroughs but found himself cut off at the pass when Girodias, who had earlier disdained *Naked Lunch*, now offered Burroughs $800 for the book. Olympia quickly rushed out an edition, done with minimal editing. Now Burroughs came to value the more chaotic, collage-like style that had been edited out of the *Chicago Review* excerpts and insisted that the Grove edition conform to the Olympia version. This cut down on Rosenthal's ability to shape the text and later led to acrimony between Burroughs, Rosenthal, and Grove.

On July 29, 1960, Allen Ginsberg stepped in, to no avail, urging Burroughs to listen to Rosenthal's advice: "Irving put a lot of work into the detail, and your last letter tends to sweep all further detail under carpet. But it won't be much work for you just to check what he did. I think book'll be better, easier to read." (Allen also did work on the text, and I recently found a copy of an invoice he submitted for eight hours of copyediting at $2.50 per hour—$20.00 due in total.) Although Burroughs acceded to some of the suggestions, he had his own ideas regarding his book's integrity. When he wrote to Ginsberg agreeing to some of Rosenthal's editorial suggestions, such as adding chapter heads, Burroughs added, "Please send more mescaline. I will send along more money very soon."

Meanwhile, I cabled Girodias on August 12, 1959, "DON'T FORGET I WANT NAKED LUNCH FOR STATES STOP DO YOU HAVE CONTRACTUAL RIGHTS STOP AND DON'T DRINK YOURSELF TO DEATH UNTIL I GET THERE."

At the outset of Rosenthal doing the editorial work, Burroughs wrote him:

> First a general statement of policy with regard to *Naked Lunch*. The Olympia edition aside from actual typographical errors is the way the book was conceived and took form. That form can not be altered without loss of life. . . . [I]t definitely is my intention that the book should flow from beginning to end without spatial interruption or chapter headings. I think the marginal headings are definitely indicated. THIS IS NOT A NOVEL. And should not appear looking like one.[87]

Burroughs now adhered to the cut-up method of composition, which he said he had adopted unconsciously in relation to *Naked Lunch*. He explained in his essay "The Cut Up Method of Brion Gysin" in *A Casebook on the Beat* that this technique had been introduced by Dadaist writer Tristan Tzara, who "at a surrealist rally in the 1920s proposed to create a poem on the spot by pulling words out of a hat. A riot ensued wrecked the theatre."[88] In other words, as Tzara suggested, an artwork would be composed by utilizing chance operations to one degree or another. Burroughs's version of this, he said, was that he sent the different parts of *Naked Lunch* to the printer in random order, so that while each section had continuity in itself, the ultimate arrangement of the pieces of the book arose by accident.

Burroughs also wanted to include an introductory note in the Grove edition explaining the background of the book, coming as it did from years of a drug addiction he had now cleaned up from, as something of a reply to critics. He put his justification like this: "I get tired of people telling me they lost their lunch reading my *Lunch*."

Aside from difficulties editing the book, there was the problem of getting copies from Olympia (which would be easier to work from rather than the original manuscript) because the government kept seizing the ones that were sent to us. As my assistant, Judith Schmidt, observed, "By this time the Customs Department must have so many *Naked Lunch*es on hand that they could easily open a bookstore to compete with us when our edition is published."

Indeed, I received a letter from the Bureau of Customs, which managed to misspell the author's name. The letter, dated August 29, 1960, read in part, "You are advised that a mail package addressed to you from _____ found to contain the following listed merchandise, has been seized as in violation of the provisions of Section 305 of the Tariff Act of 1930:—1 book "The Naked Lunch" by W. Burrough."

We had bought the rights to *Naked Lunch* from Girodias in November 1959 and even printed copies, but I hesitated to distribute the book when I was already embroiled in the *Tropic of Cancer* censorship trials. The Miller situation was still up in the air and adding more fuel to the fire by bringing out another controversial book seemed like a poor move.

As I wrote Girodias,

At this point we have legal battles over TROPIC ranging up and down the length of the country. We have employed legal firms in perhaps ten cities, leaving others to wait, and the book has been taken off sale in a major part of the United States. . . . [C]opies have been confiscated and in many places the wholesalers have kept the books but have not distributed them. Most of the trouble comes from police who intimidate the wholesalers and the actual retailers. Unless there is some sort of censorship by police intimidation and it is [a] very difficult thing to fight because in many places you cannot even prove that intimidation has taken place.

It would be absolutely suicidal to publish *Naked Lunch* at this moment—Burroughs seemed perfectly aware of that fact.

Girodias, in fact, sent Miller a copy of the Burroughs work, hoping to get a positive blurb. Miller replied in December 1960,

I've tried now for the third time to read it through, but I can't stick it. The truth is, it bores me . . . However, there's no question in my mind as to Burroughs' abilities. There is a ferocity in his writing which is equaled in my opinion, only by Céline. No writer I know of made more daring use of the language. Thinking about the law, it seems to me that the effect of Burroughs' book on the average reader—if publication were ever permitted—would be the very opposite of what the censors feared. One would have to have a diseased mind to ask for more. To read that book is to take the cure.[89]

Even with the *Chicago Review* controversy, William S. Burroughs was still not a recognized name and could not expect the attention and (relative) courtesy afforded Miller. Girodias, who was anxious for my American edition to succeed because he would receive a percentage, sent a piece by Burroughs for publication in *Evergreen Review*, writing, "It is quite essential that we rapidly establish Burroughs' reputation as a serious writer in this country." We published it as quickly as possible but this didn't stop Maurice's complaints.

He also lamented the financial consequences of the delayed publication, writing on February 21, 1961, "You certainly have valid reasons for adopting this policy [of delaying the distribution of the book] but it is quite disastrous from Burroughs' point of view and mine. I have been anxiously looking forward to the publication of *Naked Lunch* in the U.S. as one of the only imaginable means of restoring my shaky finances."

On July 21, Girodias again wrote to me frantically, "Concerning *Naked Lunch*, I must also once more ask you to let me know what you have decided. I would not like the idea of having waited one year and a half for you to publish a book, and learn at the last minute that you finally decided not to do it."

I cabled back, "PLANS PROCEEDING PUBLISH LUNCH THIS FALL."

Nonetheless, the complaints from Girodias, now happy that the book was on the verge of publication, did not stop. Burroughs had offered me excerpts from *The Soft Machine*, his follow-up book to *Naked Lunch*, and, Maurice, who was doing the novel in Paris, became incensed and complained that I was stealing his thunder, since he had already contracted to do the book and run an excerpt in his own magazine. I responded on November 13, 1961,

> Usually publishers are delighted by the chance to have a section of one of their books appear in a magazine, even if the circulation of the magazine is not too large. Usually, you have to pay for advertising, and the chance to get some free exploitation is not easily come by. Obviously in this case it is your magazine that you are protecting, and you are not concerned with the welfare of the book. Again, I think you are very silly because although I would like to think that the EVERGREEN REVIEW blankets the globe, I'm afraid that it does not. Also I think perhaps you are having some delusions of grandeur concerning your own magazine, if you believe that the section from THE SOFT MACHINE will jet propel the whole affair into the stratosphere of SUCCESS and glory. . . . If you will really think this matter over a little bit, I think you will come to Burroughs' and my point of view. You cannot consider him a slave who can only be published in your magazine.

To appease Girodias, I cancelled the inclusion of the excerpts. And although this was obviously not a result I would have wished for, I held up publication a little longer, as the *Tropic* trials dragged on. Girodias became angry and talked of buying back the copies I had already printed and offering them to Dial Press. In a letter dated December 7, 1961, I explained Grove's difficulties in relation to our censorship trials:

> When the book [*Tropic of Cancer*] is sold to the thousands of booksellers, of all description, in this country, an indemnification goes with it under which we guarantee to take up the defense for any wholesaler or retailer who might be arrested. It seems difficult for you to understand, but the arrests are CRIMINAL ones, and if someone is convicted he can go to jail—and even if he does not go to jail he suffers various penalties for

the rest of his life because of the conviction. Legal fees are expensive and these dealers cannot pay them. If we did not indemnify them, there would be <u>absolutely no sale</u>. Therefore the investment in lawsuits is a matter of necessity, not frivolity, providing one finds it important to publish the book. This same problem will also hold true for NAKED LUNCH.

More than fifty people are now awaiting criminal trial.

Burroughs was much harder to defend than Miller at that time. You could make a good case that Henry Miller was an established twentieth-century writer. But, as I say, nobody had heard of Burroughs. Lawrence had set the stage for Miller, and Miller set the stage for Burroughs. At the time we signed the contract for *Naked Lunch*, we hadn't won anything. We were right in the middle of it. Had we just gone ahead and published Burroughs it would have been a mess, because we already had all these lawsuits to contend with. That book would have proven that we were pornographers not satisfied with doing one dirty book—look, now we've got another one!

Even this did not stop Maurice's complaints and threats to go to another publisher, so I wrote back angrily on December 13, 1961, "Once again, NAKED LUNCH will be published by us. Do everybody a favor by ceasing your attempts to sell it to anybody else and stop telling us how and when to publish it here. You take care of your problems in France, we will deal with the problems here as best we can. Is this precise enough."

I put it more delicately in a follow-up letter in January:

The censorship problem has not improved—it may well get worse before it gets better. Today two local booksellers are being hauled before a grand jury right here in New York. We have our fingers crossed. . . .

A trial in Chicago has been going on for three weeks and one in Los Angles for almost as long. Only a suicidal maniac would plunge in with *Naked Lunch* at this moment—at least that is the opinion of everyone I have talked to, including Burroughs. We are not sitting on 10,000 books to spite you, believe me.

Indeed, Burroughs himself wrote me, "In any case if he [Girodias] makes any move to put *Naked Lunch* in the hands of another American publisher you can be sure it is done without my approval."

One thing that finally precipitated quicker publication was the positive reception Burroughs was receiving from the literary elite. Prompted by British publisher John Calder, who was doing yeoman work to get Burroughs known and accepted, William had been invited, along with Henry Miller, Norman Mailer, and Mary McCarthy, to appear at the Edinburgh International Writers' Conference in August 1962. Not only was Burroughs well received but both Mailer and McCarthy heaped praise on his head as being a writer of genius. This, along with my lawyer Edward de Grazia's assurance that any prosecution of *Naked Lunch* could be beaten, convinced me to publish the book.

So we announced publication on October 30, 1962.

The moment the book was out, we were hit by both negative reviews and a new round of censorship trials. As to the reviews, one of the most scandalous, because it libeled the author, appeared in *Time* magazine.[90] We consulted a lawyer, John V. Long, about the case, and he wrote that we should seek legal recourse, since the review was wrong, "1) in falsely stating that he [Burroughs] is an ex-convict, and 2) in falsely attributing his discharge from war-time military service to self-maiming for the purpose of evasion of such service." Long also bridled at the way the review casts doubts on the writer's love of country, making a perhaps disingenuous argument:

Nor would his [Burroughs's] non-conformist biography have any relevance to the amount of damages to which he would be entitled by virtue of false statements impugning his patriotism in war time. It simply does not follow that since one is or was a drug addict, he is probably unpatriotic anymore than that an unpatriotic person is likely to be a drug addict.

As for the censorship trials, we assembled expert literary witnesses, including Norman Mailer and John Ciardi. For the Boston trial, held in January

1965, we asked Burroughs himself to testify. Our lawyer Edward de Grazia prepped him with these words:

> Allen [Ginsberg] thinks you might describe how this book developed from your recordings in depth what passed through your mind, your recollections, following the apromorphine treatment and how elements of "isolation" and "alienation" got involved and how even a process of adjustment to outer world was involved, etc. I would think the material can be described as originally unconscious, made conscious through your act of creating this book, etc. and others (our psychiatric witnesses) can testify that the "horror" or "obscenity" of that unconscious material is kin to that of most people. You can perhaps relate this personal creative process to your personal drug "problem." Others may speak, as you have suggested, of "drugs" [as] the perfect American commodity. Mailer, like Ciardi, wants to talk about hell and I hope you won't feel bad if no one talks about heaven.

However, this Boston trial did not follow the normal pattern in which state authorities simply seized a book that they considered obscene. They were also prosecuting a bookseller, Theodore Mavrikos, for stocking and offering the volume for sale. De Grazia petitioned the court, protesting reasonably enough that it was unfair to prosecute Mavrikos for selling a book that was openly carried in other stores and even in the public library. Eventually, the charges against Mavrikos were dropped even though the state of Massachusetts charged that the book was obscene.

When the Boston trial finally got underway on January 12, 1965, Grove brought forth a parade of literary celebrities to testify for the defense. Ciardi testified very pertinently to complaints that Burroughs didn't really need to use such strong language, by saying that when Dante dipped the sins in excrement, he did not call it "excrement." When you are dealing with depraved subject matter, he said, you must coarsen the language.

Other writers also found religious parallels to the novel. Literary critic Norman Holland stated, "*Naked Lunch* is a religious novel about original sin. . . . If St. Augustine were writing today, he might very well write something like *Naked Lunch*." Norman Mailer played the same key, saying, "William Burroughs is in my opinion—whatever his conscious intention may be—a religious writer. . . . [The book] is a vision of how mankind would act if man was totally divorced from eternity."

Despite the lack of witnesses on the prosecution side, the judge found the book obscene. The judge stated the book was "hardcore pornography" and said the author was "mentally sick."

We appealed this ruling to the Massachusetts Supreme Court a year and a half after the Boston trial, on July 7, 1966. This court sat tight for the time being because it was waiting to see how the Supreme Court ruled on pending cases. An earlier Massachusetts obscenity case, in which *Fanny Hill* had been ruled obscene by the State Supreme Court, was now on the federal Supreme Court docket. The federal court overturned the obscenity ruling for this matter. With this and other new rulings in view, the Massachusetts court now found in favor of *Naked Lunch*, declaring it not obscene.

Still, this was not the end of *Naked Lunch*'s legal troubles. As I learned during the *Tropic of Cancer* cases, in our legal system the determination of what qualifies as obscene is left up to the individual states. While we got off in Boston, we were also prosecuted in other jurisdictions, such as Los Angeles. Here, again, booksellers were put on trial and, in this case, they were prosecuted for two books, *Naked Lunch* and Monte Steele's *The Sex Scholar*, lumping Burroughs' artistic achievement with some rather mundane sexual material in order, I suppose, to condemn the Beat writer by association. The judge in the case, however, could discriminate, and while allowing the case against *The Sex Scholar* to continue, threw out the case against *Naked Lunch*, saying that as a whole, Burroughs' novel could not be said to be without "redeeming social value."

While these trials were ongoing, I found that Burroughs, who had waited so long for his book to finally come out, was (it seemed) being stiffed by Girodias on some of his royalties. Richard Seaver—he and Fred Jordan were still my top two editors—wrote Burroughs on March 6, 1964, "I hear rumors that you have had some difficulties collecting royalties from our edition of *Naked Lunch* that we have paid to Girodias. Is this true?" Seaver went on, "Frankly, I cannot imagine how your royalties should become involved with any of Girodias' French business, since we pay royalties not directly to him, but to an agent in Switzerland." The rumors that reached Seaver had come from Paul Bowles who talked to Burroughs in Tangier.

Burroughs replied that there were indeed funds owed him, but that Girodias's financial situation was so dire, it was unlikely he would yield a cent. "[I]t is a question," he wrote, "of find a lawyer and get in line and the line is long and the till is empty. The plain fact is he spent the money to cover what he evidently considered more pressing debts and I was barely able to squeeze out of him enough to get myself back to Tangier."

Still, Burroughs remained magnanimous:

Despite my understandable annoyance with Maurice I still sympathize with his position, which could hardly be worse. More and more trouble with the French authorities, suspended sentences piling up, a twenty year publishing ban, inevitable debacle of that unfortunate restaurant venture [Girodias had opened a bistro], owing money to his staff, social security to the government, fines, lawsuits, the lot.

Once the *Naked Lunch* trials finished in our favor, we went on to publish many other books by Burroughs. Now, often as not, the headaches came not from prosecutions but from conflicts with other publishers over rights and Burroughs's over-scrupulousness. For instance, I remember a problem over *The Soft Machine* in late 1965. At the last moment Burroughs wanted a vast amount of changes to his text, after the novel had already been typeset. We acceded to his request but under protest. As Seaver wrote him on December 20, with a touch of humor:

Bill, I don't want to sound like an old St. Louis preacher, but there comes a point at which you have to write finis to the writing of a book. Before you left America, you did re-write this novel extensively and went over all our questions prior to its being sent for setting. Then, when you received galleys, your changes were so extensive (especially in your decision to lower case literally hundreds of words that had been upper case in your manuscript) that we had to junk the entire first typesetting and reset the book completely a second time.

Burroughs, though, would consider last-minute changes crucial with later books as well. When we sent him the galleys for *The Ticket That Exploded* in 1966, he asked us to put a hold on the book because of revisions he was working on:

> It really would be extremely disadvantageous to publish the book as is. The changes I am making could well make the difference between a real setback and a book that will make money. . . . I think you will agree that the original Olympia edition of *The Soft Machine* would have sold very badly indeed and that the corrections and changes made all the difference.

Once these changes had been finished and set, in April 1967, Burroughs had one final request about *Ticket*: "Everything O.K. except the photo which I have never liked . . . I am having some photos made with a studio here and will send them along toward the end of the week." The new photo arrived ten days later. Burroughs wrote that it made him look like a 1910 financier but asked that it be used on all further reprints.

In the end, Burroughs was another author who stood by me when I lost control of Grove Press. When I was forced out of the company in 1986, Burroughs, writing through his secretary, James Grauerholz, stated, "[W]e are appalled and infuriated at the treatment you have received." Grauerholz added that "In the thirteen years I have worked with William, no publisher has made more regular accountings, nor more honest, nor has paid more fairly, than Grove Press. And Grove is further distinguished from William's earliest publishers in that, unlike Olympia, there has never been any financial chicanery to blot the record."

15

Revolutionaries: *Evergreen*, Che Guevara, and the Grove Bombing

We often launched new Grove authors, such as John Rechy and Hubert Selby, in *Evergreen*. And we were now able to mingle in *Evergreen* some non-exclusively Grove authors: Jean-Paul Sartre, Allen Ginsberg, Terry Southern, Norman Mailer, Susan Sontag, Chester Himes, Edward Gorey, Charles Bukowski, and Woody Allen, for instance. Don Allen even managed to get an Albert Camus article for us about capital punishment that had been published in *Nouvelle Revue Française*. Camus won the Nobel Prize not long after I bought the article.

Evergreen was a wonderful platform for Grove, and it worked very well for a long time. Some issues were themed, such as No. 2, "San Francisco Scene," which as I have described became very well known and brought the contributors to the attention of a nationwide readership. No. 7, "The Eye of Mexico" (Winter 1959) was the only issue of *Evergreen* reviewed as a book, and quite favorably so by the *New York Times Book Review*.

This *Evergreen* came quite naturally to me, having first traveled from Chicago to Mexico in 1940 when I drove to Mexico City with a friend in an attempt to meet Diego Rivera. Trotsky was there, along with Frida Kahlo, but Rivera was away in New York.

The famous "What is 'Pataphysics?" issue was No. 13 (May–June 1960). The term was coined by Alfred Jarry for a science of imaginary solutions, or, as the *New York Times* called it, "the science of meaningful nonsense, or nonsensical meaningfulness."[91] This included pieces by Eugène Ionesco, Raymond Queneau, Michel Leiris, Boris Vian, and of course Jarry himself. "'Pataphysics relates each thing and each event not to any generality (a mere plastering over of exceptions) but to the singularity that makes it an exception. Thus the science of 'Pataphysics attempts no cures, envisages no progress, distrusts all claims of 'improvement' in the state of things, and remains innocent of any message." The scholar Roger Shattuck, who specialized in French literature, was our guest editor for the issue.

There were other important *Evergreen* issues in the early 1960s. No. 21 was "The German Scene," with contributions by Uwe Johnson, Ingeborg Bachmann, Günter Grass, and Heinrich Böll. Grove's Fred Jordan was its chief editor. No. 23 (March–April 1962) was "Henry Miller on Trial," explaining the legal issues we had faced with the publication of *Tropic of Cancer* and a resultant trial in Chicago. We continued this coverage in No. 25, with Chicago journalist Hoke Norris's report, "'Cancer' in Chicago."

The first issue published in a larger format, No. 32, got us in trouble—21,000 unbound copies of the magazine were seized by Nassau County Vice Squad detectives on April 24, 1964, at our printing plant on Hicksville Road in Bethpage, New York. A woman employed at Pegasus Press, the bindery for the magazine, tipped off a detective in the district attorney's squad, leading to the arrest of the bindery president, George Haralampoudis, on a charge of possessing and distributing obscene literature. There were some supposedly nude color photographs by Emil Cadoo in that issue, although if you looked at them you would be hard pressed to say whether anybody was nude or not. But they were beautiful and creative photographs. The whole issue was deemed lewd by the district attorney, William Cahn, because it contained "provocative and sexually bizarre poses" and "a dirty story." And the *New York Times* reported: "Warrants have been issued for the arrest of Barney Rosset, president and editor of the *Review*, and Richard Seaver, secretary and associate editor."[92]

We sued in Brooklyn Federal Court, arguing that the suppression of the magazine was unconstitutional, and on June 12, 1964, three federal judges ordered the return of the confiscated copies on grounds that the police seizure was a violation of the Fourteenth Amendment. They did not rule on the obscenity of the material. Without the magazines in their possession, the Nassau County DA claimed they would no longer be able to build a case against us, and all charges were dropped a month later. Hicksville played its name to the hilt.

●◡

In No. 77 (April 1970), we printed an excerpt, "Redress and Revolution," from William O. Douglas's book *Points of Rebellion*. This not only resulted in Justice Douglas disqualifying himself from the Supreme Court rulings on *I Am Curious (Yellow)* to avoid what could be seen as a conflict of interest, but it gave then-Congressman Gerald R. Ford ammunition to try to impeach the liberal Supreme Court justice on April 16, 1970. A group of over a hundred Democrat and Republican congressmen called for Justice Douglas's impeachment on charges of, among other offenses, "fomenting rebellion through his books and articles, writing for a pornographic magazine, [and] associating with gamblers and underworld figures."[93]

The *Washington Post*'s obituary of President Ford in 2006 explained some of the political motivations behind the failed attempt to remove Justice Douglas: "Ostensibly, it was Ford's idea to impeach Douglas because of the appearance of excerpts of a book by the jurist in the *Evergreen Review* alongside material that Ford said was pornographic. However, after he became president, Ford admitted he had been helped by John N. Mitchell, the attorney general in the first Nixon administration, who was angry about Senate rejection of two of Nixon's Supreme Court nominees."[94]

We published our last *Evergreen* issue in 1984, No. 98. It included contributions from Ferlinghetti, Beckett, Duras, McClure, and Kathy Acker. We had paid tribute to some of our most treasured contributors.

But *Evergreen Review* was reborn on the Internet in 1998, where it continues to this day.

Ernesto "Che" Guevara was killed in Bolivia on October 9, 1967, and the February 1968 issue of *Evergreen Review*, No. 51, contained a special section to commemorate his life.

The lead piece we included was a translation of a speech given by Fidel Castro at the Plaza de la Revolución on October 18, 1967, "El Che Vive!" in which Castro stated, "Che fell defending the interests, defending the cause of the exploited and the oppressed people of this continent—Che fell defending the cause of the poor and disenfranchised of this earth." While his death was a tragic loss to the anti-authoritarian movement, Castro said, the imperialists who killed him were shortsighted. "[T]hey think that by eliminating a man physically they have eliminated his thinking; that by eliminating him physically they have eliminated his ideas, eliminated his virtues, eliminated his example." On the contrary, he concluded, "[H]is death will, in the long run, be like a seed which will give rise to many men determined to imitate him, men determined to follow his example."

Che himself told the story of his part in the overthrow of the corrupt Fulgencio Batista regime in Cuba in his book *Reminiscences of the Cuban Revolutionary War*, which we excerpted in *Evergreen*. It was in 1955, in Mexico, that Che met Castro and joined the guerrilla force he was recruiting to enter Cuba. On November 25, 1956, Castro's group of eighty-two men embarked on the leaky vessel, the *Granma*, for a slow voyage to the island. They landed—starved and worn out from seasickness—on December 2 at the swampy Las Colorados beach. The bedraggled army was eventually victorious, ousting the corrupt dictator and putting the revolutionaries in power.

Once Castro's leftist government was stabilized, Che hungered for greener pastures and set off for Bolivia to join the guerrillas there. In a letter dated April 1, 1965, also included in *Evergreen*, Che wrote to Castro bidding him farewell. "I feel," he said, "that I have fulfilled the part of my duty that tied me to the Cuban revolution in its territory, and I say good-bye to you, the comrades, your people, who are already mine."

The next piece in our Che tribute was an account of what went on among the guerrillas Che led in Bolivia, reported by fledgling photographer George Andrew Roth. After a futile week accompanying the military as they hunted guerrillas, Roth hooked up with some peasants who led him to the guerrilla camp. Che wrote his own interview, both questions and answers, into Roth's notebook. He then sent his friend Tania—of whom more in a moment—to lead Roth and two journalists who had found their way to the camp, one being Régis Debray, back out of the mountains.

Debray, Roth, and the other journalist were arrested as revolutionaries by the Bolivian military and thrown in jail, and the two journalists remained behind bars. Although sentenced to thirty years, Debray was released in 1970 after Pope Paul VI and other prominent figures put pressure on the Bolivian government. While things were going badly for Debray in prison, they were also deteriorating for Che who, after two years in Bolivia, was wounded on October 9, 1967, and taken captive. Later, while under guard, he was shot through the heart. The military had planned well.

Che was a very important figure to me. Grove Press published a number of books about him, including *The Great Rebel: Che Guevara in Bolivia* by Luis J. González and Gustavo A. Sánchez Salazar, which detailed the perils and tension of Che's attempt to create an insurgency in Bolivia. The story of how we signed this book is part of the story of our attempt to secure a copy of Che's diary from the Bolivian authorities.

In March 1968 I asked a close friend, Joe Liss, who had been a top-notch correspondent for CBS News, to travel to La Paz to meet a contact we had established to obtain Che's diary from the Bolivian authorities. Liss later wrote in an unpublished report he prepared for me, titled *Notes for the Bolivian Trip on a Day to Day Basis*, that when he arrived at my office to get the plane tickets, "To my astonishment Barney handed me cash amounting to $8,500 in denominations of $50's and $100's, and told me that with this money I was expected to spend about $6,000 to get what I could of the Che Guevara diaries."

Since the Bolivian government seemed to be actively against giving any further publicity to the murdered guerrilla, this mission was undercover. Liss was to pretend he was visiting the country because he was working on a screenplay about Che. He was even to receive a phone call from a movie producer he knew, who would ask how the writing was going. As a further precaution, all communication between Liss and myself would go through his wife.

Once Liss made phone contact with a mysterious, high-ranking general named Juan Torres, he found that the general didn't speak English. So he hired a translator and set up an appointment to see him. "I explained to him that I was a film writer from New York and London and was anxious to see the Che Guevara diaries for research on a film," Liss reported.

Torres did have access to the diaries but told Liss that another American publishing company, McGraw-Hill, had also made an offer for them. Indeed, he intimated that he had already closed the deal with them.

I told Liss that I had been given the name of another contact, Gustavo A. Sánchez Salazar of the newspaper *El Diario*, who might have some information about Che's diary. Liss flew to the provincial city of Cochabamba to meet Sánchez. Although Sánchez didn't have the diary, it turned out that he and Luis J. González, yet another journalist, were writing a book about Che. Once we got a glimpse at the interesting and thorough research the two had done into Che's life and demise in Bolivia, we asked them to let Grove publish their book when it was completed, and they agreed.

It seemed possible now that Sánchez and González might be able to locate part of the diary, and they were determined to go to La Paz to hunt for it, but now a new danger arose. A radical priest the two writers brought to meet Liss had somehow learned of his meeting with the general and accused him of being with the CIA. Nothing Liss said could sway the good father, and the deal was on the verge of foundering. But this priest had been in New York and had heard of

Grove. "I told him all about the offices of Grove Press," Liss wrote in his report, "and pretty soon with my knowledge of Grove I think he became somewhat convinced that I was not a CIA agent, but a representative of Grove Press."

While Liss was on this adventure, I told him, obliquely, to expect a visit. He thought I meant that his wife was coming and I couldn't make it clear that I was using the name of his wife as a blind. So he was thoroughly surprised when he received a call from me a few days later.

Using the alias Roger Tansey, I had traveled to La Paz, Bolivia with Fred Jordan because it had become very difficult to communicate with Joe while he was there, and I had started to feel deeply concerned about him. We met Sánchez and González and made a deal for their book, which became *The Great Rebel: Che Guevara in Bolivia*. And, in addition to the six pages of the diary Liss had acquired from them and already had in hand, he was able to buy for us some eleven photos of Che. We decided to let Sánchez secure the other diary pages, which we learned had been scattered among several Bolivian generals, and send them to us.

The final hazard was getting the photos and diary pages out of the country. This turned out to be easy. As Liss explained, "Fred Jordan put them in his pocket, simple as that."

We were never able to acquire the entire Che Guevara diary, but we did publish the pages we obtained in *Evergreen*, No. 57 (August 1968), along with an illustrated feature we prepared, "Who's Who in Che's Diary."

On July 26, 1968, while the issue with the diary excerpts was hitting the newsstands, Cuban exiles bombed Grove's offices on University Place with a grenade launcher. According to a man who lived next door, a group of men in a pickup truck drove past the building and shot a grenade right through the large front window on the second floor. Pow!—better than the Bay of Pigs! It was done at a late hour, fortunately. No one was inside and nobody got hurt. I heard about the bombing shortly after it happened, 3:41 a.m., when I received a phone call from Grove's wonderful office manager, Laura Martin, who was the first Grove person on the scene. She discovered a knife tear in a poster made from our *Evergreen Review*, No. 51 cover of February 1968, the marvelous, iconic portrait of Che Guevara done by Paul Davis—it had been stabbed. That was interesting. The police were the only people in the building when Laura arrived.

The neighbor who saw the bombing told me the police hadn't taken much time to look for evidence at the scene. He also said that he had recently had a lot of trouble with his telephone; the sound was just awful. He asked an engineer friend to check it, and the friend figured out that someone had accidentally tapped into his line, which was affecting the sound level of the phone. He also said he could hear every phone call I made on my private office line, the real object of the tap.

Around that time a number of other places in New York were bombed, including an attempt at the apartment of the Cuban delegate to the UN, but they got somebody else's apartment by accident. The Canadian consulate and Japan Airlines were also bombed—groups the anti-Castro Cuban groups imagined were their enemies.

Novelist Gilbert Sorrentino, who was working as an editor at Grove at the time, described the aftermath of the bombing in the fall 1990 issue of *The Review of Contemporary Fiction*: "They wrecked one office completely, blew out the windows overlooking University Place, and made a general mess. Grove got enormous publicity out of it, 'publisher of porno-left-wing-radical-oddball-unreadable-avant-garde books bombed!' . . . Looking back on this incident, it doesn't seem that we were much affected. I mean, we came in to work, looked at the damage, chatted with the cops, and went to work."[95]

In *Evergreen*, No. 60 (November 1968) we featured "The Story of Tania: Che's Woman in Bolivia," again by González and Sánchez. This time they wrote about

Haydée Tamara Bunke Bider, who later took the name Tania—the woman who guided Roth, Debray, and the other journalist away from Che's camp. She was born in Buenos Aires in 1937 to German parents who had fled to Argentina to escape the Nazis. After the war her parents traveled back to Germany, where Tamara, as she was then called, attended university and became involved in the Socialist party. But she felt a bond with the region where she had been born. In 1960 she met Che, who was traveling with a Cuban trade delegation in East Germany. She went to Cuba the following year, changed her name, and became involved in educational and women's causes. Later she traveled with Che throughout Latin America.

Tania was killed by Bolivian soldiers on August 31, 1967, while crossing the Río Grande with eight other members of her group. The only woman who fought alongside Che in Bolivia, Tania became a feminist and revolutionary hero—Patricia Hearst even took the name Tania when she joined the Symbionese Liberation Army after being kidnapped by them in 1974.

16

Attack from Within, Attack from Without

On April 13, 1970, the Grove offices at 214 Mercer Street were taken over by a group of eight feminists in protest of what they claimed were dismissals of Grove employees friendly to the formation of a union. Among them was Grove employee Robin Morgan. Quite famous for her feminist activism, Morgan had worked as an editor for us for about two years. During that time there were rumblings about union organizing.

Fred Jordan, Cy Rembar, and I were on a visit to Denmark to screen some films when our offices were occupied. Unaware of what was happening, I called the office and reached my assistant and asked, "Everything going okay?"

"Well," she replied, "there is something special going on today. I'm on the fifth floor." Our office was on the sixth floor.

I asked, "Why?" and she said, "Well, some other people are in your office," and went on to explain that my office had been occupied by a women's liberation group.

All my personal correspondence and business records were stored in my office, where these women were barricaded. I said, "Get 'em out!"

She said, "No, they won't come out," so I said, "Go in and throw them out," and she replied, "No, nobody wants to do that."

I realized she was right.

Meantime, I was going crazy. *What are they doing while they're in there?*

I said, "Well, if none of you have enough guts to get them out, call the police." So they did. But the women requested that female cops arrest them. After an unsuccessful attempt was made to find policewomen, male cops finally went in and carried them out. They were arrested and booked.

As far as I know, the women didn't steal any documents from my office, but they certainly smashed up the place and draped flags out the window as if they'd taken over Grove Press. And there I was sitting in Denmark.

In her book *Saturday's Child: A Memoir*, Robin Morgan described how she gained access to the building at 8:00 that Monday morning. She told the security guard that she and her many friends were there to clean out her office because she had been fired the previous Friday. Morgan wrote in her book, "Once upstairs, I sever some of the elevator cables, strew Vaseline-coated thumbtacks on the stairs, lock the doors, and pour glue in the locks. Then I hang our Women's Liberation banner out the window of the executive office."[96]

They had also made a flyer with their demands which included something to the effect, "No more mansions on Long Island for boss-man Rosset and his executive yes-men flunkies, segregated mansions built with extortionist profits from selling *The Autobiography of Malcolm X*, a best-seller—and not one black welfare mother a penny better off after millions of copies made Rosset rich!"

When I came back from Denmark I found everything in chaos and the plan to unionize Grove Press in full force. As I explained in an interview published by *Smoke Signals* years later, people were marching around the building screaming, "You make all your money on obscenity; give all this money to black women of America and to Betty Shabazz."[97] Malcolm X's widow, Shabazz was a friend and seemed happy with what we were doing for her.

They also demanded a twenty-four-hour-a-day childcare center. I said, "Okay, there's an empty lot across the street owned by NYU with a fence around it. I will lead you there. And we will put up a tent." Nobody would follow me. We exchanged hostile words all day in front of the building.

Emily Goodman, a woman I had hired to be staff counsel of Grove Press *because* I wanted to be in the forefront of using women legal professionals, instead became the lawyer for the women who occupied the office. As someone who viewed himself as a champion of women's liberation, I was utterly taken aback. I found myself assailed as one of Grove's "wealthy capitalist dirty old straight white men" involved in the "scapegoating of women."

I was present in early May at the court hearing for the women who were arrested. They wanted to go to jail, and were bound and determined to do so. We went before the judge, and Emily Goodman demanded that the court return the women's fingerprints. She told the judge, "You've illegally taken our fingerprints, and we demand them back! And we want a twenty-four-hour childcare center in the courtroom right now." They had a couple of babies with them. Robin Morgan's baby was yelling and crying.

While all this was going on, I cornered the young arresting officer in an outer corridor and asked him whether it would influence him in making future arrests if we dropped the charges. He said it would not, though the DA insisted it would be a terrible tragedy if we did. Our lawyer, Cy Rembar, following up on this, asked the same policeman on the stand whether it would have any effect on him performing similar duties in the future if the charges were dropped. Again he said no. Goodman was screaming at the judge and Morgan's baby was screaming, so the judge looked around the crowded courtroom, said, "I agree with Mr. Rembar," and dismissed the case.

I think something sad happened in the feminist movement when a faction became opposed to what they considered sexist and pornographic writing. There seemed to me to be a failure to understand the nature of fantasy and creativity. Politically, it got all fouled up. If you suppress erotic art, anything that might be considered too sexual, and combine that tendency with general discrimination against women in multiple ways, you find yourself well on the way to fascism.

Years ago I was asked to debate Betty Friedan, a very well known women's rights activist of her time, about pornography, or obscenity, or whatever. We got together before the meeting and as we talked to each other we realized there was no conflict between us. We were in agreement. We became friends and our debate became a discussion and an analysis of the status quo in our society.

Besides the women's lib group, a union with a left-wing history targeted us. It all added up to an enormous outside onslaught against Grove Press. I deeply believe the FBI and CIA backed it all, and that Grove's antiwar stance had something to do with it. But I don't think the women were part of the conspiracy or consciously aware of being duped. Nevertheless, they played a vital role in bringing Grove down. We won the battle, if you want to call it winning, but we lost the war. They destroyed us. It is hard to explain it to people on the outside, but it really was the end of a fully functioning Grove Press. We lost key employees.

The union, which I believe was aiding and abetting the government effort to bring Grove down, was headed by Henry Foner of the Fur, Leather, and Machine Workers Joint Board, affiliated with the Amalgamated Meat Cutters and Butcher Workmen of North America. It was a left-wing union that had been red-baited almost out of existence during the McCarthy era. They were attempting to unionize Grove Press when no other publishing company was unionized. (The only exception was Harper & Row, which had a "company" union that was not affiliated with any independent group.) Why did they start with us if not because they were put up to it?

As I recall, the union had in its constitution a provision that you could not be a member if you believed in violence or in overthrowing the government. I believe this clause had been forced on them by the McCarthy people; otherwise the union would have been destroyed. Well, that wasn't our fault. But there they were attacking us. So we counterattacked. Jules Geller, who worked at Grove, was a Trotskyite from World War II. He was a brilliant guy and devastating because he knew exactly how to provoke what we considered the pro-union group. They supposedly adored Castro and Mao, so we made up statements that we would hang in the elevators, things like: "What Would Fidel Think If He Knew a Union That Cuts Up Animals Was Unionizing Grove?" We plastered slogans like that all over the place. The union supporters wore buttons that said "I Am Furious (Yellow)" so when I started wearing one, too, they took theirs off.

Do you want to be a member of a union in which you can't be a Black Panther? We didn't even need to say that explicitly, we just handed out the constitution to everybody who worked at Grove. There were a number of young black guys working in our book club—our manager of clerical workers had been hiring lots of young people and he made a personal thing out of hiring young radicals, many of whom were black. This was right at the moment of the Black Panther peak. The manager had treated his workers badly. They were not being paid enough, for one thing. Still, I heard one of them say, "What're they doing to us? How can we belong to a union that doesn't believe in revolution?"

It was a living hell. Every day the building was emptied out by bomb threats and fire alarms. And this union was thinking they were going to organize us and get some points out of it? We never knew who could vote in the union election, although we knew no one in management was allowed a vote. One time when they held a big union meeting at Grove, I went. I was allowed to speak because a democratic faction in the group called for the right of the opposition to particip- ate. I got up and said, "I'm firing all of you whether you win or lose," because we were running out of funds. I couldn't find out from these employees what they wanted. Unlike the feminists, the union organizers would never clearly tell me. I never got a demand.

This went on for two or three months and they finally had the election— and they were wiped out! Almost nobody voted for them. I had been sure we would lose, and had already written my speech accepting the union: *It was a good fight and we lost. Welcome. . . .* I tore it up. But in the meantime, Grove Press was critically wounded.

We were dead broke after that. At that point, 1970, we had rebuilt a big old seven-story building on Mercer Street, at enormous expense, instead of putting our money into books. The banks had assured me that real estate was a better investment even though we had a book club that was more or less thriving, a growing film distribution business, and increasing book sales. Gilbert Sorrentino recalled this period in a letter to me dated May 9, 1998:

> Reading your interview in *Paris Review* [No. 145, Winter 1997–98] reminded me that when we moved from University Place to Mercer Street, I had the flu and was out of the office during the move. When I got well, I returned to work on Mercer Street, and when I was shown my office—about three times the size of the old one, with a huge potted tree in the corner, armchairs, etc., etc., my first thought was "Who the hell is going to pay for this?" The handwriting seemed to be on the wall.

Finally we had to move back to Eleventh Street, and afterward we settled in my house on Houston Street. From then on Grove was a holding operation. For a number of years, we were actually making a little bit of money, but we had incurred debts we couldn't pay on a current basis. It took twelve years to pay them off, one month at a time. We stayed alive, but the company was just subsisting.

I brought in one accounting team after another to look at the books, and they all said, "You're broke, you're bankrupt." I didn't believe it. We went on for many years in a state of quasi-bankruptcy, and it was quite an accomplishment to keep the company going. It meant making deals with everybody to pay them ten cents on the dollar over a long period of years. Twelve years of creditors' committees. Imagine how much energy that took. You don't have much time to look for books to publish when you do that.

We entered into a distribution agreement with Random House in 1971. This enabled us to close our warehouse and make do with a much smaller staff. Random House sold the books to our accounts, shipped them, and took over the accounting functions with the stores and wholesalers. Still, we continued to shrink. In 1971 we had some thirty-five Grove employees. In 1972 there were twenty-four. By 1978, seven years after our agreement with Random House, our staff had dropped to only nine employees.

We almost had a deal with film director Francis Ford Coppola to buy Grove Press. He made an offer and I accepted it. This was just before the opening of *Apocalypse Now*, in August 1979. I first met Francis in San Francisco in 1973 when I went out to Berkeley to meet with people at the Pacific Film Archive, who were preparing a program to salute our film division. The guy who ran the PFA said, "I want you to meet Francis Coppola, he's a friend of mine." He took my wife Cristina, Cristina's sister Luisa, and me to Coppola's office, which was in a tower in a beautiful copper-roofed building. We went up to the office without being announced, and Coppola was there writing music for *The Godfather Part II* on a blackboard mounted on an easel.

At first I found him to be very cold. Someone had told me that he had been a French horn player in the San Francisco Opera company orchestra, so after a while I said, "Oh, did you know, Mr. Coppola, Cristina and Luisa's father co-founded the San Francisco Opera?" He said, "What? Let's go home to dinner," and took us to his house where he cooked up some pasta.

The whole scene at Coppola's was wonderful. His father and mother were there arguing, with Mama telling Papa, "You were a goddamn Fascist with Mussolini," and him insisting, "No, I wasn't!"

Coppola wrote me in the April of 1973:

Thanks for the copy of Graffiti, and also the Grove Press catalogue. I looked through it, and though it may sound crazy, I'd like to buy the entire library. I mean the books of course, and not the film prints. If it's possible, please bill me . . . and [send] the books to me at my home.

He had come unannounced to see me at Grove with his producer, Fred Roos, with a big manuscript by his brother August, whom he severely criticized to me. I had never heard of August but I talked to Coppola for hours about this goddamned manuscript. Francis wasn't nice to August and August wasn't nice to Francis, but there it is, he's got to take care of him and God, and could we possibly publish this manuscript. August was a professor at some college in California and he had built a museum inside another museum called a "feelatorium" or something. You went inside, I am only guessing now, and felt textures.

I read August's novel, *The Intimacy*. It was very strange, about a man who wants to experiment with his sensory feelings, so he blindfolds himself. And while blindfolded he meets a girl, but of course he cannot see her, he won't take off the blindfold. They live in a rooming house in San Francisco, but not together. The girl gets in big trouble and he saves her. We worked on the manuscript for months and published it in 1978. It was never good but it got a hell of a lot better. Francis never gave us any money for it or anything like that. I sort of liked it too . . . ultimately.

I eventually met August. He was very good-looking. In the novel he talks about his ugly brother who is a film director. It didn't hit me at first but he was putting down Francis. In addition, August had a school for young women in Francis's house. The women seemed strong and attractive, French or English, not American. Some sort of teaching was going on. Alain Robbe-Grillet even taught there. He fit in perfectly. He was a caricature of an evil person. Fascinating evil.

Then Coppola made an offer for Grove, the company itself. I said yes and our deal seemed arranged. People told me I was crazy to move to San Francisco. Meantime, Francis was buying up storefronts for more space. Fred Roos had earlier taken my son Peter and me to this big studio in Los Angeles that Coppola was going to buy, a place where Jeanette MacDonald and other stars had made movies long ago. He was doing fine until *Apocalypse Now*. I accompanied him to the premier in New York, and had a date to see him the next morning at the Sherry-Netherland. The problem was, his opening was a disaster.

When we went over to see him at the hotel, all these producers and hangers-on said to me, "What are you here for? He's not going to give you any money." I said I would leave and actually turned to go, very angry, when out comes Francis in pajamas and robe.

He sat down and said, "You know, I'm broke, Barney. Everything I have is gone."

As far as I knew, it was true that *Apocalypse Now* had cost him dearly. He said he was sorry and that was the end of it. We parted on good terms, and it took years before Coppola pulled out of his financial hole. I stayed in mine.

I continued to make frequent trips to Europe. I never failed to meet with Beckett in Paris and naturally saw Joan Mitchell at her place at Vétheuil. When her mother died in 1967 she came into a trust fund from her grandfather, with which she bought the beautiful stone house. About thirty miles north of Paris, it sat on a rise, with two acres of land. With a studio at the back, the house overlooked the Seine and a lush swathe of cultivated fields, rows of poplars, and the village's Gothic church. Monet had painted there, the gardener's cottage was once his home, and he is buried in the cemetery. The linden tree that was in the courtyard entrance, the river, the flowers, and the trees would become part of her art, just as they had for Monet.

Joan had always wanted to have a place in the country. Her arrondissement in Paris had grown increasingly dangerous as the Algerian hostilities spilled over into France. Her situation in the US had also been depressing. After the promise of the early 1960s, the assassinations, race riots, and Vietnam War made the States no longer an option, even for someone who had never been politically active. Her father had died in 1963, her mother in 1967. Frank O'Hara, who had championed Abstract Expressionism and whose friendship and correspondence were irreplaceable for Joan, died in 1966 after being hit by a jeep on Fire Island. She went through serious depressions, and her stormy relationship with Jean-Paul Riopelle did not help.

Joan was not isolated at Vétheuil. Friends visited, and Riopelle's studio, where he kept his large collection of cars, was not far away. But he usually kept his distance, rarely spent the night, and seemed to show up mainly to pick a fight. Their relationship of twenty-four years would end in 1980, leaving her unhappy but freer than she had been.

During the 1980s I saw Joan declining in health, depressed by the death of her sister in 1982 and two good friends from AIDS. Two years later Joan was diagnosed with cancer of the jaw. In 1985 she underwent hip surgery, painting the "Between" pictures between her hospital stays. Her painting was a record of her joys, her depressions, her sickness, her loves. It was astonishing to see them in person, their size and complexity. In spite of her illness and loneliness, during the last years of her life she worked with astonishing vigor and originality.

Joan's rugged, athletic, impish beauty never left her. She was surrounded by a lovely landscape, by animals, flowers, and beauty of all kinds. The house at Véutheil was usually in disorder, as if she had just moved in, but it was pleasant and, given her character, it was logical disorder. Our marriage had been difficult but separation had allowed a deep friendship to blossom. Joan was always family, wonderful with my children, and warmly accepting of my wives Loly, Cristina, Lisa, and Astrid when we visited.

After the debacle at Grove in 1971 we powered on, in the dark so to speak. I worked out of my Houston Street digs in the early 1980s. It was a comfortable arrangement and, given the fortress-like building, a hell of a lot safer. We went on publishing, but the situation was becoming untenable. We did enjoy some financially significant achievements during the decade. Most importantly, our republication of John Kennedy Toole's *A Confederacy of Dunces.*

This was a stunning publishing coup, since the book eventually won the Pulitzer Prize and became a bestseller. The novel might have never been published if Walker Percy, who was teaching at Loyola University in 1976, had not given in to a persistent caller and agreed to read a messy typescript by an unknown author who had died in 1969. Percy convinced Louisiana State University Press to publish the book in 1980, upon which it immediately attained cult status. We acquired the rights soon after and brought it out as a Grove title. Marvelous, hilarious, and weird, we loved the book yet were astonished that it took off.

We published another comic masterpiece in 1984, Kathy Acker's *Blood and Guts in High School*. Fred Jordan was always Acker's champion. But the book that really caused a sensation that year was *CIA: The Freedom Fighters' Manual*. Discovered in Nicaragua, it detailed the strategies put into place by the CIA to subvert foreign governments that were not in league with the US. The book did nothing to endear Grove Press—and Barney Rosset—to the intelligence services.

When Coppola's offer evaporated in 1979 my back was against the wall, and by 1985 Grove was faced with a desperate need to raise new money. There were monthly meetings just to decide how we could meet the payroll. Numerous offers had been made to buy the company. None of them seemed good, for one reason or another. G. P. Putnam's Sons had approached me, but I turned them down because I wanted to maintain editorial independence. So when the British publisher Lord George Weidenfeld came along telling me, in essence, "I've got this woman who has all the money in the world, and she's going to give me all I want, and I want you. You can do whatever you want, I'll give you money to run the company," I was sucked in.

The woman was Ann Getty, the wife of Gordon, an heir to the Getty oil fortune. I had known Weidenfeld for thirty years. "Known him," as I told *Small Press* in a 1986 interview,[98] not as a friend but an acquaintance. We were amicable. He came to New York in September 1984 and told me he was involved with this wonderful person, Ann Getty, who had limitless funds and wanted to be involved in American publishing. I don't know if acquiring Grove was his idea or hers, but I would guess it was his and that she approved. I imagine that her main goal was to assume a certain kind of prestige, and that becoming the publisher of Beckett and Stoppard and Pinter and Ionesco and Mamet and so on appealed to her. I in no way think that Grove Press was their only objective. But there was a promise of enormous amounts of money to do good things.

The first time I met Ann Getty I brought her a book from a Latin America series, edited by my wife at the time, Lisa Krug, called *The Other Side of Paradise*, which dealt with the domination of American conglomerates in Bermuda, Haiti, and the whole Caribbean. I said to Ann, "Do you know what you're getting into?"

She replied, "Oh yes, it doesn't bother me. We've sold all our oil to Texaco."

Well, I liked that remark. Texaco was not favorably spoken of in the book. At the same meeting I gave her an order form that included the erotic books in our Victorian Library.

She picked up on one title and said, "Oh my God, it says, *Lashed Into Lust*. I better not show this to my children—they'll all go out and buy it."

I thought both of her comments were genuine and friendly and that she understood two of the things that Grove had always stood for—a mixture of politics and a fight against the fear of eroticism, in fact a celebration of it, if you will.

We signed the $2 million deal at the Carlyle Hotel. On March 5, 1985, the *New York Times* described the details:

> . . . Lord Weidenfeld said in a telephone interview yesterday from London that he and Mrs. Getty, who are longtime friends, would seek to expand the roster of writers at Grove and "keep the character of a very literary house."
>
> It would be his first American venture, he added, and Mrs. Getty's first entrance into publishing.
>
> Mr. Rosset . . . said his company had been chronically undercapitalized and that the offer from Mrs. Getty and Lord Weidenfeld allowed a new infusion of money without loss of identity for the press. Mr. Rosset, who is president and publisher of the publicly held company, said he would retain the titles under a five-year contract drawn up with the new owners.[99]

I wrote to Ann Getty on December 20, 1985:

> It gave me such great pleasure to go to Paris to see Sam Beckett, I felt I must write to you to let you know how grateful I am for the opportunity you have provided me. Again, due to you, I was able to give to him directly almost $50,000 owed on anthology sales, performances, etc. Just being able to convey this to him made for a great trip.
>
> I hope that sometime during my next trip to Paris I can have the opportunity to introduce you to Beckett. I think it would provide a very

nice moment for us all, and it would give me great pleasure personally. Also, if you ever feel you would like to discuss this and other Grove happenings with me, I would be most happy to meet with you.

Grove's business concerns are in good hands, as you know, but nevertheless our lifeblood has been provided by you, and I sometimes wonder if you are keeping us in mind. I stand ready at any and all times to inform you of any or all of our activities.

Everything looked promising. I thought this arrangement was going to take a lot of anxiety off my mind as to how to stay afloat financially and proceed in a fashion that would enable us to afford new projects to build upon what we already had. The Gettys would assume Grove's debt, buy out Grove stock, and I would be left in charge.

Soon I learned this was not to be the case. I had visions of starting up *Evergreen Review* again, with the young John Oakes, who had recently joined the team, and Ann's son Peter Getty, then a student at Harvard. Peter was a kind of macho kid whose aesthetic interests were in punk rock, war heroes, and assorted third-rate writers. He was also a paranoid anti-Marxist. For an heir to an immense fortune he was pretty pathetic—borrowing money for bus fare or lunch while his mother was shopping for a jet airplane.[100]

Weidenfeld was an astonishing, cigar-chomping hippopotamus with small feet, bulging eyes, exquisitely tailored suits, and a puzzling Austrian accent. He and Ann Getty—slim, girlish, coquettish with red fiery hair—made an odd couple. At the 1985 American Booksellers Association Convention, we organized a dazzling booth. Weidenfeld lodged himself in a perilously conventional folding chair, and held forth. Ann was busy flirting here and there, looking for famous authors. It wasn't exactly the usual Grove event.

There were some other interesting highlights during the early days of Grove/Weidenfeld. Ann Getty threw a party at the Getty mansion, with luxurious refreshments and a speech in which she extolled both presses and looked forward to a fertile future in publishing. Everyone applauded. Under the direction of publicity manager Ira Silverberg, an old buddy of William Burroughs', we held wild nightclub parties, supposedly to celebrate the publication of our books. The meetings with the board that was technically running the press became thornier, louder, and more unpleasant. None of the members had a feel for what Grove represented in American publishing, nor did they have the least sense of the creative. What they were looking for were safe bets, accepted standards of presentation, money-making names.

I spent a lot of time running back and forth—I lived on the bottom two floors of the townhouse where the Grove offices were located—trying to make sense of a situation that had turned nasty. Even liquor did little to soften the pain, and I saw it would be a short time till the end came, and come it did.

I was politely removed from my duties as editor-in-chief in April of 1986. The five-year period was cut short, violating the agreements in the contract of sale, and I was thrown out. I should not have been surprised. Weidenfeld was a master mesmerizer. He had a great talent for taking you in and making you feel immune. He told me exactly what he was going to do to everyone and then he did it to me. That in a nutshell was that. But it took only a year for the corporate marriage to hit the skids, as reported in the *New York Times* on April 10, 1986:

AN OUSTER AT GROVE PRESS RAISES WRITERS' IRE

Barney Rosset has been removed as president and chief executive officer of Grove Press, the avant-garde book publishing company he founded in Greenwich Village in 1951, and news of his ouster immediately sparked complaints from authors and literary agents.

"We are making the change because we are now merging the service departments of our publishing companies," said Lord Weidenfeld, the British publisher who with Ann Getty, his American partner, bought Grove Press last year. The two also started Weidenfeld & Nicolson, named after Lord Weidenfeld's British house, which will publish its first list this September.

Lord Weidenfeld said that Mr. Rosset has been offered the position of senior editor, so that he can concentrate on acquiring new books. However, Mr. Rosset said yesterday that he was "too stunned and traumatized" to know whether he would accept.

As word of Mr. Rosset's ouster spread yesterday, a number of writers and literary agents signed a letter of protest decrying "the impersonal corporate hand" that led to the move. It also called for Mr. Rosset's reinstatement or, barring that, asked Grove's new owners "to allow the company to be bought by more interested owners."

. . . Lord Weidenfeld also described as "absolutely ridiculous" suggestions that he was bringing corporate power to bear on Grove or was contemplating altering its unique character.

"It has nothing to do with corporate power," he said. "We want to make the two companies more efficient by merging the sales force and distribution, and we want to give Barney a chance to acquire new authors and do what he has always done best."

Mr. Rosset, 63, learned that he was being replaced last Thursday afternoon at a board of directors meeting attended by Lord Weidenfeld and Mrs. Getty. He said that he immediately offered to repurchase Grove for $4.5 million, but was told that the company was not for sale.[101]

When I was informed I was being thrown out, I turned to the man sitting next to me at the meeting, Marc Leland, who worked for the Gettys, and said, "I don't get it. Am I hearing straight? I'm no longer running Grove Press?"

As I remember it, he basically said, "Oh, you knew that. You knew the day you signed that contract we were going to throw you out as soon as we could." I never received an explanation, but I know I was judged too iconoclastic to remain at the helm of the company. A clause in my contract had stipulated they could replace me as president and demote me to senior editor, a position that could carry a great deal of power. But they hadn't given me those powers. The first thing that happened after I was thrown out as president was that I was told I could not go to editorial meetings, could no longer acquire books, I could not sign checks, and, later, could not even attend the American Booksellers' convention for Grove.

Fred Jordan had the job of telling the staff, in a meeting in his office, that I had been relieved of my duties and that he was now in charge. He had met with the board and they had appointed him chief officer of Grove. It was impossible for me to contain myself, but rage as I did, nothing came of it.

Weidenfeld brought in Dan Green, who had worked with Simon & Schuster, to take over the hands-on operation. When Green learned that I had a complete library of Grove Press books in my home in the Hamptons, he dispatched a truck and workers to pack up my private library. An arrogant—and illegal—move. There was obviously going to be a fight.

Some of the staff met with me at dinner and decided to come up with a petition signed by editors in the industry and the Grove authors—among them Samuel Beckett, William, S. Burroughs, Robert Coover, John Rechy, and Hubert Selby, Jr.—claiming that without me Grove Press would die. The petition was organized by my wife Lisa and the enthusiastic John Oakes, who made dozens of calls soliciting signatures. It was released to the *New York Times*, which published an article on the situation. But it soon became evident that when you are up against Big Money you are doomed.

In June we mounted a $7 million lawsuit against Weidenfeld and Getty. Two months later they countersued, delaying things as much as possible. It was obvious they were preparing for a long drawn-out battle. They had a bevy of high-powered lawyers who could spend months or years on such a case. We had spent about $35,000 in court costs and legal fees to defend *Lady Chatterley's Lover*. When we defended Henry Miller we were faced with 60 separate court actions because I had offered to defend anyone prosecuted for selling *Tropic of Cancer*. We ended up spending $250,000 before the US Supreme Court ruled in our favor. The Miller battle nearly bankrupted Grove and forced me to seriously consider selling the company. This time around could be even more ruinous. I couldn't afford to pay lawyers for a protracted suit. It would cost millions and eat up my life, and Weidenfeld and Getty knew it.

A few months later, Weidenfeld appointed Aaron Asher as Grove's new publisher, infuriating Fred Jordan who was shoved aside with no excuse. Cold, efficient, professional, and full of himself, Asher had worked for a wide variety of publishers and soon took charge of things, with weekly editorial meetings, strict procedures, and no bullshit.

The Getty team was afraid of alienating the famous Grove writers—understandably so, since they were the lifeblood of the firm. Asher even flew to Paris to meet with Beckett and returned with a full account of their meeting. According to Fred, Asher referred to Beckett as "Sam," and described in detail their conversation, during which Beckett told him, "I can't write anymore for you." Asher thought he meant he was finished with writing, but what he actually meant was that he couldn't write anymore for *Grove Press*. Asher hadn't the slightest idea that Beckett and I were friends of long standing.

I was promised that if the Gettys came in there would be a great deal of money made available to buy new manuscripts, books, and so on, and I would have a contract to stay there and it all seemed very appealing. But I was wrong. And when I left they started pouring money into Grove. Weidenfeld and Getty had won a victory of sorts, but eventually it would become evident that Grove Press was foundering, buoyed solely by its backlist, which they could hardly depend on forever.

Publishing in the US had suddenly evolved into an industry of huge conglomerates. The Germans especially entered the field with an eye on genre-based books with an assured market, avoiding anything "marginal"—the radical, the controversial, or stylistically original—and pouring money into backing established writers whose sales were guaranteed, while taking a portion of blockbuster profits to produce a few quality books, poorly advertised, as a kind of sop to culture. It became harder and harder for smaller houses, including Grove, to compete. This represented a different kind of censorship, one based on money, more than the censorship and repression of the so-called obscene. Most outstanding writers, and still more second-rate writers, entered academia. Even the craft of writing had become industrialized.

The turn of events at Grove certainly did not change my feelings about the books themselves. I liked the Grove books as much as ever, but I still felt terribly disappointed. Beckett wrote in *Stirrings Still*, "Head on hands half hoping when he disappeared again that he would not reappear again and half fearing that he would not."[102] Perhaps Sam was speaking both for himself and for me. In any case, I was not about to give up, let alone disappear.

It was essential to start again. In 1986 I took a deep breath and started Rosset & Co. and on March 10, 1987, Blue Moon Books began business. Blue Moon would publish an array of generally erotic novels in a classic small format, but also works of astounding literary merit. It flourished for years. I felt that I was moving into a distinguished niche, one of the survivors of an era that was fast becoming part of the history of American publishing—the struggles finished, the names fading.

In 1990, the Getty/Weidenfeld venture into American publishing would peter out and Grove Press was put on the auction block. As far as I know, we—a conglomeration of other small publishers I trusted along with a foreign investor—made an offer that was three times more than anyone else. Grove was worth, let's say, $2 million. We offered eleven. Simon and Schuster was the only other company that made a big offer. I think they offered eight but, quite properly, wanted to see Grove's financial details. I knew then that Simon and Schuster would ultimately withdraw, and they did. So, there was no other bid but my own—which was five times more than the company was worth—and it was still rejected. There would be no buyer. Allowing me to take over my old company would have been too much for them to stomach.

On October 30, 1991, Joan died in Paris, after a long period of illness and depression. Now that both Sam Beckett and Joan were gone, I felt once more that an epoch had passed, heightened by my divorce from Lisa who had gone through so much with me and Grove Press. But there would be some compensation for personal sadness and reduced professional activity. My close and caring relationship with Kenzaburō Ōe was a bright spot, and a fight was looming over the rights to Beckett's *Eleuthéria*.

17

My Tom Sawyer:
Kenzaburō Ōe

At Francis Parker, we students read *The Good Earth* and other books by the already famous Pearl S. Buck, the American author who had been raised in China, and who had been one of the first literary figures to introduce Americans to Asian literature and culture. We also read translations by Arthur Waley, the greatest translator of Chinese poetry of his time, possibly ever. Also at Francis Parker our eighth-grade teacher, Sarah Greenebaum, introduced us to Chinese history, telling us about the Ming dynasty, among others. The reading of André Malraux's *Man's Fate* and Edgar Snow's *Red Star Over China* in the next few years only helped to cement my interest in and fascination with Asian literature and culture.

Back in the Chicago World's Fair of 1893, the Emperor of Japan contributed a stunning Japanese Pavilion. In the 1940s, after many of the other structures from 1893 no longer stood, my Francis Parker friend Teru Osato and her mother helped take care of the Pavilion, making sure it didn't fall into ruins, while at the same time Teru's father was jailed in a sort of internment camp in Chicago.

There wasn't much translation of Asian literature between the two World Wars, not until the Japanese became our enemies during World War II. Then as an important part of wartime intelligence, the US Armed Forces undertook a big translation program and that effort, among other things, eventually brought to light post–Word War II authors. At that time, Alfred A. Knopf was the biggest publisher of Asian literature in this country.

Donald Allen introduced me to Donald Keene, a friend he had met while they were both studying in a US Navy program, and a man who became the foremost Western authority on Japanese literature. In 1955, we published his small book, *Japanese Literature: An Introduction for Western Readers*, which had originally been published in Great Britain by John Murray in their Wisdom of the East series.

We commissioned Keene to edit a collection of Japanese literature, which ended up being published as two volumes: *Anthology of Japanese Literature: From the Earliest Era to the Mid-Nineteenth Century* (1955), dedicated to Arthur Waley, and *Modern Japanese Literature: From 1868 to Present Day* (1956). UNESCO was a sponsor, which was very helpful, as it lent its reputation to our books, and we also received help through a Ford grant.

It was not until 1965, though, that the well known translator Thomas Fitzsimmons approached me about the young poet and author, Kenzaburō Ōe, who would become one of Grove's most influential authors and, equally important, a close friend of mine. Fitzsimmons suggested that I get in touch with John Nathan, who he thought was the translator for the job. Nathan lived in Japan as a student from Harvard on a scholarship and would go on to become one of the greatest scholars of Japanese modern writing.

I wrote to Nathan and he was not long in responding to my letter. On May 7, 1965, he wrote:

I would very much like to translate into English a novel by Kenzaburō Ōe, the author of *Lavish Are the Dead*, which you apparently received in the mail. To my mind, Ōe is the most exciting novelist in Japan today, and his latest and best novel, *Kojinteki na Taiken*, would certainly be well received in America. Would Grove Press be interested in such a venture? If you are in any way interested, I shall be glad to furnish you with more information about Ōe and his novels.

I certainly was interested, and asked him to contact Ōe to see if he would be agreeable to Grove's publishing the translation, pending agreement on the actual terms. It took some back and forth before the thing was settled.

June 15, 1965

Dear Mr. Rosset:

. . . You may know that I completed in January a translation of a Mishima Yukio novel that Knopf will publish in September [*The Sailor Who Fell from Grace from the Sea*]. Harold Strauss had been pressuring me for months to do the next Mishima book and I had been hedging. The book fails to excite me but my personal relationship with Mishima made it very difficult for me to refuse. In several of my letters I had asked why Knopf continued to ignore Ōe Kenzaburō and I had received various unsatisfactory answers. After several months of fencing with Harold Strauss about Mishima I got annoyed and asked you if Grove Press would be interested in *Kojinteki Na Taiken*. It seemed like a long shot at the time, and I was surprised and very pleased when you wrote that you wanted to do the book. Then, in a letter dated May 14, Harold Strauss suggested, to my amazement, that Knopf would take on Ōe if I opted for him rather than Mishima. . . .

I had now received two favorable replies in two days; the situation called for a choice and it seemed obvious that Ōe himself was the person to make it. I assured him that I would go along with whatever he decided. Finally, Ōe chose Knopf; primarily, I think, because other Japanese writers such as Abe Kobo had reminded him that Knopf has been more receptive to Japanese writers than any other American publisher. But Ōe insisted that *Kojinteki Na Taiken* should be the first book, and I agreed. I wrote Knopf what Ōe had decided, mentioning that Grove Press was also interested in *Kojinteki Na Taiken*. Harold Strauss replied by return mail that Ōe's terms were acceptable. I informed you of our decision and the matter seemed closed.

Then, on June 9, Ōe appeared with your cable and announced that he had changed his mind. Again I agreed. Frankly, I more than agreed; I was pleased. At any rate, you will by now have received Ōe's cable accepting your offer; and I will assume, unless I hear otherwise from you, that Grove Press plans to publish my translation of *Kojinteki Na Taiken*. I am tremendously enthusiastic about this book and hope you begin work on it toward the end of this month.

I look forward to your reply.

Sincerely,
John Nathan

Ōe's own letter came shortly after Nathan's:

22 June [1965]

Mr. Barney Rosset,

Today I received your second telegram. I accept your offer with great pleasure. As an admirer of your Evergreen books splendid "Doctor Sax" it is a genuine honor to accept your offer.

When I received your first telegram, I answered "Agreed" by return of telegram. I think there was some trouble in the way of telegram delivery. This summer I am invited as a participant of Harvard University Summer Seminar. I will spend four months in the U.S. . . . I leave Japan at 5th July.

Sincerely yours,
Kenzaburō Ōe

Doctor Sax is, of course, the novel by Jack Kerouac that we published in 1959.

I was totally surprised when Kenzaburō Ōe chose Grove over Knopf in the end. I had thought it was a done deal, an upsetting one, but I'd been ready to move on. Soon after signing Ōe, I knew we had added a great author to the Grove list. Little did I know then how important a writer he would become to me personally, second only to Samuel Beckett.

●⌣

In 1965, Ōe was invited to the United States to study with Henry Kissinger, who was at that time the director of the Harvard International Seminar. This was the seminar he mentioned in his letter of June 22. In Ōe's words, from an interview he gave in 1999 at the University of California at Berkeley, "I was in a seminar with Mr. Kissinger. Mr. Kissinger said in the goodbye party, with a very malicious smile, 'The very wicked rabbit makes a smile in the cartoons, Mr. Ōe's wicked smile.' . . . I am not a wicked person. Against the policymaker, sometimes I make a wicked smile."[103]

He wrote to me several times during the course of the seminar:

[1965]

Mr. Barney Rosset,

I arrived at Cambridge Monday. Before my departure I spent some pleasant nights with Neitham [i.e., John Nathan] and Mr. Donald Keene. Especially Mr. Donald Keene was very pleased to know my acceptance of your offer. I am so much encouraged by him. Now in Japan the ouvres complets of Henry Miller is very impressive. I am always under the influence of him. I believe Henry Miller is the best prosaist of our times like many admirers of him in Japan.

I am very impressed by what you have done against the censorship. In Japan we are tortured by the censorship and the self-censorship of publishers especially about Sex and Emperor.

From now I will stay here two months in Harvard. And from the beginning of September I intend to spend a few weeks in New York, then I hope to visit you. That is [a] very exciting plan for me . . . .

Sincerely,
Kenzaburō Ōe

July 18, '65

Mr. Barney Rosset,

. . . In this Harvard International Seminar with 40 participants from East and West I am reading "Huckleberry Finn" and "Invisible Man" and others. And we are discussing about "the roles of novels in the age of tension" and "the tension" itself. But I am always silent or independent because of my poorest English.

Sincerely,
Kenzaburō Ōe

After the Harvard seminar was over, Ōe came to New York City. I told him I wanted to videotape him—videotapes were a brand-new phenomenon—and the next thing I knew, I saw Akio Morita, the co-founder and chief executive of Sony, walking to our office on Broadway between Ninth and Tenth Streets, carrying in his arms this very heavy hunk of equipment. It was a videotape prototype, and he carried it up the stairs personally. Unbelievable! As it turned out, Ōe said they did it because they were afraid of him. Sony was a very anti-union company, and Ōe was known as a great organizer in Japan. He told his wife, Yukari Itami, the younger sister of Juzo Itami, the acclaimed director of such films as *Tampopo*, *The Funeral*, and *A Taxing Woman*, to call Sony and get after them to get me the machine. I guess you can say they thought it was best to just give Ōe that machine.

In the 1999 interview he did at the University of California at Berkeley, Ōe said:

> I was born in 1935 in a small island of the Japanese archipelago. I must emphasize that the war between U.S.A. and Japan began when I was six years old. And then at ten years old, I saw the war finished. So my childhood was during the wartime. That is a very important thing. . . . I didn't read many books before nine years old. . . . But one day, there was some discussion between my grandmother and my mother. And my mother got up very early in the morning . . . and she went to the small city of our island through the forest. Very late at night she returned. She gave a small doll to my sister, and some cakes for my younger brother, and she took out two pocket books. . . . I found Mark Twain's *Huckleberry Finn*. I didn't know the name of Mark Twain, the name Tom Sawyer or Huckleberry Finn, but my mother said—and this was the first talk between my mother and I about literature, and almost the last talk. She said, "This is the best novel for a child or for an adult. Thus your father said. . . . I brought this book for you, but the woman who made the barter with the rice between us said, "Be careful. The author is American. Now the war between U.S. and Japan is going on. The teacher will take the book from your son. [Tell him] that if your teacher asks you who is the author, you must answer that Mark Twain is the pseudonym of a German writer."[104]

I was very pleased when, in a letter, Kenzaburō called me his "Huckleberry Finn," and did so repeatedly thereafter. I could love him forever for that statement alone.

December 18, 1965

Dear Barney,

I remember of you and your splendid family and something very warm is stirred within me. I can not imagine in the future I can find out the other publisher who is genuinely kind and understanding like you. In Japan I am a rather flattered writer, but always I find out a kind of hostility against my publishers. So it was a surprise for me that I could experience true being at ease and delight in your family and office. I can't look at the picture of Peter, Christine [i.e., Cristina] and you (also of Suki [our dog]) without feeling a kind of sorrow which I often felt when the best part of my youth passed. The summer was one of my best summer. I thank you very deeply and thank your splendid family. Also I remember a strong feeling of pride that my publisher provides very good staff like Mr. Jordan and Mr. Seaver.

Returning to Japan, I began to continue an activity against the Japan–Korea treaty and I published a long essay about this problem, but as usual, we Japanese leftists were defeated. I am very much anxious about the future of us and Koreans and also I did a pleasant (of my feeling) work. I published a short essay about the censorship which I mentioned about your activity against the censorship. I try to translate some parts of that.

"Grove Press began entirely alone the dubious war, and Grove Press has fought the lonesome war surely authentically and continued it. Mr. Barney Rosset and his staff have a sure opinion and a strong attitude about 'dangerous books.' I am very proud of myself because they are going to publish my book."

. . . I and my wife are very glad to welcome your family in Japan. . . .

Kenzaburō Ōe

My wife Cristina and I traveled to Tokyo for three weeks in March 1966, where we met Yukio Mishima and his wife Yoko, and visited with Ōe and his family. Mishima told us about a short film he wrote and co-directed, *The Rite of Love and Death*, now known as *Patriotism* based on his short story of that title, about an army lieutenant who, unable to follow orders to execute fellow soldiers who had attempted a coup, instead commits hara-kiri with his wife. (This would turn out to be the only film he directed.) We featured stills from *The Rite of Love and Death* in *Evergreen*, No. 43 (October 1966) along with the story, and in No. 45 (February 1967) we published Ōe's "The Catch." I also arranged to publish Mishima's play *Madame de Sade*, which was translated by Donald Keene. Mishima sent me a letter on April 24, 1966, to discuss details of these projects, and concluded with this ominous sentence: "My life in Tokyo is deadly busy as always as you might imagine since you visited here. People here are just eating the flesh of each other." Four years later he would commit suicide.

We also met translator John Nathan for the first time during this Tokyo trip. An ex-polio victim, he nonetheless looked big, hale, and hearty. He'd met and gotten married to a lovely and talented Japanese woman, the artist Mayumi Oda. Both became good friends of mine.

A couple of months after my return to New York, Ōe wrote to me on May 3, "After your departure I became very deeply depressed and I found I have been getting little by little the authentic feeling of old Japanese folk who feels every saying good-bye as a transformed death. But thanks to the airplane that safely landed you and Christina [sic] I am now recovering. Your stay in Japan was one of the most wonderful thing for me for those years."

By the time Grove published Ōe's novel *A Personal Matter* and his story "Ague the Sky Monster" (in *Evergreen Review*, No. 54), Ōe had already won the Tanizaki Prize, one of Japan's most prestigious literary distinctions, for the *The Silent Cry*. He shared the prize, in 1967, with his friend and fellow novelist Kobo Abe.

June 16, 1968

Dearest Cristina,

Yesterday I received your letter about the hepatitis of Barney and another sad news about R. Kennedy. I am very much upsetted and unhappy to hear about Barney's disease. And I waited until the midnight and made two telephone call to New York to ask Mr. or Mrs. Rosset. But I couldn't reach both of you. I am thinking two possibility.

1) Barney is well and at East Hampton
2) Barney is worse and at Hospital.

And I hope to know how Barney is as soon as possible. Yesterday I couldn't sleep and so much drunken, and alone in my room I was watching that beautifully and genuinely human portrait of Barney in *New York Times*. I, now in Tokyo very often, find out myself who is imitating the way of behavior of Barney . . . walking . . . talking . . . and feeling happy or sad and everything. I feel Barney became one of a very few human being that is truly important for me. Now with your letter I am truly scared.

Cristina honestly speaking I don't have so much reason to live on. I am very deeply disappointed about our political situation, and I am from the very pessimistic family. "Pooh" [Ōe's son] is important. Literature is also important especially when I am working on a new novel. But I have very few friends that are truly important. Then I can't forget the word Barney said to me in the last night at Black Circle. Then I felt I was going very sentimental, so I said good-bye to Barney and Cristina when John and Mayumi was leaving there.

I sincerely need Barney who is healthy and who is always fighting
. . . and who is like he is every time.

With Love and hope Kenzaburō Ōe.

For you and Tansey and Peter I sincerely pray (to some even leftist God!) Barney's recovery and for myself I pray (to God anyway, I am not against God) his recovery, not only as a publisher but as a human being. I need him.

On October 14, 1994, it was announced that Kenzaburō Ōe had won the Nobel Prize in Literature, the fourth Grove author to do so. (Pablo Neruda, Octavio Paz and, of course, Samuel Beckett, are the earlier winners followed by Harold Pinter in 2005.) Kenzaburō told the *New York Times* that he was shocked at the news, although I was not.

By this time, the management at Grove Press had changed, and the present publisher, Morgan Entrekin, who had been very friendly toward me, called upon hearing the news and profusely thanked me for having left Grove a wonderful legacy, namely the three Ōe books I had published which the company, now known as Grove/Atlantic, still had in print. Entrekin made me two enticing offers. The first was an invitation to attend the Nobel Prize ceremony in Stockholm two months hence. The second was a request to have me co-publish with the new Grove any untranslated Ōe novels that I might be able to present to them. In a letter on October 24 of that year, I told Ōe about these invitations, and detailed some of the memories we had shared over the past thirty years:

This offer made a very strong impression on me—in many ways as I am sure you will understand. It meant in some ways finding things past—Ōe in New York, Ōe in East Hampton, both of us crying over a film depicting the death of Che Guevara, a little Olympus camera for Peter, Pooh and Yukari on the train to Osaka. The lovely inn where I was enchanted by, but afraid of the strange bath filled with hot water. Ōe's "animal" which stands today on Astrid's lawn [Astrid Myers, my last wife].

Ōe replied on October 30, "I thank you deeply for your moving letter. It was the best voice from the other side of the planet. If you publish my novels with John Nathan again, it is the best fruit of the Prize. And I hope to meet in Stockholm soon."

So, along with Ōe's translator John Nathan and two Grove executives, Entrekin and Joan Bingham, my wife Astrid and I traveled to Stockholm for the Nobel festivities, arriving late on the evening of December 6.

There were lunches and parties all week. At a lunch hosted by Kenzaburō's Swedish publisher, Karl Otto Bonnier, two days before the ceremony, I finally encountered Kenzaburō. The next day Astrid and I were invited to Kenzaburō's hotel room, where I was able to spend more time with him. A Japanese film crew was in attendance, and John Nathan and I were also part of the interview. We spent two wonderful hours with Kenzaburō telling stories to an appreciative audience.

The award ceremony itself was held on December 10 in the Stockholm Concert Hall. I videotaped the festivities. In his Nobel Lecture, Ōe spoke of his work: "Herein I find the grounds for believing in the exquisite healing power of art. . . . As one with a peripheral, marginal, and off-center existence in the world, I would like to seek how . . . I can be of some use in a cure and reconciliation of mankind."[105] After the ceremony we were all bused to the impressive City Hall for a banquet, followed by a formal ball complete with a thirty-five piece orchestra. It was an exhilarating four days.

Grove did follow through with the offer made to me by Morgan Entrekin, and they have published three Ōe novels since the Nobel was announced. I was also approached by a translator from the Netherlands, Luk Van Haute, who wanted to do a translation of Ōe's highly controversial *Seventeen*, which told the fictionalized story of the young, right-wing assassin who in 1960 had killed the chairman of the Socialist Party. The novella had appeared in a literary magazine in Japan, *Bungakukai*, and caused a storm of protest from reactionaries.

Seventeen had never appeared in book form, and Ōe did not want a full version translated, but he was willing to combine the first half with another novella called *J*. My new company, Foxrock, published these two works in one volume, with Van Haute's translations, in 1996. The *Los Angeles Times* reviewer Richard Eder aptly characterized the plots of both works in the volume as examples of how a "materialistic and decadent society gives rise to an act of grotesque extremity." He concluded that Ōe's message is "by no means simplistic" and "is beautifully and darkly related."[106]

My friendship with Ōe is also "by no means simplistic" since it involves so many strands—and so many years—of mutual interest, respect, and heartfelt generosity.

18

Eleuthéria

In May 1986, a tribute to Samuel Beckett was held in Paris on the occasion of his 80th birthday. Beckett was not interested in attending any of the festive ceremonies or readings of his work, but he did get together at the bar of the Hotel PLM with a group of old friends, including myself. I am afraid I put something of a damper on the occasion, because I couldn't help but tell people about my new and unenviable position, having been unceremoniously fired from Grove Press.

Sam said he felt badly about me and wondered what my next step would be. I told him I would have to consider starting a new publishing company. He believed every author of mine should offer me an unpublished manuscript. In the weeks following, I met with Sam a few more times and we discussed what he might have to give me. One possibility was an early unpublished novel, *Dream of Fair to Middling Women*. But, considering his idea further, Sam felt that because this book was something of a roman à clef it would not make a very good choice;

some of his characters were thinly veiled portraits of people who were still alive. Instead he decided to give me his first play, *Eleuthéria*, and he immediately set out to translate it. Two days or so later Marguerite Duras followed Sam's lead and offered me *The Man Sitting in the Corridor*. I published it in 1991. Sam and Marguerite turned out to be the only authors who offered me work to publish, so that was as far as that project went.

But the translation of *Eleuthéria*, written forty years before, proved too much for Sam. In June 1986 he wrote that he didn't have the energy to translate the play after all. Besides, he told me, he detested it: "I had completely forgotten *Eleuthéria*. I have now read it again. With loathing. I cannot translate it. Let alone have it published. Another rash promise. . . . I'll try to try writing something worth having for you."

Eleuthéria always had something of a star-crossed history.[107] Back in 1948, Sam wrote his friend Thomas MacGreevy that "*Eleuthéria* is dithering, dithering, and beginning to be spoken of a little. I think it will see the boards in time even if only for a few nights." And in March 1949 he mentioned it again: "I've finished a second play *En Attendant Godot*. And I am now typing it up. . . . I submitted the first play, *Eleuthéria*, for the Prix Rivarol, which has not yet been awarded as far as I know."

Sam's wife Suzanne took both *Eleuthéria* and *Godot* with her when she made the rounds of Paris theaters, trying to interest one of them in a production. In 1950, she gave director Roger Blin both plays to consider. At first Blin was inclined toward putting on *Eleuthéria* but the cost of production ruled against it. *Eleuthéria* had seventeen characters, a massive numbers of plots, and called for a complicated, divided stage. *Godot*, by contrast, had only four characters, two of whom were bums who didn't require much in the way of costuming. After the enormous success of *Godot*, *Eleuthéria* was put away, although—significantly—not destroyed. Indeed, Sam kept the original and the manuscript notebooks that accompanied it, which he later bequeathed to various universities.

Having years later once more set *Eleuthéria* aside, Sam let me know he had written another piece, much shorter, to replace it. It was *Stirrings Still*, which as I have mentioned was dedicated to me, and I published it in 1988.

Robert Scanlan of the Beckett Society wrote to me from Harvard that one of the last things Sam said to him before he died was, "Be good to Barney. He's been through a rough time at Grove Press."

Having been given the great present of *Stirrings Still*, I forgot about *Eleuthéria* until four years after Sam had passed away. Then the literary scholar Stan Gontarksi began prodding me about this play, which both of us thought of as an important addition to the Beckett *oeuvre* that should see the light of day and eventual theatrical production. Not anticipating too much trouble, I wrote to Sam's executor, Jérôme Lindon, in 1993.

I was aware that Lindon had given *Dream of Fair to Middling Women* to Richard Seaver at Arcade Books for posthumous publication. The people depicted in the novel were, like Sam, deceased by this time, so Lindon deemed it appropriate to go ahead and publish the book. The problem was, for me, that he never offered me the chance even to look at it.

As I wrote him on March 2, 1993: "I've been puzzled . . . that I had never been informed about . . . much less offered a chance to publish the book myself." Making the insult worse, Eoin O'Brien's foreword to the novel alluded to the fact that at one point Sam "was considering how best to help a friend to whom he wished to give a text for publication," namely, *Dream*. The unnamed friend was, of course, me. And offering the novel to someone else could certainly be interpreted as a breach of faith with Sam. I further said in the letter to Lindon, "The conclusion from O'Brien's foreword seems inescapable; once it was time to publish *Dream*, it should have been offered to Sam's American publisher as Sam himself directed in 1986. This was certainly his intent."

I then asked Lindon to do the right thing in the case of *Eleuthéria*. He said I could not publish the work because it would violate the letter of Sam's wishes. This claim rang very hollow indeed, given Lindon's blatant disregard for Sam's wishes with regard to *Dream*.

Sam's heir, his nephew, Edward Beckett, with whom I had a very friendly relationship, wrote me on April 21, 1993, to say, "I feel this is getting out of hand; you must know that there is no question of *Eleuthéria* being published without the Estate's consent. . . . I beg you not to pursue this matter any further; it will do good to no one."

I dropped the idea of publishing *Eleuthéria*. For a while.

Over the years *Eleuthéria* occasionally reared its head. Ruby Cohn writes in her book *Back to Beckett* that *Eleuthéria* had been accepted by Jean Vilar for the Théâtre Nationale Populaire on the condition that it be cut to one act, which Sam refused to do.

Stan Gontarski also mentions in *The Grove Companion to Samuel Beckett* that *Eleuthéria* was announced for publication by Les Éditions de Minuit in 1952 and then withdrawn by Sam.

Grove even had a copy of *Eleuthéria* in its possession: Sam referred to it in a letter to my assistant Judith Schmidt, dated February 7, 1963, saying, "Please hold both original and copies of *Eleuthéria* and *Mercier and Camier*."

After his Nobel Prize was announced in 1969, Sam felt pressure to publish old things, such as the story collection *More Pricks Than Kicks*, originally issued in 1934 in England by Chatto & Windus. He wrote to his English publisher, John Calder:

> Some days ago I had a letter from [Grove editor Richard] Seaver saying "they could wait no longer to publish M. P. T. K." I answered that this was against my wish. But in the last few days pressure on all sides has grown so strong—and I was so tired, that I capitulated. You may therefore proceed with trade edition of this juvenilium. I also capitulate for "Premier Amour" and *Mercier et Camier*—but not for *Eleuthéria*.[108]

Sam had a habit of changing his mind about the publication of earlier works. In 1964 we had been in the midst of the publishing process for *More Pricks Than Kicks* when we received the following letter:

> I have broken down half way through galleys of *More Pricks Than Kicks*. I simply can't bear it. It was a ghastly mistake on my part to imagine, not having looked at it for a quarter of a century, that this old shit was revivable. I'm terribly sorry, but I simply have to ask you to stop production. I return herewith advance on royalties and ask you to charge to my account with Grove whatever expenses whatever entailed by this beginning of production. . . . Please forgive me.[109]

He then reversed himself again and allowed us to publish the collection in 1970. Today *More Pricks Than Kicks* is considered among Beckett's major works and is tremendously admired, especially the story "Dante and the Lobster."

Sam also did this with *Mercier and Camier*. In a 1960 letter to my assistant, he wrote, "This is just to say that I am opposed to the publication in English of *Mercier et Camier*, also to the publication of any other extracts." But fifteen years later, in 1975, he allowed us to publish it.

The original *Eleuthéria* manuscript, in the Beckett collection at the University of Texas library, contains this note written in Sam's hand: "Prior to Godot. 1947. Unpublished. Jettisoned." And in March 1969, Sam wrote on a photocopy of the play: "Never edition of any kind if I can help it." He and his favorite theater director, Alan Schneider, also discussed the play in a pair of 1975 letters. Schneider told Sam in a letter dated April 27, 1975: "Did you hear about some off-off-Broadway group saying it was going to do ELEUTHÉRIA (in English!) next fall?" Sam replied on May 4, 1975, "We must prevent *Eleuthéria* at all costs."

But he allowed the *Revue d'Esthetique* to publish excerpts from the play in 1986, and in 1988 he also authorized the publication of dialogue from *Eleuthéria* in *Beckett in the Theatre: The Author as Practical Playwright and Director: From Waiting for Godot to Krapp's Last Tape* by Dougald McMillan and Martha

Fehsenfeld. So the door was not firmly closed, and I have no doubt that Sam would at last have changed his mind and allowed us to publish *Eleuthéria*, too.

I waited a year, and tried the subject of *Eleuthéria* again with Lindon and Edward Beckett. They remained vehemently opposed to the idea, but I felt strongly that *Eleuthéria* should be brought forward. So I arranged for a staged reading at the New York Theatre Workshop on September 26, 1994. Edward told the *New York Times*, in a long article by Mel Gussow, that the reading was "not only illicit but morally disgraceful," that his uncle "always opposed its being published in book form, its being translated into other languages, or its being performed in any way whatsoever. All those who might be a party to this New York event, which deliberately transgresses the will expressed by Samuel Beckett, would of course expose themselves to legal proceedings."[110]

After the *Times* publicity, the New York Theatre Workshop asked for a $25,000 bond to hold the reading, so at the last moment we shifted theaters, requesting the audience, actors, and press to walk with us to a new location. I wanted to echo Orson Welles' twenty-one-block walk with his audience of 600 from the Maxine Elliott Theater to the Venice Theater when his production of Blitzstein's *The Cradle Will Rock* had to be moved at the last minute. Our reading was at the Mime Theater, a small space in the building where I lived. Thirteen actors read the play to 100 invited guests. The reading was also covered by the *Times*, although Gussow wrote that his photographer was not allowed to film the reading. Our fault.

As a result of my part in the staged reading, on October 13, 1994, Edward Beckett and Jérôme Lindon fired me from my position as US agent of the Beckett Estate, an appointment Sam gave me after my ouster from Grove in 1986 and the source of a major portion of my income.

But in January 1995 came a reversal. Lindon sent me a two-line fax asking to see a copy of an English translation of *Eleuthéria* I had commissioned by the playwright, poet, and novelist Michael Brodsky, who made his living as a French-to-English translator at the United Nations.

The next day there was another fax: "I persist in thinking that Sam would not have wanted *Eleuthéria* to be published. Yet as I see you are staunchly bent on publishing your translation, I bring myself to grant you that publication right for the United States."

So with my partners, John Oakes and Dan Simon of the Four Walls Eight Windows publishing house, we put *Eleuthéria* into print. Mel Gussow reviewed the book quite favorably in the *Times* on June 25, 1995: "Those who regard Beckett as a minimalist may be surprised by the ebullience of his first play." And he called it a "valuable addition to Beckett's body of work [that] will be of interest to anyone concerned with the author's art and with exploratory theater. De-jettisoned, *Eleuthéria* has found its freedom."[111]

In France, Lindon beat us to publication with his own edition of *Eleuthéria* in the original French. Faber and Faber published an edition in England, commissioning a different translator, Barbara Wright.

During the summer of 2007 a friend found an Internet reference to a 2004 performance of *Eleuthéria* that had been staged in Iran. This astounded and excited me, as it seems to be the only instance of this play actually being performed *anywhere* in the world. I found a contact name and quickly sent off an e-mail. A reply came from the co-director and translator of the project, Vahid Rahbani, who in the meantime had relocated to Montreal, where he was attending the National Theatre School of Canada. He was glad to hear from me: "It is really interesting to receive an e-mail from you. A close friend of Beckett. I am so lucky! I wish you could have been there to see our production of *Eleuthéria*, which was a great challenge for me and my group. As far as I know our production is the only professional performance of this brilliant play." He referred me to the website of his theater company, Naqshineh, where stills of his *Eleuthéria* production could be found. An accomplished film and theater director, Vahid had also put on productions of *Waiting for Godot* in Iran and Paris, Ionesco's *Rhinoceros* in Iran, and Pinter's *Ashes to Ashes* in Toronto. He told me he was eager to publish his translation of *Eleuthéria* in Farsi.

I think he was right. I don't know about any other full productions of the play. There was an English-language reading in 1998, beautifully done and jointly sponsored by the French and Irish cultural sections of the respective governments in 1998. The reading, which verged on being a full-fledged acted production, was staged by the SCENA Theatre's Robert McNamara at the elegant French embassy in Washington, DC. Two additional readings were performed, one at the National Arts Club and the other at the Classic Stage Company, both in Manhattan.

How I would love one day to see a full production of *Eleuthéria* myself. What a fulfillment that would be. After all, it's been my life's work to bring books, films, plays—art!—to the world, no matter the obstacles. As I always said to critics, naysayers, and those who would stand in the way: *No pasarán!*

19

A Nightmare in the Stone Forest

It is November 5, 1996. I am sitting next to my companion of many years, Astrid Myers, on Thai Airlines flight 103, the 1,200-mile daily jitney from Bangkok to Kunming in southern China. How much more comforting it would be to be back in a Bangkok bar, taking the opiate of female beauty, than approaching Kunming with its too-many memories. This is the 51st anniversary of my war. Kunming was my battleground. They should package this trip for old warriors and call it the Hemlock Tour.

Months before the trip I had been tending eastward. I had placed three of my own photographs of Thai bar dancers in a single frame, then encrusted the frame with layer upon layer of gold paint—I labored on this fantasy in my Astor Place live/work loft, absorbedly working the pigment with an array of brushes, amid the office noises of my slender structure of book publishing. The central photograph of my gold triptych shows a woman's midsection twisting upward in the dark like a candle flame. Women in the left and right panels are etherealized by "rare lamps with faint rainbow fans," like those at the Mabbot Street entrance to James Joyce's "nighttown."

My Nighttown is a superimposition of many cities. Beyond the golden entrance is the full inventory of my fears and loves—seven decades worth. In my Nighttown the Chez Paree—the great Chicago nightclub of the 1930s—adjoins the brothel clubs and restaurants of liberated Shanghai, post-war Paris, Hamburg, New York, and Bangkok. The streets of La Paz and Havana turn sharply into Greenwich Village. Like Joyce's, my Nighttown contains reproachful ghosts, the ghosts of Chou En-lai, Mao Tse-tung, and Edgar Snow; the names of women pulsate there, wives and near wives, Nancy, Gale, Joan, Loly, Ann, Cristina, Lisa, Kim, Astrid; here are also famous and anonymous comrades in arms, Muddy Rhule and Fred Jordan, Maurice Girodias, Haskell Wexler, Heinrich Ledig-Rowohlt and Dick Seaver, Wallace Fowlie, Horace Gregory, Henry Miller and Sam Beckett. Nighttown is an evanescent soldier's camp adjoining an ascendant American publisher's reserved suite at the Frankfurt Book Fair. It is fraught with the ambushes of wartime and of peacetime—with danger, combat, and yearning.

As the plane sets down, my first glimpse of Kunming reminds me that I never loved it. I remember a large sign at the hot springs of the Health Spa: BOYS WILL NOT BATHE WITH GIRLS. Kunming was a "Thou Shalt Not" place. We disembark, and I linger on the runway, looking for the "rusted hulks of WWII planes" which my guidebook advertises. I photograph a number of planes—but not the old ones. How empty and glum this airfield looks now.

After going through cheerless lines at customs, without any help or direction, we take an unmarked taxi. The sullen female driver acknowledges only the name of the hotel—KING WORLD—to which we have told her to take us. The boulevard along the way is drab, the landscape somewhat between a construction project and a slum. There is traffic, but what a contrast to the bustle and life of Bangkok.

Kunming is still a "Thou Shalt Not" place. The only touch of sensuality is a pair of chic, good-looking young women in our hotel elevator. When we get in, the elevator stalls and re-opens. Framed in the door is a stunning Chinese-gowned woman. She speaks a few harsh words and a policeman appears. He pulls the frightened women next to us out. When we arrive at our floor, an attendant stands at the elevator, hands folded primly before her face, an obsequious house-cop making sure that we go *straight* to our room.

My apologies to such heroes of my youth as John Steinbeck, André Malraux, Chou En-lai, and that Depression-era Robin Hood, John Dillinger, but visiting Communist countries can be bruising to one's youthful ideals. The malaise which quickly invades me here is just what I experienced shortly after the war, when I traveled to Czechoslovakia with my soon-to-be wife Joan Mitchell. I had just made my first and only feature film, *Strange Victory*, an angry reminder to America that we still faced the enemies of racism and fascism at home. Taking the film to newly Communist Prague, I encountered the same veiled hostility as today in Kunming, the same sense of being watched. At the Prague airport, customs agents overstepped when they tried to confiscate my cognac. I knew that our supply of cognac and powdered Nescafé would dictate the duration of our visit. "No cognac, no film" was my answer. "I'll turn and go home." They gave in. I was in the grips of what might be called the "Ninotchka paradox." I loved pleasure as much as justice. Lincoln Steffens, the famous muckraking journalist, was asked why, praising the Russian proletariat as he did, he lived on the French Riviera. "I'm too old to move there," he answered, seeing no contradiction.

Our request made to the front desk for a newspaper other than the free handout in the lobby was answered with a curt "Go to the foreign bookstore." We were directed to a neighborhood where a scrim of old Kunming clung to the riverfront, its bricks, quays, shingles, and foliage completely hemmed in by steel towers. There were no newspapers in the bookstore to which we had been directed, but among an array of books of the "Teach Yourself Business French" variety there were four or five heavily-annotated, paperbound novels, including D. H. Lawrence's *Lady Chatterley's Lover.*

Now, carrying my new Chinese *Lady Chatterley*, I walked slowly back to my hotel room. What was it they were saying in the copious notes? Was someone in one of these towers of glass straining over the text, piercing such obscurities as "Pentecost," "madonna-worship," "phallus," "Cannes," and "hopeless anachronism"?

I did not expect to be welcomed by rifle salutes, but no one we met seemed remotely aware of Kunming's past. Amazingly, the travel agents here have no maps. "And Kweiyang?" I ask. I remember Kweiyang as being 500 kilometers or so to the east, eighteen hours away by jeep, but the town appears to have fallen down a deep ravine. The place I considered my war home had apparently been excised from both foreigners' itineraries and local memories, despite being the birthplace of the current president, Jiang Zemin. The party-line newspaper, *China Daily*, reports that Zemin visited Kweiyang, where he distributed bedding to impoverished farmers still living in thatched huts. He reached the town via "wriggling mountain roads" just as I had 50 years earlier. So much for my dreams of social progress under the leadership of Mao and Chou En-lai. They had absorbed a nightmarish tinge.

The following morning Astrid made an excursion without me to the "Stone Forest" limestone peaks outside Kunming, of which my guidebook said, "As twilight comes in, the forest of limestone pillars seems grey and forbidding. The paths become a maze and you suddenly wonder if you can find your way out." Charming. My war experience made me regard such formations as presenting risks of ambush. But Kunming is a petrified forest in itself, and every hour I spend in this ascending pile of steel and glass grows more suffocating and distasteful.

When Astrid returns we walk in the city and see a rare sign of independent life, a gang of young men loitering on the sidewalk, hawking large knives that I suspect are both their merchandise and their arsenal. Thugs or no, I like them. When they see my camera they run up and hug us.

Walking back to our four-star hotel, along Beijing Boulevard about midday, we stop for a red light at a busy intersection. A serious, intelligent-looking man, neatly attired in a student or professional way and holding a child of about three in his arms, cautiously approaches.

"Would you like something to read?" he asks, very quietly. Then he says, "I have been arrested."

He puts down the child, opens a small black leather briefcase and hands me a photocopy of a handwritten document. I take it and, unasked, hand him a 100 yuan note, worth about twelve US dollars. He accepts it, whereupon I thank him and wish him good luck. A bit surprised, he gently lifts up the child and moves silently away as we continue across the street. The whole incident seems to last no more than a minute.

The document proves to be a complaint against brutal political corruption, where the victim who reports a crime to the local police is caught in a Kafkaesque maze. I think that Boeing, GE, and the Chinese Communist Party are building an unholy alliance here. Sentences leap out—quotes from a student leader, Li Peng: "*Today's government is crueler than Guo Ming Dang's* [Kuomintang] *government, seventy years ago. . . . that government only used high pressure water to disperse students. But in Tian An Men* [Tiananmen Square], *the police used guns. . . . In this society, money talks. If you want to do something, enough money is very important.*"

This chimes with my memories. I wrote a letter to my parents in 1946 that is applicable today, omitting only one name: "Where we are dead wrong is our policy in China. The Central government in China are the biggest bunch of grafters and crooks I have ever seen. Chiang Kai-shek is nothing but a fascist in my estimation. . . . Important Chinese civilians and military men lived like kings, with new cars, the best of homes, the best of everything."

Back at the King World Hotel I feel even more disgust for the huge, expensive, and deserted lounge area, the joyless luxury designed for business junkets. My fear mounts as I stare from the hotel window, which overlooks the corner where we received the document. The busy thoroughfare holds a lone, slow truck. Two dim streetlamps fend off a sea of darkness. Even under the Japanese bomb threats of 50 years ago, we had not extinguished the city to this degree, having enough cheer and bravado to light fires in the street and keep the wine flowing.

As I fall asleep I sense an unmistakable panic, which progresses into a dream.

It is a nice summer evening in East Hampton in the 1950s. Norman Mailer is here, looking young, healthy, and calm. Bill de Kooning is around, and so is Franz

Kline. I agree with Mailer that we need not search for the best party of the evening, that old constant preoccupation. It does not seem so pressing now. We are beyond that. Grown up.

And now I hear that we were lucky to miss the "right party," or "the orgy" as someone has mysteriously referred to it. The party had gone wrong. Two hundred fifty four people have died I am told. I rush to my hotel room's TV, turn on the news to get the details. But there is no CNN, no news.

And now I am being told a brash populist is opportunistically restaging the disaster, for profit, right now at Madison Square Garden, which has been transported to the center of Kunming. Crowds are lined up outside the hotel, waiting to enter, but fires have broken out. People are burning to death. I chase the hired cameraman, trying to help him. He bursts into flames! Can I help him or is he already dead? I am paralyzed. I must try.

The nightmare peaks. The fear has become intolerable. I am half-awake, shame and horror following close upon the dream. I am tortured by my dereliction, my indecision in going to the aid of the cameraman. I hoped his swift destruction would relieve me of responsibility. But he has survived the first bonfire. The dream resumes.

I run toward him across the Kunming slum. This Lower East Side vacant lot, this Kunming/Manhattan plot of cursed real estate. There are murderous drug dealers and there are outdoor fires, and there is the hapless cameraman. A structure is collapsing on him. Now he must be suffocating, dying. But is he? I have to check, move toward him, free him from the collapsing timbers and debris. But will I escape this killer mob?

My fear is all-enveloping. I wake up.

I look at the desolation called Kunming, desperate to leave. Another day here and I would be out looking for that hapless guy who gave me the manuscript. Soon we would both be in trouble, real trouble.

It took me thirty-five years to even partially decipher the story which had transported me to Kunming, to Shanghai, and back. At the time I naively believed that this was the magical circuitry of art and life, *Red Star Over China* and *Man's Fate*, two milestones of my emotional life. It was not until I obtained my intelligence files under the Freedom of Information Act that I would learn anything of the dense fog in which my destiny had unfolded. That I was probably sent to China to get me out of the way. That I was under constant, absurd suspicion, first of "treason" and then of "disaffection." That I had been inducted into and then expelled from the OSS without being informed of either event. That my "premature anti-fascism" was held against me. The gulf between my ardor to contribute and the government's misgivings about me was unbridgeable. The OSS Washington personnel chief was aghast that his counterpart in China had taken me on. What a blunder! The Army had sent me to Kanchapara, the end of the line. I had only gotten into action by replacing a suicide. And now I was in the OSS? Why didn't the officer in China check *his* files before making rash personnel decisions? That would have taught him what he was dealing with.

I had enlisted in the Army in the summer of 1942. Certainly by the late spring of 1943, but probably much sooner, Army Intelligence had singled me out for investigation. A report charged that I was in "mail communication with persons who are under suspicion as possible espionage agents for Japan." Another further identified those persons as being "two Japanese girls in New York City" and then gave their names and addresses.[112] It also said: "H.D.C. & Fourth Army, Presidio of San Francisco, Ca., discloses information indicating possible Communist sympathies of subject." In another report, requested by the Assistant Chief of Staff of G-2, Military Intelligence, War Department, Washington, DC, dated May 28, 1943, my twenty-first birthday to be exact, a background check was requested: "Character of Investigation: Espionage." The profile of me read:

> Characteristics: Over-emotional; highest consideration of others, highest integrity; independent; great self-confidence; sarcastic; ruthless behavior in high school; courageous; aggressive; lacks spirit of compromise; lacks judgment.
> Miscellaneous: Subject is left-handed.

When our plane takes off from Kunming Airport the following day, for the return to Bangkok, there are no Zeros stalking us. I am heading back to

Nighttown. Perhaps I will see the shades of Valerie and Ferral[113] at the weekend market, laughing as they buy a new birdcage and a fighting cock to put in it. And of course I will have a drink with Tony at the bar of the Shangri La or the Oriental. Perhaps at the Asia Bookstore on Silam Boulevard I will bump into the aristocratic and handsome Chou En-lai. I have bad news for him.

End Notes

All notes were written by the editors.

Quoted text without annotation from Barney Rosset's personal or business correspondence is from the Barney Rosset papers, 1841–2011, Rare Books and Manuscripts, Butler Library, Columbia University (hereafter, BRP) and/or the Grove Press Records, Special Collections Research Center, Syracuse University Libraries (hereafter, GPR).

> http://findingaids.cul.columbia.edu/ead/nnc-rb/ldpd_7953908/summary
> https://clio.columbia.edu/catalog/7953908
> http://library.syr.edu/digital/guides/g/grove_press.htm

1 Barney Rosset's (BR) extensive historical research on the Tansey murder trials, including contemporary newspaper reportage, court transcripts and prison photographs, in addition to genealogical research on the Tansey family, is collected at BRP.

2 Burton Holmes, *The Olympian Games in Athens* (New York: Grove Press, 1984).

3 Sono Osato (born 1919) became a noted dancer with the American Ballet Theatre and a Broadway actress.

4 Adler and BR corresponded regularly during Rosset's school and war years. Grove published Adler's short fiction collection *Souvenirs Fresh and Rancid*, which focuses on his career as an educator, in 1983. Their letters and de Grazia's interview are collected at BRP.

5 This report is in BR's FOIA file at BRP.

6 BR's FOIA file at BRP details the exhaustive FBI investigation of his early life. His school archive includes yearbooks, school newspapers, report cards and even Greenebaum's version of *Robinson Crusoe*.

7 This FBI interview is among BR's papers at BRP.

8 Henry Miller, *Tropic of Cancer* (New York: Grove Press, 1961), 12. Rosset's essay is at BRP.

9 Adler's comment is from an unpublished interview with Edward de Grazia. This and BR's Haskell Wexler correspondence are at BRP.

10 White House usher during the FDR and Truman years, Claunch (1899–1978) was appointed Government Secretary to the United States Virgin Islands by Eisenhower.

11 Produced by BR and completed in the summer of 1948 with documentarian Leo Hurwitz (1909–91, *Native Land, The Plow that Broke the Plains*) as director, the didactic and unabashedly leftist *Strange Victory* mixes dramatic scenes with newsreel footage and equates racial politics in post–WWII USA with those of Hitler's Germany. The film's critical failure and commercial neglect ended BR's intended career in film: "The *Star* review . . . was one of the few good ones. A favorable article about Leo which focused on

how he got his inspiration for the film and his professional and personal life ran on the opposite page. I crawled back to my hotel room almost physically sickened by the lack of business, the bad review, and Leo's article. In my room I broke down and cried and cried. The tensions of the whole affair had reached the breaking point. I felt isolated, a failure, and I wanted to annihilate myself. But it was the climax of my *Strange Victory* experience. Then I began to feel better. I stopped sobbing, dried my eyes, and staggered back over to the theater. I knew. The run was a disaster." This excerpt, from a chapter on *Strange Victory* edited from the manuscript on which *Rosset* is based, is at BRP.

12 This quote is from Benn's preface to *The Lucky Chance* (1687).

13 From Berryman's Introduction to Matthew G. Lewis, *The Monk* (New York: Grove Press, 1952).

14 Al Silverman, *The Time of Their Lives: The Golden Age of Great American Book Publishers, Their Editors and Authors* (New York: Truman Talley Books, St. Martin's Press, 2008), 44.

15 Leo Edelstein, *Pataphysics: Pirate Issue*, 2001. http://www.pataphysicsjournal.net/catalogue.html.

16 The BR/Beckett correspondence is collected at BRP and GPR.

17 This chapter is adapted from BR's essay "Beginning to End: Publishing and Producing Beckett," in S. E. Gontarski, ed., *A Companion to Samuel Beckett* (Wiley & Blackwell, 2010), 49. Works sourced for this chapter are Kevin Brownlow, *Hollywood: The Pioneers* (New York: Harper Collins, 1979); Alan Schneider, *Entrances* (New York: Viking Press, 1986); and Amos Vogel, *Film as a Subversive Art* (New York: Random House, 1974).

18 Samuel Beckett, *Waiting for Godot* (New York: Grove Press, 1954).

19 Samuel Beckett, *Endgame* (New York: Grove Press, 1958).

20 Samuel Beckett, *Krapp's Last Tape and Other Dramatic Pieces* (New York: Grove Press, 2009), 9.

21 Samuel Beckett, *The Collected Shorter Plays* (New York: Grove Press, 1984).

22 Portions of this section are adapted from BR's 2001 essay "On Samuel Beckett's Film," *Tin House* 6 (3).

23 Kevin Brownlow, "Brownlow on Beckett (On Keaton)," *Film West* 22. http://ireland.iol.ie/~galfilm/filmwest/22brown.htm.

24 Schneider's recollection of the production is also discussed at http://www.apieceofmonologue.com/2010/06/alan-schneider-samuel-beckett-film.html.

25 Samuel Beckett, *The Complete Short Prose* (New York: Grove Press, 1996), 265.

26 S. E. Gontarski, "An Interview with Michael McClure," *The Review of Contemporary Fiction: Grove Press Number*, Fall 1990, 119.

27 This was not done lightly. Jacob Brussel, who released a pirated edition of *Tropic of Cancer* in New York in 1940, spent three years in prison for publishing pornography.

28 For this exchange and other BR source materials, see S. E. Gontarski, ed., *The Grove Press Reader: 1951–2001* (New York: Grove Press, 2001).

29 US Postal Service official Charles Ablard had written Barzun and MacLeish during the initial investigation, asking if they believed *Chatterley* was pornographic. For this

background and the authoritative legal perspective on all the Grove Press trials, see Grove attorney Charles Rembar's *The End of Obscenity: The Trials of Lady Chatterley, Tropic of Cancer & Fanny Hill* (New York: Harper & Row, 1968).

30 Rembar, 61.

31 Ibid., 63.

32 From legal argument by Saul J. Mindel, general counsel for the US Post Office. Rembar, 65.

33 Ibid., 51, quoting from *Roth v. United States*, 1957.

34 Ibid., 64. Also see Raymond T. Caffrey, "Lady Chatterley's Lover: The Grove Press Publication of the Unexpurgated Text," *The Courier* 20.1 (1985): 49–79.

35 Ibid., 69.

36 Ibid., 75, from the record. Also see Caffrey.

37 Ibid., 79.

38 Ibid., 96, from the record.

39 Ibid., 110–11, from the record.

40 Ibid., 114.

41 Ibid., 117.

42 Ibid., 118.

43 Ibid., 139.

44 Much of this chapter was adapted by Barney Rosset from an introduction written by Ed Halter at Rosset's suggestion, based largely on extensive interviews with, and information and files provided by, Rosset, around 2001. Their intention was to have the introduction accompany a collection of film writings he had proposed from *Evergreen* edited by the two of them, to be published by Rosset's Foxrock Books; in the end Foxrock was unable to publish the collection (recently released by Seven Stories Press as *From the Third Eye: The Evergreen Review Film Reader*). Writes Halter:

"We may never know how Barney got from asking me to revise that introduction numerous times to inserting large parts of it into his autobiography, without my knowledge, after we had stopped working together. He was often difficult to work with, given to changing his mind and opinion, but he was also incredibly generous with his time and advice, and he and Astrid and I had some great times together. I fondly remember bringing my 16mm projector over so we could watch some ancient silent porn films he had found in his storage. While other writers might bristle at having their work recycled in such a fashion, for me it's a strange kind of honor, and a weird souvenir of an intense but formative time in my life spent working with Barney Rosset."

45 A. H. Weiler, "International Projects in Prospect," *New York Times*, September 8, 1963, X9. http://query.nytimes.com/gst/abstract.html?res= 9E0DE1DF143BE033A0575BC0A96F9C946291D6CF.

46 https://www.youtube.com/watch?v=6AzmhorISf4.

47 Also see http://idiommag.com/2012/04/amos-vogel-life-as-a-subversive-art/.

48 B. Greely, "'Evergreen' Vidmag for Cassettes Piloted, With All the No-Nos for TV," *Variety*, December 2, 1970.

49 Vincent Canby, "What Godard Hath Wrought," *New York Times*, March 29, 1970, 77.

50 See Edward de Grazia and Robert K. Newman, *Banned Films: Movies, Censors and the First Amendment* (New York: R. R. Bowker, 1982).

51 Earl R. Hutchison, *Tropic of Cancer on Trial: A Case History of Censorship* (New York: Grove Press, 1968), 93.

52 Also see Ibid., 57.

53 Also see Ibid., 59.

54 Also see Ibid., 59.

55 "Tropic of Cancer Scores a Victory," *New York Times*, June 14, 1961, 21. Also see Hutchison, 59 for complete article.

56 Hutchison, 60.

57 Ibid., 63.

58 Ibid., 63–4.

59 Ibid., 196–7.

60 Ibid., 65.

61 Ibid., 65.

62 See GPR and Hutchison, 68.

63 Hutchison, 82.

64 Ibid., 80–2.

65 Ibid., 82.

66 Anthony Lewis, "The Most Recent Troubles of *Tropic*: A Chapter in Censorship," *New York Times*, January 21, 1962, 210.

67 Hutchison, 92.

68 Hoke Norris, "*Cancer* in Chicago," *Evergreen Review*, Vol. 6, No. 25, 1962.

69 Henry Miller, *Tropic of Cancer* (New York: Grove Press, 1961).

70 William Lockhart and Robert McClure, "Literature, the Law of Obscenity, and the Constitution," *Minnesota Law Review* 38 (Mar. 1954).

71 In addition to quoted issue of *Evergreen Review*, see Paul Molloy, "He Questions the Merit of 'Tropic,'" *Chicago Sun-Times*, March 16, 1962, 20.

72 Hutchison, 103.

73 378 U.S. 184, *Jacobellis v. Ohio* (No. 11). Argued: March 26, 1963, Decided: June 22, 1964 173 Ohio St. 22, 179 N.E.2d 777, reversed.

74 John Calder, "The Transatlantic Connection," *The Review of Contemporary Fiction: Grove Press Number*, Fall 1990, 146–9.

75 Maurice Girodias, *Une journée sur la terre* (Paris: Editions de la différence, 1990). This, the second volume of Girodias's autobiography, has not been translated into English. The quoted translation is presumably by BR. The first volume of the autobiography, *The Frog Prince*, was published by Random House in 1988.

76 Jacqueline Duhême's hand-illustrated and -colored letters to BR are among his papers at BRP.

77 Peter Singleton-Gates, *The Black Diaries: An Account of Roger Casement's Life and Times with a Collection of his Diaries* (Paris: Olympia Press, 1959 and New York: Grove Press, 1959).

78 Mirra Alfassa (1878–1973).

79 S. E. Gontarski, ed., "Barney Rosset Interviews Giangiacomo Feltrinelli, WNET Radio [1959]", 3–4.

80 Ann Charters, ed., *Beat Down to Your Soul: What Was the Beat Generation?* (New York: Penguin Books, 2001).

81 Translation source of this quote is unknown. Pivano's introduction in Italian first appeared in the 1960 Feltrinelli edition.

82 Jack Kerouac, *The Subterraneans* (New York: Grove Press, 1959).

83 Jack Kerouac, "Written Address to the Italian Judge," *Evergreen Review*, Volume 7, Number 31 (New York: Grove Press, 1963).

84 Ken Jordan, "Barney Rosset: The Art of Publishing II" (an interview with Ken Jordan), *The Paris Review*, 145 (Winter 1997): 171–215.

85 John Ciardi, "The Book Burners and Sweet Sixteen," *Saturday Review*, June 27, 1959.

86 186 F. Supp. 254 (1960). *Big Table, Inc. v. Carl A. Schroeder*, United States Postmaster for Chicago, Illinois. No. 59 C 1382. United States District Court N. D. Illinois. June 30, 1960.

87 William Burroughs, *Naked Lunch: The Restored Text*, eds. James Grauerholz and Barry Miles (New York: Grove Press, 2001), 249.

88 Thomas Parkinson, ed., *A Casebook on the Beat* (New York: Crowell, 1961). Also see William S. Burroughs and Brion Gysin, *The Third Mind* (New York: Seaver Book/Viking Press, 1978). http://www.writing.upenn.edu/~afilreis/88v/burroughs-cutup.html.

89 This correspondence is collected in the Grove papers at Syracuse University. Also see Ted Morgan, *Literary Outlaw: The Life and Times of William S. Burroughs* (New York: Holt, 1988), 328–9.

90 For an excerpt from the *Time* review, see Morgan, 349–50.

91 Lewis Nichol, "In and Out of Books," *New York Times*, May 15, 1960, BR8.

92 http://www.nytimes.com/1964/04/25/evergreen-review-seized-in-nassau-as-being-obscene.html?_r=0.

93 *Sarasota Herald Tribune*, April 20, 1970.

94 http://www.washingtonpost.com/wp-dyn/content/article/2006/12/27/AR2006122700528.html.

95 S. E. Gontarski, ed., "Working at Grove: An Interview with Gilbert Sorrentino," *The Review of Contemporary Fiction: Grove Press Number*, Fall 1990, 104.

96 Robin Morgan, *Saturday's Child: A Memoir* [Electronic Resource] (Open Road Media, 2014). Also see print edition (W. W. Norton, 2001).

97 http://smokesignalsmag.com/3/barney.html.

98 "An Interview with Barney Rosset," *Small Press*, Vol. 3, RR Bowker, 1986.

99 http://www.nytimes.com/1985/03/05/arts/grove-sold-to-ann-getty-and-british-publisher.html.

100 For further details on this period see John Oakes, "The Last Days of Grove," *The Review of Contemporary Fiction: Grove Press Number*, Fall 1990, 175–8.

101 http://www.nytimes.com/1986/04/10/arts/an-ouster-at-grove-press-raises-writers-ire.html.

102 Samuel Beckett, *Stirrings Still* (New York: Foxrock, 1998).

103 Harry Kreisler, "Art and Healing," interview with Kenzaburō Ōe, April 16, 1999, Institute of International Studies, University of California at Berkeley http://globetrotter.berkeley.edu/people/Oe/oe-con1.html.

104 Kreisler, "Art of Healing."

105 http://www.nobelprize.org/nobel_prizes/literature/laureates/1994/oe-lecture.html.

106 http://articles.latimes.com/1996-08-11/books/bk-33107_1_kenzaburo-oe.

107 For an excellent contemporary assessment of the *Eleuthéria* controversy, see "You Call this 'Freedom'? The Fight to Publish and Produce Samuel Beckett's First Fulllength Play" by Stephen Graf, *New England Theatre Journal*, 25, pp 71–92.

108 Anthony Cronin, *Samuel Beckett: The Last Modernist* (New York: Da Capo, 1999), 547.

109 This letter is in the collected BR/Beckett correspondence at RBMB and at Syracuse.

110 http://www.nytimes.com/1994/09/24/theater/a-reading-upsets-beckett-s-estate.html.

111 http://www.nytimes.com/1995/06/25/books/waiting-for-eleutheria.html.

112 As detailed in the FOIA files at BRP, during his World War II service BR was investigated by US Intelligence for his association with his childhood friends the Osato sisters, Sono and Teru, who were married to men serving in the US Armed Forces. In addition to being considered possible Japanese collaborators, the Osatos were accused of engaging in prostitution. The first charge was unfounded, and the second scurrilous. An official US Intelligence letter ending the investigation is at BRP.

113 The lovers in Malraux's *Man's Fate*.

Acknowledgements

Writing this autobiography spanned many years, and in that time numerous people worked with Barney in all capacities—scanning photos, typing, filing, researching, editing—and all the tasks and changes that have gone into a final manuscript. I wish that I could recall all the staff and interns and volunteers who helped to shape this book. Unfortunately I cannot. But I want all to know how much Barney and I appreciated their time and commitment and willingness to do whatever needed to be done. I am deeply grateful.

I would also like to thank those whose commitment and support were especially helpful in moving this manuscript forward. It was an ongoing, intensive project from beginning to end. And now we have reached the light at the end of the tunnel.

My thanks go to Guy Baldwin; Edward Beckett, executor, Estate of Samuel Beckett; Tony Bly; Steven Brower; William Bryant; Jim Feast; Jules Geller; Joy Glass; Mary Kaplan and the J. M. Kaplan Foundation; Kathy Kiernan; Elena Landriscina; Sandy Meehan; Richard Milazzo; Caroline Milne; Laura Morris, archivist, Joan Mitchell Foundation; Brad Morrow; Lucy Mulroney, Special Collections Research Center, Syracuse University; Michelle Myers; Suresh Nayak; Catrina Neiman; New York State Foundation of the Arts; Karla Nielson, Rare Book and Manuscript Library, Columbia University; C. S. O'Brien; John Oakes; Kenzaburō Ōe; Lois Oppenheim; Ignacio Ponce de Leon; Chantal Rosset; Elisabeth Scharlatt, Algonquin Books; Margarita Shalina; Rami Shamir; Frank Shouldice; Nat Sobel; Robert N. Solomon; Jerry Tallmer; Jim Wade; and Ramsi Woodcock.

—*Astrid Myers Rosset*
East Hampton, New York
February 2016

Portrait by Astrid Myers Rosset.

Appendix A
Timeline

1922   May 28: Barnet Lee Rosset Jr. born at Michael Reese Hospital, Chicago, IL

1925   Feb. 12: Joan Mitchell born in Chicago

1928   July 21: maternal grandfather Roger Tansey dies

1930   June 13: maternal grandmother Margaret Flannery Tansey dies

1931   Attends Camp Kawaga, Minocqua, WI (summers 1931–33)

1932   Father buys Metropolitan Trust Co.

1934   January 21: Date of earliest intelligence report on BR obtained through Freedom of Information Act (FOIA)
        Attends Cheley Summer Camp, Estes Park, CO (summers 1934–36)

1935   Enrolls at Francis W. Parker School, Chicago
        Travels to Hawaii with parents

1936   Creates the *Sommunist*, later *Anti-Everything*, school newspaper with Haskell Wexler

1937   July: Visits Europe with parents. England, France, Italy, Switzerland
        December: Sent as delegate to the American Student Union at Vassar College

1938   First class with Alfred Adler, most important teacher in school life
        Arrested for speeding on March 11, according to FBI

1939   Wins three events at Private School Track Championship

1940   Graduates from Francis W. Parker School. President of senior class and co-captain of football team with Haskell Wexler
        Enrolls at Swarthmore College

1941   Buys *Tropic of Cancer* at Gotham Book Mart, New York City
        "Henry Miller vs. Our Way of Life" essay
        Transfers to University of Chicago after completing academic year at Swarthmore. Leaves after one quarter
        Signs protest to US President and Congress against existing or proposed legal restriction on Communist Party or individual Communist activities
        Francis W. Parker class reunion

Arrested for speeding on August 2, according to FBI
Transfers to UCLA

1942   Enlists in US Army
Inducted at Camp Grant, IL and assigned to Camp Adair, Corvallis, OR where the 96th Infantry Division is training. Spends eight months in Company I, 383rd Infantry Regiment
Marriage of Nancy Ashenhurst and Haskell Wexler

1943   Graduates from Officer's Training School in VA as Second Lieutenant
Signal Corps Pictorial Service. Assigned to Army Pictorial Service and receives training at Army Film School in Astoria, NY. Accredited as Photographic Unit Commander
Correspondence from Teru Osato intercepted by Army Intelligence
Shipped out from Newport News, VA. Arrives in Bombay, India after a forty-three day trip

1944   Arrives in India. Sent to Camp Kanchapara, thirty miles outside Calcutta, awaits assignment
Transferred to 164th Signal Photo Company in New Delhi, India
Orders to go to Kunming, China
Kweiyang

1945   Recommendation is made for Bronze Star for his role in the capture of Liuchow Airfield
Recommendation disapproved
December 27: Arrives in New York Harbor after twenty-two day trip via Suez Canal, Mediterranean Sea, and the Atlantic Ocean

1946   March 29: Discharged from US Army, returns to Chicago
Resumes friendship with Haskell Wexler and Nancy Ashenhurst
Meets Joan Mitchell in bar
Enrolls at University of Chicago
Briefly a member of Communist Party
Travels to Mexico to visit Joan Mitchell

1947   Moves to New York City
Establishes Target Films at 1600 Broadway
Production of *Strange Victory* begins
Joan Mitchell graduates from Art Institute of Chicago and moves in with BR in Brooklyn

1948   Joan Mitchell moves to Paris, BR joins her there for the month of August
Strange Victory premieres in NYC on September 24
BR and JM travel to Prague, return to Paris at Christmas

1949   BR and JM drive to Spain to see Guernica
        BR and JM are married at Le Lavandou, France
        Return to NYC, residing at Chelsea Hotel before renting a small apartment on
        West Eleventh Street

1950   Works at the American Association for the UN as a volunteer while seeking
        employment at UN
        BR and JM move to 57 West Ninth Street

1951   Enrolls at New School for Social Research, NYC
        Break with JM
        Robert Phelps and John Balcomb sell their shares in Grove Press to BR and
        father for $3,000

1952   B.A. from New School
        Divorces JM on May 13
        Meets Donald Allen at Columbia University publishing class
        Purchases East Hampton, NY home designed by Pierre Chareau for Robert
        Motherwell

1953   August: marries Hannelore (Loly) Eckert
        Moves Grove Press from Ninth Street to 795 Broadway
        Meets Samuel Beckett and Jean Genet in Paris
        Beckett correspondence begins

1954   Father Barnet L. Rosset Sr. dies on September 5

1955   Son Peter Rosset born

1956   First issue of *The Evergreen Review* published
        Divorces Hannelore (Loly) Eckert

1959   JM relocates to France
        Rejects Tolkein's *The Hobbit*
        Interviews Italian publisher Giangiacomo Feltrinelli concerning censorship on
        WNET Radio

1961   Arrives in Brooklyn to be arrested for publication of *Tropic of Cancer*; grand
        jury refuses to indict

1962   Chicago *Tropic of Cancer* trial

1963   Testifies at obscenity trial for Kerouac's *The Subterraneans* on behalf of Feltrinelli

1964   Produces Beckett's *Film.* Beckett visits BR in NYC
        Naked Lunch trial

1965   Marries Cristina Agnini

1966	Purchases film distributor Cinema 16 for $49,500
	Purchases Mid-Century Book Club
1967	Daughter Tansey Rosset born
	Moves Grove Press to 53 East Eleventh Street
	BR and Fred Jordan travel to Bolivia after execution of Che Guevara
1968	Grove Press offices bombed
1969	Son Beckett Rosset born
	Lectures at University of Michigan, "The Case Against Censorship"
	Grove Press financial peak, 163 titles published
	Grove purchases building at corner of Bleecker and Mercer Streets
1970	Grove offices occupied by female activists
	Grove unionization bid fails
	Grove Press v. Maryland State Board of Censors re: *I Am Curious (Yellow)*
1971	*Evergreen Review* ceases publication
	US Supreme Court upholds Maryland ruling declaring *I Am Curious* (Yellow) obscene
	Agreement with Random House to distribute Grove Press, Black Cat, and Evergreen hardcover titles
1972	Grove downsizes to twenty-four employees
1975	Submits FOIA request to CIA for records relating to Grove Press and/or BR
1979	Divorces Cristina Agnini
	Richard Avedon photographs Samuel Beckett and Beckett Rosset in France
	Travels to Vétheuil, France with Lisa Krug, daughter Tansey, and son Peter to visit Joan Mitchell
	Mother Mary Tansey Rosset dies
1980	Henry Miller dies on June 8
	Marries Elizabeth (Lisa) Krug
1982	Daughter Chantal Rosset born
1985	Sells Grove Press to George Weidenfeld and Ann Getty for $2 million. Grove is a public company and payment is to stockholders
1986	Leaves Grove Press
	Receives original typescript of Beckett's *Eleuthéria* in Paris
	Files $7 million lawsuit against Weidenfeld and Getty, who counter-sue
	Starts Rosset & Co., Inc.
1987	Delivers commencement address at Hampshire College
	Starts Blue Moon Books

1988   Wins PEN publisher citation

1989   Censorship battles with Rev. Donald Wildmon and his American Family
        Association, Waldenbooks, and K-Mart
        Beckett dedicates *Stirrings Still* to BR
        Publishes *Stirrings Still*, Beckett refuses to work further with Grove Weidenfeld
        Beckett dies on December 22

1991   Divorces Lisa Krug

1992   Joan Mitchell dies on October 30

1993   Fight with Beckett estate to publish *Eleuthéria* begins

1994   Relieved of position of US theatrical agent for Samuel Beckett
        BR and Astrid Myers attend Kenzaburō Ōe's Nobel Prize ceremony
        Establishes Foxrock, Inc.

1995   Foxrock publishes first book, Beckett's *Eleuthéria*

1996   Returns to Kunming, China with Astrid Myers

1998   Return of *The Evergreen Review* as an Internet publication. Website established

1999   Named by French government Commandeur de l'ordre des arts et des lettres

2001   Grove publishes *Grove Press Reader*

2002   Exhibition of China photos from WWII, Janos Gat Gallery, NYC

2007   Marries Astrid Myers

2012   Dies on February 21 in New York City at age 89

Appendix B

Grove Press Milestones

1954   Samuel Beckett, *Waiting for Godot*
        Jean Genet, *The Maids* and *Deathwatch*

1955   Frederico Garcia Lorca, *Poet in New York*

1956   Donald Keene (editor), *Anthology of Japanese Literature*
        Khushwant Singh, *Train to Pakistan*

1957   *Evergreen Review*, No. 1 (Barney Rosset, ed.)
        Evergreen Review, No. 2, *San Francisco Scene* (Donald Allen, ed.)

1958   Antonin Artaud, *Theatre and Its Double*
        Eugene Ionesco, *The Bald Soprano, et al.*
        Jack Kerouac, *The Subterraneans*
        Alain Robbe-Grillet, *The Voyeur*

1959   Brendan Behan, *The Hostage*
        e. e. cummings, *100 Selected Poems*
        D.H. Lawrence, *Lady Chatterley's Lover*
        Juan Rulfo, *Pedro Paramo: A Novel of Mexico*
        The Eye of Mexico, #7 (Octavio Paz, ed.)

1960   Donald Allen (ed.), *The New American Poetry*
        Samuel Beckett, *Krapp's Last Tape*

1961   Samuel Beckett, *Happy Days*
        Henry Miller, *Tropic of Cancer* and *Tropic of Capricorn*
        Pablo Neruda, *Selected Poems of Pablo Neruda*
        Octavio Paz, *The Labyrinth of Solitude*
        Harold Pinter, *The Birthday Party* and *The Room*
        Edgar Snow, *Red Star Over China*
        Evergreen Review, No. 21, *The German Scene*

1962   John Arden, *Sergeant Musgrave's Dance*
        Jorge Luis Borges, *Ficciones*
        William S. Burroughs, *Naked Lunch*
        Robert Gover, *One Hundred Dollar Misunderstanding*
        John Rechy, *City of Night*

1963   Samuel Beckett, *Complete Poems in English and French*
          Bertolt Brecht, *Mother Courage*

1964   Eric Berne, *Games People Play*
          Bertolt Brecht, *The Threepenny Opera*
          Rolf Hochbuth, *The Deputy*
          Hubert Selby, Jr., *Last Exit to Brooklyn*

1965   Franz Fanon, *Wretched of the Earth*
          Joe Orton, *Entertaining Mr. Sloane*
          Pauline Réage, *Story of O*
          The Marquis de Sade, *Justine*
          Malcolm X, *The Autobiography of Malcolm X*

1966   Bertolt Brecht, *The Good Woman of Setzuan* and *Caucasian Chalk Circle*
          Mario Vargas Llosa, *The Time of the Hero*

1967   Jorge Luis Borges, *A Personal Anthology*
          Tom Stoppard, *Rosencrantz and Guildenstern Are Dead*

1968   Che Guevara, *Che Guevara Speaks*
          Vaclav Havel, *The Memorandum*
          Kenzaburō Ōe, *A Personal Matter*
          Vilgot Sjoman, *I Am Curious (Yellow)* (film distributed by Grove Press)
          Evergreen Review Reader

1970   Samuel Beckett, *Endgame*

1977   David Mamet, *American Buffalo*

1981   John Kennedy Toole, *A Confederacy of Dunces*

1984   Kathy Acker, *Blood and Guts in High School*

Appendix C

Grove Press financials, 1964–1984

	net revenue	net expense	net income
1964	$1,009,172	$925,484	$83,688
1965	$1,614,655	$1,306,318	$308,337
1966	$2,318,653	$2,070,073	$248,580
1967	$3,784,493	$3,465,620	$318,873
1968	$7,162,232	$6,978,588	$183,644
1969	$14,294,152	$14,073,679	$220,473
1970	$10,576,845	$12,086,995	($1,510,150)
1971	$4,201,129	$8,421,950	($4,220,821)
1972	$4,835,036	$5,510,007	($674,971)
1973	$3,221,525	$3,006,173	$215,352
1974	$2,883,655	$2,545,940	$337,715
1975	$3,171,412	$2,580,788	$590,624
1976	$2,635,201	$2,379,199	$256,002
1977	$2,293,704	$2,287,524	$6,180
1978	$2,436,053	$2,835,779	($399,726)
1979	$2,387,111	$2,104,052	$283,059
1980	$2,274,392	$2,187,723	$86,669
1981	$3,113,350	$3,110,048	$3,302
1982	$3,021,786	$2,961,517	$60,269
1983	$3,304,601	$3,225,748	$78,853
1984	$2,798,227	$2,715,965	$82,262
totals	**$83,337,384**	**$86,779,170**	**($3,441,786)**

Appendix D
Barney Rosset: A List (delivered on BR's 77th birthday)

Soon after Barney Rosset's 75th birthday party in 1997, his companion Astrid Myers made a list of some of the things he "likes extremely." It is a curious list, yet a revealing one: playing pool, Korean women, tennis, rum and Coke, spanking, Victorian erotica, dogs, *Man's Fate* (Malraux), photography, Thailand, fried chicken, and three-bean salad. He also likes rearranging furniture, strippers, bars at three in the morning, primitive and naive art, and Samuel Beckett. A catalog of the things he heartily dislikes would be even longer. Astrid names only a few: rudeness, zaftig women, Rudy Giuliani, spicy foods, and Chicago. The list should be extended, for he very definitely dislikes certain whole sections of civilization (as an eighth-grader he published a newsletter called *Anti-Everything*) and in particular, any form of oppression: instruction manuals, Don't Walk signs, automatic transmissions, smoke and dust, the religious right, politicians, and practically everyone with whom he has been forced to have business relations. Rosset is shy, daunting, imposing, quick-tempered, courageous, and morbidly sensitive. He has a talent for adapting himself to uncongenial surroundings, and much of his life has been spent in passionate rebellion against censorship laws that people of milder temperament learned to endure and to eventually ignore. At 77 he has a few loyal friends, a somewhat longer list of bitter enemies, and has published more than a dozen authors of such quality as to assure him a permanent place in the history of publishing.

— Mike Topp

Appendix E
A Brief History of this Book

The late Barney Rosset, dean of combat publishing, scarred veteran of too many battles over the word to enumerate, must have chuckled appreciatively when considering this book's evolution, and the many editors and publishers involved along the way.

That the memoir was necessary was never in doubt. Any serious student of American culture from the post-World War II era right up into the 1970s knows that were it not for the indefatigable Rosset, our lives would be very different. That one person fundamentally reshaped the way we think, perhaps more than any other in the modern era: he unleashed upon us *Lady Chatterley's Lover*, the intellectual puzzles of Beckett, Genet, Pinter, Ōe, Robbe-Grillet, Ionesco, and Stoppard; the *Tropics* of Miller, the outrages of Burroughs and Rechy, and so much more—Amos Tutuola, Octavio Paz, the fabled *Evergreen Review*, the groundbreaking film *I Am Curious (Yellow)* . . . that in the 21st century, the idea of "normal" sexuality has changed so much owes not a little to Rosset's pioneering, joyous exploration of such concepts. And he did so not as part of a larger organization, but as an independent, perhaps the most fiercely independent publisher since Aldus Manutius, he of the Venetian Renaissance (and the man who invented italics).

For Rosset, publishing wasn't only a matter of styling a work and presenting it to the public. Every book was a battle, and he was the pirate captain exhorting his crew to slaughter. In fact, the list of censorship obstacles overcome by Grove Press under his tenure is so extensive, it might be argued that the company was more likely to publish a book if it was somehow "forbidden."

Who was this restless iconoclast? What motivated him? How did he assemble the world-changing list of artists and thinkers he did? Those of us in the publishing industry want to know, as do scholars of the period. And so, a few decades back, not long after the Gettys ousted him from the leadership of Grove,

Barney set to work. He amassed a vast collection of letters, photographs, films, interviews and notes (packing at least two dozen large three-ring binders), and with the help of long-suffering assistants and various family members attempted to organize it all. But trying to put a living Barney Rosset into the pages of a book was like trying to stuff a sun into a Volkswagen Beetle. Things kept popping out, and there were frequent and grand explosions. Much was destroyed. Survivors were traumatized. All amusing to witness from a distance, but never fun to be in the midst of. Hundreds and hundreds of pages were dictated and transcribed; thousands of pages edited and re-edited; thousands of photocopies were made. Drafts were written and discarded; at least fifteen different freelance editors, and at least four experienced publishers (not including Barney himself) wrestled with this project.

The book couldn't be completed to his satisfaction. And this was true to the man: "contentment" was not in his vocabulary. He was forever hiring, firing, and rehiring his employees; renovating, refinancing, and replanting. Anything marked as finished was dead; anything living involved change, challenge, and revision, revision, revision.

I worked with Barney in the 1980s—he gave me my first job in publishing—and we stayed in touch in the post-Grove years. He was one of the most exciting people I'd ever met: yes, he was impatient, unpredictable, and a bit scary, but he also crackled with laughter. The man was either brooding, laughing, or raging. From afar, I observed the memoir slowly become a spiky, intractable thing, not unlike its subject: as an editor and publisher, of course I wanted to work on the project, but as an ex-employee of Barney's, and as someone who had worked with him closely on Beckett's *Eleuthéria* and an anthology of the *Evergreen Review*, I doubted any publisher could collaborate with him on his memoir while he was alive.

When the autobiography came to OR Books via the good graces of Barney's Estate, it was in quite different form. It seemed to us to reflect the publisher's electric personality only in flashes. It had been pruned to death. We went back to Barney's papers in the archives of the library at Columbia University and put back in much of what had been taken out. The voice is authentically Barney's. We think the result, while not a complete portrait of the man, provides insight into who he was and what he did.

We thank Barney's family—Astrid Myers Rosset and Barney's children Peter, Tansey, Beckett, and Chantal—for their trust. C. S. O'Brien deserves particular thanks for his extraordinary research and restorative efforts, as does Elisabeth Scharlatt of Algonquin Books, for her patience.

— John Oakes for OR Books

Index

FROM FOXROCK

IN PARTNERSHIP WITH OR BOOKS

Eleuthéria
Samuel Beckett
ISBN 978-1-68219-017-3 PAPERBACK
ISBN 978-1-68219-018-0 E-BOOK

Stirrings Still
Samuel Beckett
ISBN 978-1-68219-011-1 PAPERBACK
ISBN 978-1-68219-012-8 E-BOOK

The Man Sitting in the Corridor
Marguerite Duras
ISBN 978-1-68219-013-5 PAPERBACK
ISBN 978-1-68219-014-2 E-BOOK

Seventeen and J: Two Novels
Kenzaburō Ōe
ISBN 978-1-68219-015-9 PAPERBACK
ISBN 978-1-68219-016-6 E-BOOK

For more, visit EVERGREENREVIEW.COM